BRISTOL RECORD SOCIETY'S
PUBLICATIONS

General Editors: MADGE DRESSER
                 PETER FLEMING
                 ROGER LEECH

VOL. 59

RECORDS OF BRISTOL CATHEDRAL

RECORDS OF BRISTOL CATHEDRAL

EDITED

BY

JOSEPH BETTEY

Published by
BRISTOL RECORD SOCIETY
2007

ISBN 978 0 901538 29 1

The Bristol Record Society acknowledges with thanks the continued support of Bristol City Council, the University of the West of England, the University of Bristol, the Bristol Record Office, the Bristol and West Building Society and the Society of Merchant Venturers.

The Society exists to encourage the preservation, study and publication of documents relating to the history of Bristol, and since its foundation in 1929 has published fifty-nine major volumes of historic documents concerning the city. All the volumes, together with their authoritative introductions, are edited by scholars who are experts in their chosen field.

Recent volumes have included: *Africa and the Eighteenth-Century Slave Trade to America* (Vols. 38, 39, 42 and 47); *The Goldney Family: A Bristol Merchant Dynasty* (Vol. 49); *William Worcestre: The Topography of Medieval Bristol* (Vol. 51); *The Topography of Medieval and Early Modern Bristol* (Vols. 48 and 52); *The Diary of Sarah Fox* (Vol. 55); *The Pre-Reformation Records of All Saints' Church, Bristol* (Vols. 46, 53 and 56); *Bristol Probate Inventories* (Vols. 54 and 57) and *Robert Sturmy's Commercial Expedition to the Mediterranean 1457–8* Vol. 58.

Forthcoming volumes will include The Topography of Medieval and Early Modern Bristol, Part 3; Bristol Probate Inventories, Part 3, and the Bristol Hearth Tax Returns.

In return for the modest subscription, members of the Society receive the volumes as they are published. The subscription for private members is £10 per annum, for UK institutions £12.50, and for overseas membership £15.

Subscriptions and enquiries should be made to the Secretaries, c/o The School of History, University of the West of England, St Matthias Campus, Oldbury Court Road, Bristol BS16 2JP

Produced for the Society by
4word Ltd
Unit 15 Bakers Park, Cater Road
Bristol BS13 7TT

CONTENTS

ACKNOWLEDGEMENTS

The help received in the preparation of this volume is gratefully acknowledged. The Dean & Chapter of Bristol Cathedral gave permission for their records to be published, and the Dean, the Very Revd Robert Grimley, and Canon Peter Johnson, have been a constant source of encouragement and support. The staff of the Bristol Record Office have been unfailingly helpful, and I am particularly grateful to Anne Bradley for her invaluable help and advice. Assistance has also been received from Michael Richardson, Hannah Lowery and Nicholas Lee in the Special Collections section of Bristol University Library, and from Jane Bradley and the staff of Bristol Reference Library. Thanks are also due to Martin Crossley Evans, Madge Dresser, Prof. Christopher Elrington, Peter Fleming, Francis Greenacre, Philippa Johnson, Roger Leech, John Lyes, Elizabeth Sabin, Warwick Rodwell and Alan Rome for their assistance. I have derived much benefit from earlier work on the Cathedral archives. Isabel Kirby's <u>Catalogue of the Records of the Diocese of Bristol</u> (1970) has been an essential guide, and likewise the studies produced by Arthur Sabin, Elizabeth Ralph, Canon John Rogan and Michael Q. Smith.

Joseph Bettey

EDITORIAL NOTE

Introductory material and editorial commentary are printed in italics. The original spelling and capitalisation of documents have been kept, but abbreviations have been extended. Some punctuation has been added for the sake of clarity. Wherever possible, the meaning of obsolete words or terms, the modern form of aberrant place-names, and the dates of saints' days have been added within square brackets. Uncertain readings are followed by (?). Dates are given as they appear on documents, with the year beginning on 25th March until 1753. References for the location of each source appear at the beginning of the entry.

ABBREVIATIONS

A.P.C.	Acts of the Privy Council
B.G.A.S. Trans.	Bristol & Gloucestershire Archaeological Society Transactions
B.R.O.	Bristol Record Office
B.R.S.	Bristol Record Society
Cal. S.P. Dom.	Calendar of State Papers, Domestic (1856–1972)
Great Red Book	E.W.W. Veale, ed., Great Red Book of Bristol, Bristol Record Society, IV, VIII, XVI, XVIII, 1931–53
Hist. MSS Comm.	Royal Commission on Historical Monuments
Hockaday Abstracts	Abstracts of Ecclesiastical Records relating to Bristol & Gloucestershire compiled by F.S. Hockaday
L & P Hen. VIII	Letters & Papers, Foreign & Domestic, of the Reign of Henry VIII
Nicholls & Taylor	J.F. Nicholls & John Taylor, Bristol: Past & Present, II, (Ecclesiastical History), Bristol, 1881
Oxford D.N.B.	Oxford Dictionary of National Biography
T.N.A. (P.R.O.)	The National Archives (Public Record Office)

LIST OF ILLUSTRATIONS

INTRODUCTION

The diocese and bishopric of Bristol was founded by order of Henry VIII in 1542, with the former Augustinian abbey as its cathedral. The monks' quarters and abbot's lodge provided accommodation for the bishop, dean, cathedral canons and other members of the establishment. This volume brings together extracts from the major documentary sources relating to the history of the cathedral from its foundation until the triumphant success of the ambitious proposal to re-build the nave which was completed in 1877. The documents include the sources relating to the dissolution of the Augustinian abbey, the creation of the new diocese and cathedral, religious life under successive bishops, deans and canons, the relations with the city of Bristol, and the vicissitudes of the cathedral building, its furnishings and precinct. As well as Charters, Statutes, correspondence, miscellaneous administrative records and copious material relating to the management of the cathedral estates and properties, the archive of the Dean & Chapter also includes a complete series of Chapter Minutes from 1663, with some material from 1542, and annual accounts or <u>Computa</u> for most years from 1550. A great deal of information also survives concerning successive changes to the fabric of the cathedral and about its restoration during the 19th century.

The Augustinian abbey was founded in 1140 by Robert Fitzharding, later Lord Berkeley, on his estate at Billeswick, just outside the walls of Bristol and on the high ground across the river Frome from the town. It is probable that the site for the abbey was chosen because of its association with St Jordan who, according to ancient tradition, was one of the 40 monks who accompanied St Augustine to Canterbury in 597. In 603 he is alleged to have accompanied St Augustine on his journey to meet with Christians from Wales on the banks of the Severn, possibly at Aust. St Jordan remained in Bristol, and later was buried near the site where the abbey was to be founded. His tomb and the chapel built over it became the centre of religious worship and veneration. Whatever the truth of this legend, it is certain that throughout the Middle Ages there was a chapel dedicated to St Jordan on the open space later to be known as College Green. Here the abbey was founded in 1140. Through its connection with the wealthy Berkeley family, the abbey was well-endowed with extensive properties, estates and appropriated parish churches in Bristol, Gloucestershire, Somerset, Wiltshire and beyond. This meant that by the time of its suppression by Henry VIII's commissioners in 1539, the abbey, although not in the same league as the immensely rich and ancient Benedictine abbeys such *as Glastonbury, St Peter's, Gloucester or the nunnery at Shaftesbury, was nonetheless a wealthy institution with widespread properties; it enjoyed an annual income of more than £700 to support eighteen canons and their servants, and to maintain a fine, richly-furnished church. It was by far the richest and most important ecclesiastical establishment in Bristol* [*For details of the abbey's history see* Joseph Bettey, St Augustine's Abbey, Bristol, Bristol Historical Association, 1996; *for St Jordan see* David Higgins, From the Catacombs of Rome to College Green, Bristol, Bristol Historical Association, 2007].

FROM AUGUSTINIAN ABBEY TO ANGLICAN CATHEDRAL

The inheritaunce of this transitorye worlde hath all these noughty properties rehersed, and manye worse, townes and towres, castels and manours decayeth continuallye, and where noble men have dwelled, nowe dwelleth dawes and crowes, the vawtes [vaults] and rouffes [roofs] be so ruinous, that no man dare well come under them: Where is Troye? Where be the olde Emperies and monarchies of the Assirians, of the Caldeis, Medes, Persies, and of Rome, whose Emperours had under them in maner all the worlde, for theyr tyme? Where is the devotion that noble men and ryche marchauntes hath had to magnifie and encrease Goddes service to his honoure? If God had not preserved our mooste Gratious Soveraigne Kinge Henry the eyght, whiche by his princelie zele, love, and devotion to God, hath erecte this Cathedrall Churche of Bristowe, and manye other suche within this Realme, God knoweth what case divine service should have bene in.

[from a sermon preached in Bristol Cathedral soon after its establishment in 1542 by Roger Edgeworth, one of the first canons. Janet Wilson, ed., <u>Roger Edgeworth Sermons very fruitful, godly and learned</u>, (1993)].

The process which was to lead to the suppression of the abbey started in 1534 when Parliament passed the Act of Supremacy, which effectively abolished Papal power in England and gave to Henry VIII the title of 'the only Supreme Head in earth of the Church of England'. A requirement of the Act was that all adults, including monks and nuns, should take an oath upon the Holy Scriptures that they acquiesced in the repudiation of Katherine of Aragon, agreed with the royal marriage to Anne Boleyn, and that they would give allegiance to the children of that marriage, as well as accepting the royal supremacy over the Church. On 9 September 1534, the abbot of St Augustine's William Burton, together with 18 canons, met in the Chapter House and signed the acknowledgement of royal supremacy.

No doubt the abbot and canons saw no alternative in the face of royal power and the pressure that was put upon them to give their assent. Their solemn acceptance of the royal supremacy, however, left them with little defence against the upheavals which were so soon to follow. During 1535 Henry VIII's principal minister, Thomas Cromwell, instituted a series of inquiries into the wealth of the religious houses and into the way in which they performed their duties. The first careful survey into the wealth and income was to produce the Valor Ecclesiasticus *of 1535 which revealed for the first time the enormous wealth of the Church. For some unknown reason or oversight, Bristol was omitted from the* Valor Ecclesiasticus, *but the surviving late-medieval accounts of income from the abbey estates and from appropriated parish churches and other sources show annual receipts of more than £700 for the support of the abbot and 18 canons.*

Since St Augustine's, Bristol was omitted from the Valor Ecclesiasticus, *it is particularly useful to have detailed surveys of its properties and income at the end of the Middle Ages. The following table shows the property which the monastery possessed in Bristol and the income it derived from it during 1491–2; the properties included houses, shops, inns and a water-mill. Oblations were the offerings made by visitors to the abbey, and were low in 1491–2, probably because of controversy and tension between the abbey and the townsfolk of Bristol over their respective rights, which had resulted in a lawsuit. The bulk of the abbey's income was derived from its properties in the surrounding area, and from parish churches 'appropriated' to the abbey which thus became the rector of the parish and took a considerable proportion of the tithe, appointing a vicar to attend to the spiritual welfare of the parishioners. The profits of trade included sales of malt and bread by the abbey.*

G. Beachcroft & A. Sabin, eds., 'Two Compotus Rolls of St Augustine's Abbey, Bristol', B.R.S., IX, 1938, 63, 84–5

A. Sabin, ed., 'Compotus Rolls of St Augustine's Abbey, Bristol', B.G.A.S. Trans., LXXIII, 1954–5, 192–207

Estates and Income of St Augustine's Abbey, Bristol during the later Middle Ages

	Annual Value in 1491–2		
	£	s	d
Property in Bristol	99	9	11½
Appropriated churches in Bristol (All Saints', St Nicholas, St Augustine the Less)	6	8	8
Oblations and fees	1	2	6½

Property in Gloucestershire

Horfield	Ham
Almondsbury	Hill
Cromhall	Stone
Arlingham	Bevington
Berkeley	Swanshanger
Blacksworth	Wanswell
Codrington	Barton Regis
South Cerney	Ashleworth

Property in Somerset

Leigh (Abbotsleigh)	Pawlett
Portbury	East Harptree

	£	s	d

Rowberrow   Stanton Drew
Baggeridge

Property in Dorset
Fifehead Magdalen

Property in Wales
Penarth
Peterstone

Appropriated churches
Gloucestershire
     Almondsbury   Filton
     Ashleworth   Horfield
     Berkeley –Herons   Kingsweston
     Elberton   Wapley
Somerset
     Clevedon   Tickenham
     Pawlett   Weare
     Portbury
Wales
     Penarth   St Mellons
     Peterstone   Marshfield
     Rumney
Dorset
     Fifehead Magdalen
Devon
     Halberton

	£	s	d
Annual value of manors, lands and appropriated rectories outside Bristol	595	3	10½
Profits of trade in 1491–2	65	16	2½
Total net income in 1491–2	768	1	3

As well as the detailed inquiry into the wealth of the Church, commissioners were also appointed to investigate the manner in which the monasteries were conducting their affairs. The commissioners were in no doubt that they were expected to produce evidence of laxity, neglect of vows, failure to live up to monastic ideals and scandalous behaviour which could be used to justify at least a partial suppression and confiscation of monastic wealth by the Crown. As Thomas Fuller was to write a century later:

> *'they were men who well understood the message they went on, and would not come back without a satisfactory answer to him that sent them, knowing themselves were unlikely to be no losers thereby'* [T. Fuller, Church History of Britain, (1655), 1837 edn., II, 214]

The commissioner who came to St Augustine's was Richard Layton, a young, energetic and ambitious priest, anxious to rise in Cromwell's service. He evidently found nothing amiss at St Augustine's, since had he done so he would assuredly have reported it to Cromwell. His cynical and contemptuous attitude towards the monks and canons, and his total disbelief in the relics which were treasured by the religious houses is clear from the report which he sent to Cromwell from St Augustine's, Bristol, writing early in the morning on St Bartholomew's Day [24 August] 1535. He was not above fabricating evidence of irregularities and grossly exaggerates the misdeeds of the prior of Maiden Bradley. His disappointment at not finding anything scandalous to report on from the Charterhouse at Hinton, near Bath, nor from Bruton and Glastonbury, is very evident from his letter. Likewise, he appears to have found nothing at all to criticise at St Augustine's.

L. & P. Hen. VIII, IX, 1886, 168;
T. Wright, <u>Letters Relating to the Suppression of the Monasteries</u>, Camden Society, XXVI, 1843, 58–9

Richard Layton to Thomas Cromwell, 24 August 1535

Please it your Mastership to understand, that yesternight late we came from Glastonbury to Bristol at St Austins, where we begin this morning, intending this day to dispatch both this house here, being but xiiii canons, and also the Gaunts where be iiii or v. By this bringer, my servant, I send you relics, first two flowers wrapped in white and black sarcenet that on Christmas eve, at the very hour that Christ was born, will spring, bud and bear blossoms, saith the prior of Maiden Bradley. You shall also receive a bag of relics wherein you shall see strange things, as shall appear by the scripture, as God's coat, Our Lady's smock, part of God's supper, part of the stone on which Jesus was born in Bethlehem (belike there is in Bethlehem plenty of stones and some quarry there making mangers of stone). The scripture of every thing shall declare you all; and all these of Maiden Bradley, where there is a holy father Prior, and has but vi children, and but one daughter married yet of the goods of monastery, trusting shortly to marry the rest. His sons be tall men waiting upon him, and he thanks God he never meddled with married women, but all with maidens the fairest could be gotten, and always married them right well. The Pope, considering his fragility gave him licence to keep a whore, and he has good writing under seal to discharge his conscience, and Mr Underhill to be his ghostly father, and he to give him full remission, etc.

I send you also Our Lady's girdle of Bruton, red silk, which is a solemn relic sent to women travailing, which shall not miscarry in childbirth. I send you also Mary Magdalen's girdle, and that is wrapped and covered with white, sent also with great reverence to women travailing, which girdle Matilda the Empress, founder of Farleigh, gave unto them, as saith the holy father of Farleigh. I have crosses of silver and gold, some which I send you not now because I have more that shall be delivered me this night by the Prior of Maiden Bradley himself. Tomorrow, early in the morning, I shall bring you the rest, when I have received all, and perchance shall find something here.

In case you depart this day, it may please you to send me word by this bringer, my servant, which way I shall repair after you. Within the Charter house have professed and done all things according as I shall disclose you at large tomorrow early. At Bruton and Glastonbury there is nothing notable; the brethren be so strait kept that they cannot offend, but fain they would if they might, as they confess, and so the fault is not in them.

From St Augustines without Bristol, this St Bartholomew's day, at iiii of the clock in the morning, by the speedy hand of your most assured poor priest.

Richard Layton

One result of Layton's visit to St Augustine's was that on his departure he ordered the abbot, William Burton, that neither he nor his canons should go outside the precincts of the abbey, that the monastic rule should be strictly observed and that no lay persons, especially women, should be allowed inside the abbey. These were orders which he issued to all the monastic houses he visited. At Bristol, however, they produced a protest from the abbot, who wrote a servile letter to Cromwell asking for the restrictions to be relaxed.

T.N.A. (P.R.O.) SP 1/96, fols 32–3

A letter from the Abbot of St Augustine's, Bristol, to Thomas Cromwell in the early Autumn of 1535

Right honourable Mr Secretary, Principal Visitor under the King's most royal majesty, supreme head of the church of England next under God in earth. So it is that the reverend and discreet man Master Doctor Layton by his great authority lately visited us at the King's monastery of St Austins where he left at his gentle departing with me and my brethren certain injunctions somewhat hard and strait to be observed and kept. Wherefore I most heartily desire your good mastership to grant to me and to my officer chamberlain licence and liberty to go and to ride to see good order, custom, and manner to be kept within the lordships of the said monastery at times convenient for the profits of the same. Secondly I heartily pray you to give me licence and liberty to walk to my manor places nigh to Bristol for the comfortable health of my body and for the saving of expenses. Thirdly I beseech you that I may walk within the circuit of the monastery, that is to say within the Green and Canons Marsh next adjacent to the precincts of the said monastery. Furthermore both I and my brethren instantly prayeth, desireth, and beseecheth your good mastership to grant to me power to give them licence some times to walk, three or four together, the juniors with the seniors (refraining the town) about the hills and fields to recreate their minds and to lax their veins, whereby they may be more apt to continue both night and day in the service of God. Yet we most heartily desire you to suffer us to have some poor honest woman to keep us if any pestifer[ous] plague or distress of sickness do fall amongst us, as it hath been there of long consuetude....

Throughout the country during the years 1536 to 1539 many monasteries were suppressed or succumbed to pressure from Cromwell and his commissioners to 'voluntarily' surrender their houses with all estates, property and buildings to the

Fig. 1   The Chapter House c1170, together with its entrance from the cloister,
is the finest example of Romanesque architecture in Bristol. It was used for all formal
meetings by the Augustinian canons, and it was here that the abbey was surrendered
to Henry VIII's commissioners on 9 December 1539. It continued to be used by the
Dean and Canons of the cathedral for their Chapter meetings.
(Photograph: J. Britton, <u>History & Antiquities of Bristol Cathedral</u>, 1830).

*Crown. In Bristol, however, St Augustine's remained untouched. On 21 February
1539 the abbot, William Burton, wrote another obsequious letter to Cromwell,
thanking him for his great goodness to the abbey and sending him a gift of 20 nobles
(£6 13s 4d). Clearly, the Augustinian canons at Bristol hoped that their house would
be allowed to continue. This optimism seemed to be justified, for when William
Burton, who had been abbot since 1525, died in July 1539, a licence was granted by
Cromwell for the election of a successor, and Morgan Gwilliam, who had been the
prior, became abbot on 24 August 1539. It may be that there was already some
understanding with Cromwell's commissioners that the house would be surrendered
without protest, for Morgan Gwilliam had been abbot for little more than three
months when the end came. On 9 December 1539 the abbot and 11 canons
surrendered the house to the Crown*
[J.H. Bettey, <u>The Suppression of the Monasteries in the West Country</u>, 1989,
70–94].

T.N.A. (P.R.O.) Aug. Office Misc Book 494 f 47

9 December 1539 Certificate of Commissioners

Late monastery of St Augustine's nigh Bristol
Clear yearly value of all the Possessions belonging to the said late monastery spiritual & temporal over and besides £70 -3–4 in fees and annuities granted to divers persons for term of life = £692 -2 -7

Pensions assigned to the late Religious dispatched:

Morgan Gwilliam late abbot	£80 per annum	
Humphrey Heymond prior	£8 ,, ,,	
John Rastell, student	£8 ,, ,,	
John Carye	£6–13–4	
Henry Pavye	£6	
William Wrington	£6	
William Underwood	£6	£151–6–8
Nicholas Corbett	£6–13–4	
Richard Hill	£6	
Richard Oryell	£6	
Richard Kersey	£6	
Richard Hughes	£6	

And so remaineth clere = £540–15–11

Records and Evidences remain in the Treasury and Audit House there, the keys whereof remain in the custody of Richard Poulett Esq. Receiver
The Church, Houses and Buildings committed to the custody of Manning the King's farmer there
Lead remaining on the church, aisles, chapels, dormitory, chapter house, Frater, cloister and other lodgings there esteemed to be 130 foders [a fodder =19_ cwts]

Bells in the steeple there X
Jewels reserved to the use of the King's majesty:
   Mitres garnished with silver gilt ragged pearls and counterfeit stones
   Certain garnishing of vestments of silver gilt duameld and set with small pearls
   Plate of silver reserved to the use of the King's majesty:

Silver Gilt	229 ounces	
Silver parcel Gilt	151 ounces	526 ounces
Silver White	146 ounces	

Ornaments Goods & Chattels sold by the Commissioners   £103–13–7

Payments to the late religious and servants dispatched:
   To 11 late Religious persons of the King's majesty's reward   £21
   To 46 persons being officers and servants of the late
   monastery for the wages and liveries   £42–2–0

Debts owing by the said monastery:
    To divers persons of the towns of Sarum and Bristol
    for victuals, cloth, wax, salt, wine and spices had
    of them to the use of the late monastery   £58–10–2

Payments:
    To Walter Denys knight, Surveyor and receiver of the
    lands of the late monastery for arrears of his fee   £14–0–0
    To Nicholas Thorne of Bristol, merchant   £60

Patronage of Churches belonging to the said late monastery:

Bristol: St Nicholas
                        All Saints
                        St Leonards
                        Little St Augustines

Gloucestershire   Almondsbury
                        Berkeley Herness
                        Ashelworth
                        Wapley

Somerset   Poulett
                        Portbury
                        Tickenham
                        Clevedon
                        Weare
                        Roborough

Wilts	Fifehead	Glamorgan	Penarth
Devon	Halberton	Berks	Finemere
Monmouth	Rumney		

Like many other monastic buildings and their precincts, the site, church, cloisters and other buildings of St Augustine's were rapidly leased to a new owner. This was William Greensmith, yeoman, of Hampton, Middlesex and Joan his wife, who were granted a lease of the whole property on 14 March 1541. This included the abbey church and its precinct, including the cloisters, houses, orchards, gardens and ponds, 32 acres of marsh along the river which were known as Canons Marsh, and pasture land on St Michael's Hill which consisted of several enclosures known as Cantock's Closes. William Greensmith's lease of the property was short-lived, for a year later it was cancelled by the Crown, in order to implement the decision to create a diocese of Bristol, complete with a cathedral.

The Creation of the Cathedral and Diocese of Bristol

Throughout the Middle Ages the major part of Bristol, the area to the north of the river Avon, was part of the large diocese of Worcester. The suburbs south of the river were within the diocese of Bath and Wells. In 1541 Henry VIII's government, as some recompense for the vast wealth which had been confiscated from the religious houses, established five new dioceses. One of these was the diocese of Gloucester, which included Bristol, north of the Avon, with the Benedictine abbey church of St Peter in Gloucester as its cathedral. A year later, in 1542, apparently as an afterthought or possibly because of pressure from prominent Bristolians, a new diocese of Bristol was created and Bristol was for the first time declared to be a city. A further reason for creating a diocese of Bristol may have been the fact that the town was regarded as a centre of religious dissent and had experienced fierce controversy during the 1530s between the supporters of reform and those who wished to uphold traditional doctrines. The new diocese consisted of all the parishes within Bristol, both north and south of the river, together with some adjacent parishes in south Gloucestershire, and the parish of Abbots Leigh which, as its name implies, had been a possession of St Augustine's abbey. Since these parishes were considered insufficient, the county of Dorset was taken from Salisbury diocese to become part of the new diocese of Bristol. The nearest part of Dorset is more than 40 miles from Bristol, and moreover, many of the Dorset parishes remained as 'peculiars' of the Dean of Salisbury cathedral and were thus exempt from episcopal supervision. This administratively-impossible arrangement was to remain in existence until 1836. For the cathedral of the Bristol diocese the former Augustinian abbey church was chosen, and the bishop's mansion and houses for the cathedral clergy and other members of the establishment were situated within the former monastic buildings.

The new cathedral church comprised only the chancel, transepts and side-chapels of the former Augustinian abbey. A major project to replace the twelfth-century nave with a larger structure had been begun by Abbot John Newland (abbot 1481–1515). Abbot Newland's <u>Chronicle</u> records that by the time of his death in 1515 the foundations of the new nave had been laid, and the new walls on the north and west sides had reached as high as the sills of the windows. Soon afterwards the old nave was demolished, but completion of the new nave had to wait until the later 19th century [J. Rogan, ed., <u>Bristol Cathedral: History & Architecture</u>, 2000, 36].

To accommodate the cathedral services and congregation within the truncated building, the high altar, bishop's throne and quire stalls were moved eastwards into what had been the Lady Chapel. A new quire screen was erected two bays east of the crossing, and the congregation was confined within the west end of the former quire. The new screen was from the former Carmelite friary and was given by Thomas White, a Bristol merchant. Most of it was destroyed during the 19th century restorations, but the surviving fragments contain the initials T W, together with the royal coat of arms of Henry VIII, and the arms of Prince Edward beneath the initials P E. The Berkeley chapel served as a vestry for the clergy. A solid wall was built west of the transepts to close the arch leading to the former nave. The small, self-contained church resulting from this reorganisation of the interior space was little larger than a college chapel. To listen to sermons the whole congregation moved west of the solid screen and into the space created within the two western bays of the chancel and in the transepts where a pulpit was installed. This cramped, inconvenient situation remained unchanged until the 19th century.

From the 1580s houses were built on the site of the former nave, and other houses for the canons and cathedral staff were crowded around Lower College Green, south of the cathedral, while successive bishops occupied the former abbots' lodging. These dwellings, like the former abbey, were supplied with water from a spring on Brandon Hill which was piped to a cistern and conduit in the centre of the cloisters. The cathedral records contain numerous entries concerning the care of the spring, the building which had been erected over it and the maintenance of the pipe and cistern [B.R.O. DC/E/11/1]. The former abbey burial ground to the north of the cathedral remained open and soon became known as College Green. On the Green stood the chapel of St Jordan, which was used as a schoolroom, together with an open-air pulpit. Leases granted by the Dean and Chapter in 1595 include references to 'the premises commonly called the Scholehouse in St Augustine's Greene and a certen place there called the Pulpitt and all the trees growinge in the same place called St Augustine's Greene' [B.R.O. DC/E/1/1/c, fol. 99v].

A slightly earlier and more detailed description of the Green emerges from the evidence provided concerning a skirmish which occurred there in 1579 between the retainers of two local gentlemen, Sir John Young and Hugh Smyth. The matter was treated seriously by the Elizabethan government, and the parties involved were summoned before the Court of Star Chamber. Evidence was given by numerous witnesses including Thomas Pynchinge, curate of St Mark's hospital and Christopher Pacye, a canon of the cathedral. The depositions of these and other witnesses are long and repetitive, but their evidence
concerning the Green can be summarised as follows:

> *All the witnesses agreed that the Green had been the burial ground for the abbey, and recalled that human skulls and bones had been found there, particularly when trees had been blown down in a storm. They also remembered that stone coffins and coffin-lids had been discovered, notably 'a coffyn of free stone near to a chappell called St Jordan his chappell which is now the Grammar School'. The witnesses also mentioned the pulpit or preaching place in the Green which was still in use. Canon Christopher Pacye, who had known the Green for more than 50 years, described it as an ancient pulpit 'where preachinge hath byn and yet is used'.*

[T.N.A. (P.R.O.) STAC 5/S14/26; STAC 5/S24/12. Joseph Bettey, 'Feuding Gentry and an Affray on College Green, Bristol, in 1579', B.G.A.S. Trans., 122, (2004), 153–60].

When the cathedral was established in 1542 the early Reformation changes had made little difference to the services of the Church. The Latin mass continued, the furnishings and decoration of churches remained unaltered and the clergy were still not permitted to marry. The major disruption of the ancient forms of worship and ecclesiastical organisation did not come until after the death of Henry VIII in 1547. The arrangements made for the new cathedral clearly envisaged a group of clergy living a communal life together with singing-men, choristers, schoolmasters, almsmen, servants and provision for charity very much like the Augustinian abbey which it replaced. Henry VIII clearly intended that the daily liturgy in the new cathedral should be accompanied by music and choral singing. The new foundation is described as a 'college' or community of clergy, a name which was to remain attached to the cathedral for many years and is still used for the open area north of the cathedral which was the former abbey cemetery and the site of St Jordan's chapel.

By the Foundation Charter of 4 June 1542 the new establishment was to consist of a Dean, six Canons , six Minor Canons, (one of whom was to be the Precentor and another the Sacrist), one Deacon, six Lay-clerks, one Master of the Choristers, two Masters of the Grammar School, four Almsmen, one Sub-Sacrist or Sexton, one Porter and Verger, one Butler and two Cooks.

The fact that that the first bishop, Paul Bush, was a former monk of Edington priory in Wiltshire and the first dean , William Snow, was an Augustinian canon from Bradenstoke, Wiltshire, no doubt ensured that during the early years of its life the cathedral community closely followed the pattern of life which had for so long been established by the religious houses. The original intention is evident from the details of the stipends allocated to the various members of the cathedral establishment on 10 June 1542.

T.N.A. (P.R.O.) E 135/24; B.R.O. DC/A/6/2/1; DC/A/7/1/1
L & P Hen. VIII 1542, 443 (9); 1093 (60); 1154 (60)

The booke of the erection of the kinges new college att Seynt Austen in Bristowe wt the names & porcon of lyvinge assigned to the Busshopp & all other officers appoynted for the accomplisshement of the same

Bishop	Paul Busshe bacheler of divinitie late rector of Edington	£100		
Deane	Wm Snowe late prior of Bradstok	£60		
6 prebendaries	John Gough DD	£20		
	Roger Edgeworthe DD	£20		
	Henry Morgan LLB	£20		
	Roger Hewez LLB	£20		
	Richard Browne LLB	£20		
	George Dogeon BD	£20		
6 petycanons there				
	Thomas Alen with 40 s for the sextons office	£12		
	John Browne	£10		
	William Penne	£10		
	John White	£10		
	John Dier	£10		
	William Bowden	£10		
Gospeller	John Somer	£6	13s	4d

Epistoler	Richard Bowier	£6	13s	4d

Singingmen	John More			
	Thomas Sexten			
	Nicholas Crepulgate	£6	13s	4d
	John Morgan			
	John Bedell			
	John Archarde			

Master of Quoristers	Thomas Sennes	£10		

6 Quoristers	John Tyson			
	Raphe Snowe			
	James Bonyfante		66s	8d
	Thomas Escourte			
	William Hungerford			
	Edmund Killinge			

William Edon schoolmaster	£13	6s	8d
Richard Lee usher	£6	13s	4d

4 poremen decayde in the kinges warres
orr in his grace's servyce

Richard Cooke			
John Rutter			
John Phillippes			
Adam Williams each	£6	13s	4d

Yearly in alms to pore householders	£20	

For making and mending highways	£20	

Repairs	£53	6s	8d

William Button steward of lands	£6	13s	4d
Griffyn Tyndale auditor	£10		
John Colyns porter for wages and diet	£6	13s	4d
Robert Brewer, butler	£6	0s	0d
William Nutte 'chiffe cooke'	£6	0s	0d
David Apwatkyn under cook		66s	8d
Thomas Cutter 'the catour there'	£6	0s	0d

Extraordinary charges	£20	

All charges £5570 over and beside the bishop's portion

there is added to bear tenths	£57		
first fruits	£28	10s	0d

So to bear all charges and bear tenths and first fruits
it may please the King's Majesty to endow the church
with   £655 10s 0d
Item bishop's portion before not charged with £34 6–8
to him allowed for the tenth   £366 13s 4d

     Total   **£1022** **3s** **4d**

[signed] Richard Ryche

Statutes of Bristol Cathedral 1544, translated by Canon J.P. Norris in 1870

Although the Foundation Charter establishing the cathedral was published on 4 June 1542, it was not until 5 July 1544 that the Cathedral Statutes were issued. The 38 Statutes laid down rules for all aspects of the life of the cathedral, dealing with its property, personnel, governance, alms-giving, worship, sermons and discipline. It is clear from the Statutes that the King envisaged a community of clergy, with their lay assistants and servants, living together in a fashion not greatly differing from a medieval monastic house. They were to live a communal life, and eat at a common table. Their major purpose was to be the maintenance of a constant service of prayer and praise to God. Some details of this original scheme did not long survive the religious changes which rapidly followed Henry VIII's death in 1547. Major modifications followed the licence allowing the clergy to marry, since this inevitably disrupted the idea of a communal life. The introduction of simpler services in English in place of the Latin Mass, and the legislation ordering the removal of statues, lights, figures of saints in stained glass, all brought changes to the cathedral community. Nonetheless, the Statutes remained in force and continued to regulate most aspects of the life of the cathedral. The Statutes were in Latin and it was not until 1870 that Canon John Pilkington Norris, an accomplished classical scholar, produced an authoritative translation in English. They are too long to reproduce in full, but the following extracts are taken from Canon Norris's translation.

B.R.O. DC/A/7/1/5

Letters Patent 4 June 1544

......

Henry the Eighth, by the grace of God, of England, France, and Ireland, Defender of the Faith, and supreme head upon earth of the Church of England and Ireland: to all sons of holy mother Church, to whose notice this present writing shall come, greeting.

Whereas it has seemed good unto us, and to our nobles, and to our whole senate, styled the Parliament, moved hereunto, as we trust, by God Himself, to suppress and abolish, and convert to better uses, the monasteries now existing throughout the kingdom, for their grave and manifold enormities, and for divers other good causes and reasons; judging it more conformable to the Divine will, and more for the interest of Christianity, that where ignorance and superstition used to prevail, there the pure worship of God should flourish and the holy Gospel of Christ should be diligently and sincerely preached; and that, for the greater increase of the Christian faith and piety, the youth of our kingdoms should be instructed in good literature, and poor persons be ever maintained; we have erected and constituted in the place of those monasteries divers churches, whereof some we will to be called Cathedral churches, and others Collegiate churches: for the better rule and government whereof, we have caused the following Laws and Statutes to be prescribed, which the Dean, and the Canons of both orders, as well as the other officers and poor who shall belong to the said churches, ought to submit unto and obey, and be ruled and governed by the same, as being decreed and ordained by ourselves; which if they shall observe, a great increase of piety in this kingdom will, as we trust in God, accrue; and then our expectation and prayer in erecting those churches for the honour of Almighty God, and the increase of the Christian faith, and in furnishing the same with divers orders of officers, will in no wise be disappointed.

Statute I
The Number of those who are to be maintained in the Cathedral Church of Bristol.

In the first place, we decree and ordain, that there be for ever in the said church one Dean, six Canons, six Minor Canons, whereof one shall be a Sacrist, another shall be Deacon, another Sub-Deacon; six Lay-Clerks, one Master of the Choristers, six Choristers, two Masters to instruct the boys in grammar, whereof one shall be the Head-Master, the other the Under-Master; four poor people to be maintained at the charges of the said church; one Under-Sacrist, one Door-keeper, who shall also be Verger, one Butler, one Cook, one Under-Cook.

Statute II
Of the Qualifications, Election, and Admission of the Dean.

Statute III
The Dean's Oath.

Statute IV
Of the Office of Dean.

Whereas it behoves a Dean to be vigilant (like the eye in the body, ever looking out for the rest of the members); we will and ordain, that the Dean, for the time being, shall with all diligence govern, and shall influence, chide, convince, and beseech the Canons, and all other officers of the church, instant in season and out of season, as one that watcheth for the good of the flock committed to his charge. Let him particularly take care that divine services be performed with all decency, that sermons be preached upon the appointed days, that the boys be fruitfully instructed, that alms to the poor be distributed, and that he do himself faithfully discharge all those duties wherewith he is intrusted.

Moreover, it is requisite, that the Dean, as often as he is resident, do maintain a sober and competent household, and relieve the poor with alms; and herein we charge him upon his conscience, that he set an example of honesty and frugality in all things. If the Dean be so miserly as to cause remark, the Bishop shall correct him; and if the

Canons be so, the Dean shall reprehend them. He shall also correct and punish according to the statutes, all others, who shall be blameworthy and slothful in their duties.

Statute V
Of the Visitation of the Lands.

Statute VI
Letting of Lands & Tenements on Lease.

Statute VII
Concerning the surrendering of Goods to the Dean

Statute VIII
Concerning the Residence of the Dean

We will and ordain, that the Dean shall always reside in his own church, except some lawful impediment prevent him. ....
Moreover, we grant leave to the Dean to be absent from our Church one hundred days, consecutive or inconsecutive, in each year, to visit his cures and other benefices, if he hath any, and to dispatch his own other private businesses. ......

Statute IX
Of Obedience to be yielded to the Dean

Statute X
Concerning the Qualities, Election, and Admission of the Canons.

Statute XI
Of a Canon's Oath

Statute XII
Of the Residence of the Canons

From the outset it was recognised that the Canons might hold other appointments in the Church, and the Statute allows them leave of absence for 80 days each year 'to visit their cures or other benefices, if they have any, and to mind their private concerns.

Statute XIII
Of Sermons to be preached in our Church.

Because the Word of God is a lanthorn unto our feet, we ordain and will, that the Dean and our Canons – we beseech them by the mercies of God – be diligent, in season and out of season, in sowing the Word of God, as elsewhere, so more especially in our cathedral church.

And we will, that every Canon shall every year make four sermons at least to the people in the church aforesaid, in English, either by himself or by others, and that upon the Lord's Days; to wit, once between the Nativity of Christ and the Feast of the Annunciation of the Blessed Virgin Mary [*25 March*]; once between the Feast of the Blessed Virgin Mary and the Nativity of John [*24 June*]; once between the Nativity of St John and the Feast of Michael [*29 Sept.*]; and once between the Feast of Michael and the Nativity of Christ; so that almost no one Lord's Day in the whole year shall pass without a sermon. Also, we will, that the Dean, either by himself or by his proxy, shall preach every year, in our English tongue, at Easter, upon Corpus Christi day, and at Christmas.

....

Statute XIV
Of the Canons' Table.

Statute XV
Of the Salary of the Dean and Canons.

The Dean was to receive £27 per annum, and each Canon was to receive £7 16s 8d per annum.

Statute XVI
Of the Election of Office Bearers.

Statute XVII
Of the Office of Sub-Dean.

Statute XVIII
Of the Office of a Receiver.

Statute XIX
Of the Treasurer's Office.

Statute XX
Of the Quality, Election, and Admission of the Minor Canons.

This statute ordered that there should be six Minor Canons and Six Lay Clerks together with a Deacon and Sub-Deacon. They were to be men skilled in singing so that God might be worshipped 'with hymns, psalms, and continual prayers'.

Statute XXI
Of the Oath of the Officers.

Statute XXII
Of the Residence of the Officers.

Statute XXIII
Of the Precentor & his Office.

We decree and ordain, that by the Dean or, he being absent, by the Sub-Dean and the Chapter, out of the Minor Canons, one older than the rest, and eminent among them, both for behaviour and learning, shall be chosen Precentor; whose office it shall be, decorously to direct the singingmen in the church, and to lead the rest and be their guide by voice, that no discord may arise in the chanting. He shall be obeyed, in all that concerns the business of the choir, by all the Minor Canons and Clerks, and others who shall sing in the church; whatever he shall direct to be read or sung, they shall promptly obey.

Beside, he shall truly and impartially mark the absence from Divine service, as well of the Dean and Canons, as of all who serve in the choir; of which absence he shall give a true account every fortnight in the chapter-house, before the Canons there present.

And if any of the minor Canons or Clerks shall give a reason of his absence, it shall prevail, if the Dean or, in his absence, the Sub-Dean approve it.

He shall also see that the books for the service of the choir be well cared for and preserved. And, in fine, as oft as he shall be absent from our church he shall substitute a deputy, who shall faithfully perform the Precentor's office.

All which, by a solemn oath he shall promise that he will faithfully perform.

Statute XXIV
Of the Sacrist & Sub-Sacrist.

Statute XXV
Of the Choristers & their Masters.

Statute XXVI
Of the Boys' Masters in Grammar.

Statute XXVII
Of the Poor Men & their Duty.

This laid down the tasks to be performed by the four poor men who were to be nominated by the Crown from former royal servants or soldiers 'oppressed with want and poverty, broken down, or maimed in the wars, weakened with age, or any other ways disabled, and reduced to want or misery'. They were to be maintained at the cathedral, and were expected to take part in the daily services and to work on cleaning the church, tolling the bells, lighting the candles and other such duties.

Statute XXVIII
Of the Inferior Officers of the Church.

Statute XXIX
Of the Common Table of all the Officers.

Orders for the common dining arrangement of Minor Canons and all other members of the cathedral community.

Statute XXX
Of the Vestments of the Officers called Liveries.

........All Minor Canons, and the Upper Grammar Master, four yards of cloth for their gowns, at 5s. per yard. The Deacon, Sub-Deacon, each of the Clerks, the Lower Grammar Master, shall receive for their garments three yards of cloth, at the rate of 4s. 6d. And the other officers, that is, the Sub-Sacrist, Butler, Door-Keeper, and the Cook, every one shall receive for himself three yards of cloth for his garments, at the price of 3s. 4d. Each of the Choristers, and the Sub-Cook, for their garments, two yards and a half, price 3s. 4d. Lastly, each of the poor men shall receive for his garments three yards of cloth, at 3s 4d. .....This cloth and these livery garments, the Dean or, in his absence, the Sub-Dean, together with the Receiver for the time being ought every year to provide; and they shall deliver to every one their portions of cloth before Christmas, that they may celebrate the birth-day of our Saviour Jesus Christ with new clothes and renewed spirits: but the poor men shall always wear on the left shoulder of their gowns a rose made of red silk; and when they go either into church or elsewhere abroad, they shall every where walk in the said gowns.

Statute XXXI
Of the Salaries of the Officers in our Church.

We ordain and will, that out of the common stock of our church, beside their commons and liveries before assigned, certain stipends be paid quarterly to all the officers of our church, by the Treasurer, by equal portions, in manner following: that is, to each Minor-Canon for his share, £5 2s. To the Head Grammar Master, £8 8s. 8d. To the Master of the Choristers, £5 7s. To the Lower Grammar Master, 59s. 2d. To the Sub-Deacon, 59s. 2d. To the Sacrist, 26s. 8d. To every Clerk, 59s. 2d. To the Butler, 58s. To the Door-Keeper, 58s. To the Cook, 58s. To the Choristers, 15s. To each of the four poor Men, £6 3s. 4d. To the Sub-Dean, 26s. 8d. To the Precentor, 26s. 8s. To the Steward or Clerk of the lands, 53s. 4d. To the Auditor, 53s. 4d. To the Sub-Cook, 26s. 6d. To the Sub-Sacrist, 23s. 4d.

Statute XXXII
Of the Celebration of Divine Service.

This ordered that 'constant prayers and unceasing supplication' should be offered, 'and that every day the praise of God may be celebrated with song and rejoicing'. Unlike the Augustinian canons, however, the clergy, lay-clerks and choristers were not obliged to sing their offices by night.

Statute XXXIII
Of the Common Treasury & Keeping of the Seal & Muniments.

Statute XXXIV
Of the Audit of the Accounts every Year.

Statute XXXV
Of Correcting Excesses.

Statute XXXVI
Concerning Alms.

Generous contributions were to be made to charity, including £40 per annum to be distributed for the poor and needy, and £20 per annum to be given for the repair of highways and bridges. Alms were also to be given to the poor living on the lands and properties of the Dean and Chapter 'lest our church seem always to be reaping from its estates and never sowing'.

Statute XXXVII
Of Keeping Chapters.

Chapters to be held at least once a fortnight.

Statute XXXVIII
Of the Visitation of the Church

There is no work so piously begun, so prosperously continued, or so happily consummated, which is not soon undermined by carelessness, and subverted by negligence. There are no statutes so sacred, and firmly made, but in length of time they pass into oblivion and contempt, if there be not constant care and zeal for religion. And that this may never happen, or ensue in our church, we, trusting in the faith and diligence of the Bishop of Bristol for the time being, have constituted him to be the Visitor of our cathedral of Bristol, willing and commanding, that according to his Christian faith, and earnest zeal for religion, he watch, and take care that those statutes and ordinances which we have made for our church be inviolably observed; that the possessions, and the spiritual as well as temporal affairs may flourish in a prosperous state; that the rights, liberties, and privileges, be preserved and defended. ....

Moreover, we will, that the Dean, at the common charges of the church, prepare and set before the Bishop visiting, and attended with eight persons, two entertainments at most within the lodgings of our church. ....

THE BISHOP, DEAN AND CANONS OF
THE NEW CATHEDRAL

Paul Bush, the first Bishop of Bristol

Paul Bush (1490–1558) was born at Dilton, near Westbury, Wiltshire, the second son of William Bush who leased a farm and fulling mill from the monks at Edington Priory. His elder brother, John, continued to live at Dilton throughout his life, but Paul was educated at Edington and Oxford. He graduated B.A. in 1518, and remained at Oxford where he established a reputation in the study of theology and medicine, and for Latin poetry. In 1525 he returned to the priory at Edington, and during the next few years produced several theological and devotional books. In 1538 he became head or 'rector' of the priory, but a few months later was obliged

Fig. 2 The medieval pulpitum or screen which came from the Carmelite
friary and was erected in the cathedral soon after its creation in 1542. This drawing by
J.H. Clarke of 1830 shows the west side of the screen, with the organ of 1683, the
figures of the prophets in the niches and the stairway to the pulpit. The screen was
removed during the re-ordering of c1860.
(© Bristol's Museums, Galleries & Archives)

to surrender the house into the hands of Cromwell's commissioners. When the
diocese of Bristol was established on 4 June 1542, Paul Bush was chosen to become
the first bishop, and was consecrated on 25 June 1542.

Although he was a considerable scholar and theologian, Paul Bush's career at
Oxford and as a monk at Edington had not equipped him to deal with all the
pressures of his new and unwieldy diocese. He seems to have spent much time in the
peaceful seclusion of his manor house at Abbots Leigh rather than in the episcopal
mansion beside the cathedral in Bristol. Certainly several of his surviving letters
and documents were endorsed as written 'from my maner of Lyghe' or 'In manerio
nostres de Lighe'. He was conservative and traditional in his religious views,
although he supported the introduction of the Bible in English and accepted with
some misgivings, the Books of Common Prayer of 1549 and 1552. When clerical
marriage was permitted after 1547, Bush was quick to take advantage of the new
freedom. His wife was Edith Ashley of Monkton Up Wimborne, Dorset. The Ashleys
were a land-owning family, and Paul Bush's sister, Margaret, was married to one
of Edith Ashley's brothers. In 1550–51 Bush was forced to face a demand to
surrender Abbots Leigh to the government. John Dudley, Earl of Warwick and later
Duke of Northumberland, had triumphed over Edward Seymour, Duke of Somerset,

for control of the young King, Edward VI. Now he needed to reward his supporters, among them Sir George Norton who desired the episcopal manor of Abbots Leigh. In the face of this threat to the endowments of his bishopric, Paul Bush began to grant long leases of the episcopal manors. In this he was following the precedent set by late-medieval abbots in their unsuccessful attempts to avoid royal confiscation of their properties. In January 1548 Bush granted a lease of his valuable manor of Ashleworth (Glos.) to Thomas Seymour, Lord Sudeley, for 70 years. The manor of Minsterworth was leased to Sir John Thynne and Cromhall manor was granted to Thomas Throckmorton. The bishop's manors and lands in the lower Severn valley, including the rich manor of Almondsbury, were also leased to laymen for long terms. Other leases were granted to members of his own and his wife's family. In June 1550 he leased the Dorset manor of Fifehead Magdalen to Henry Ashley of Wimborne St Giles for 80 years, and later in 1550 he leased the manor of Horfield to another of his wife's relatives, John Hawles of Monkton Up Wimborne (Dors). Earlier, while Paul Bush was head of the Bonhommes' house at Edington, he had appointed his elder brother, John Bush, to the post of steward of the monastery's estates in Wiltshire. As bishop of Bristol he granted a lease of the manor of Abbots Leigh to his brother in 1550. Such leases, however, counted for little with the Duke of Northumberland, a ruthless Tudor nobleman, and the pressure upon Paul Bush to surrender the manor of Abbots Leigh continued unabated. With the support of the Dean and Chapter of his cathedral, Bush delayed matters for as long as he could. Finally, in February 1551, he was summoned before the Privy Council, but he still refused to yield up the property of his bishopric. The record of the Privy Council meeting gives an account of this dramatic encounter, and of the remarkable bravery with which Bush faced all the majesty of the Privy Council in the splendid palace at Greenwich.

The Bishop's Dispute with the Privy Council 1550–1

Letter to the Bishop of Bristol in January 1552

A.P.C. NS, 3, 1550–2, 210

A lettre to the Busshop of Bristoll, mervaileng that he hathe not graunted the Kinges Majesties request toochinge the manour of Lie, consideringe he was offred sufficient recompence, and therfore the Kinges Majestie eftsones requireth him not to denye it, &c.

This daie the Busshop of Bristoll was before the counsaill tooching his aunswere to be made to the Kinges Majesties request for Sir George Norton, knight, who desired upon reasonable recompence to have of the Busshop the manour of Lie, in Somerset, which manour the same Bishop affirmed that he had graunted in lease unto his brother [John] Bushe. Marie, he saied he had don it upon this condicion, that if his successour, the Busshop that hereaftershallbe, woll dwell upon yt him self, that than Busshe shulde suffer him to have it, taking of him recompence for the chardges alreadie bestowed upon it, which he thought had cost him cc ^{li} above the rent lymited in his lease. And albeit that the Counsaill perswaded the Busshop as muche as was possible to tender the Kinges Majesties request in this case, yet wolde he in no wise yelde therunto, but departed, refusing to commune of the matter.

The Tudor government was not deterred by Bush's adamant refusal to discuss the matter, and soon after the bishop, together with the Dean and Chapter of the cathedral, received a sharp reminder of the Privy Council's power. The Council wrote to remind the recalcitrant clerics that it was the King's own wish that they should relinquish ownership of Abbots Leigh, with a strong hint that harsh penalties would follow any further refusal, leaving them in no doubt as to what they must do.

B.R.O. DC/E/1/1

...Nothing doubting of your good conformitie in that behalf hath willed us on his Majesties behalf to make request unto you for possession. Wee doe therefore desire and pray you with convenient diligence to procede thereunto, and advertisinge us of your doinges, wee shall not fayle to make report to his highness of your redy mynde and good disposcion to the satisfaction of his Majesties requests accordingly

Your loving Frendes

On 2 May 1551 Paul Bush surrendered ownership of Abbots Leigh to the Crown, reserving some rights in the manor during his lifetime, but with the reversion to Sir George Norton. Shortly the grant was ratified by the Dean and Chapter in the cathedral Chapter House in the presence of Edmund Gorges and Hugh Denys, the local commissioners or agents for the Duke of Northumberland. The power and ruthless determination of those who rose to the top positions in Tudor governments is well illustrated by this ceremony. The long history of the Bristol Chapter House can have witnessed few scenes more humiliating to the Church dignitaries than this, as the Duke of Northumberland's men compelled them to sign away one of the endowments of the diocese [Joseph Bettey, 'St Augustine's Abbey and the Manor of Abbots Leigh', in Joseph Bettey, ed., <u>Historic Churches & Church Life in Bristol</u>, 2001, 98–108].*

Bush apparently welcomed the restoration of Catholicism by Queen Mary in 1553, but was in an impossible position as a married bishop, even though his wife died in October 1553 and was buried in Bristol cathedral. Bush resigned his bishopric and became rector of Winterbourne in south Gloucestershire. There he lived in considerable style with several servants, resuming his earlier life of scholarship. In the seclusion of Winterbourne Paul Bush revealed his true feelings in a notable defence of Catholic doctrines. This was addressed to Margaret Burgess, the wife of a local clothier, who had shocked him by her ignorance of the traditional teachings of the church and was entitled <u>A brefe Exhoration</u>. The book contained a spirited defence of the Mass and of the doctrine of the Real Presence against 'the rasshe fantastycall myndes of the blynd and ignorante'. He died at Winterbourne on 11 October 1558, and was buried near his wife at the east end of the north aisle of the cathedral. The inscription on her grave is no longer visible, but read 'Of your charyte pray for the soule of Edith Bushe, otherwise Ashley, who deceased 8 October 1553'. Paul Bush's tomb was erected according to his instructions and depicts him as a scantily-clad, emaciated figure, lying on a rush mat, holding a *pastoral staff and with his head resting on a jewelled mitre, under a low classical canopy. The Latin inscription reads:*

> *'Hic jacet Dominus Paulus Bushe, primus huius ecclesiae episcopus qui obit xi die Octobus Anno Domini MDLVIII, aetatis suae LXVIII, Cuius Animae Propitietur Christus, Amen'*

His will shows his continuing attachment to the Catholic faith, as well as making elaborate arrangements for his funeral.

Paul Bush's will

T.N.A. (P.R.O.) P.C.C. Reg. 3 Welles

In the name of the Father and of the sonne and of tholly Goost Amen. The xx ^{ti} Daye of September in the yere of our lorde Jesu Christe M^l vc.lviij^{ti} I Paule Busshe late bisshopp of the Cittie of Bristowe, and presently parsonne of Winterbourne in the Countie of Gloucester, being in helthe of bodie and parfite off mynde and remembraunce praise be to allmighti god doo ordaine and make this my last wille and testament in manner and fourme as herafter followith, that is to say. First I commentd and bequeath my soule to allmighti god my moost merciful saviour Jesus Christe Who hath redeamed the same with the price of his moost preciouse bludde. And by vertue therof I doo faithefullie hoope thorough his great mercye that he will deliver me from thandes and Wicked mallice of my mortall enemy the devill and all his Sathanicall power. Beseching the blessed virgin and mother of our Saviour Jesu Christe and all thollye company of heaven to praye with me and to praye for me. Secondlie allso when it shall please allmighti god to take my soule out of this wretched and fallible World I bequeathe my bodie decentlie to be buryed in the northe side of the hie aulter of the Cathedral Church of Bristowe fast by the side of thaulter there standing now; and there a tombe of free stone to be made to helpe to cloase in the said aulter in thisle there. Item I give and bequeathe iiij^{or} markes of laufull monney of Englande to be paide in allmes uppon the poore peple the daye of my buriall, and so muche more at the daye of my monnethis mynde in penny doole. Item I wille that the Deane of the Cathedrall Churche of tholly Trinitie in Bristowe being present in the quyer there at Dirge and Requiem masse the daye of my buriall (singing the saide Requiem masse) to have iijs. iiijd. for his paynes. Item I give to everye prebendarye of the same churche being there present in the like fourme twoo shillinges. Item I give to every ministre there being present of the same churche, and preest in like fourme xijd. And to every secular minister viijd. And to every chorester being there present iiijd. Item I give to my parrishe preest off Winterbourne, and to the parrishe preest of Frampton Cotterell to eche of them vs. to conducte my bodie in their surplesses to the Cathedrall Churche of Bristowe, and to eche of their clerkes bearing the crosse in their surplices to the said Churche xxd. Item passing by the Churche of Stapleton my bodie there pawsing whiles the preest of Stapleton saith De profundis and castith hally water uppon it to have viijd. For his labour. Item I give to xx^{ti} of the poorest housholders Within my parishe off Winterbourne vjd to eche house. Item I give to the under sexten or belringer of the Cathedral Churche of Bristowe xijd. Item imprimis I geve and bequeath to my suster

Elizabeth Busshe, my brother John Busshes wif whose soule Jesu pardon vili. xiijs. iijd. of lauful monneye of Englaunde and my golden ringe with the turkes, and also my skarlett ryding Chymer. Item I give to my nevewe John Busshe my brothers heire apparraunte my signett of gold graved with a boore to remayn alwaies to his right heires as inheritaunce. And to my Nece Isabel my hoope of gold. Item I give my nephew William xxxs. of money. Item I give to my nephew Edwarde xxs. of money. And to my Nece Isabell my said nephewes wif, I geve xxs. of money and my longe Chamblett gowne. Item I give to my Nece Elizabeth Busshe my brothers naturall daughter my gold ringe graven with theis Wourdes, Sub potestate viri eris, and my longe damaske gowne. Item I give to my godsonne Peter Bussh xls. of money. Item I geve to my cousen Katherine Wiltshire xs. Item I give to my cousen Anne Okes tenne shillings. Item I geve to my brother in lawe John Jaques of London and to my naturall suster Margery his wife all that my due debits Which Marye Herbertes Wife vnto Mathewe Herbert late deceased owith vnto me the saide Paule the daye of the making herof uppon the condemnation for the rentis of my late parsonnages Porteburye Tikenham and Cliven. Item I give unto Oswalde Barteley of Edington my olde servante xs. for a token of remembraunce. Item I give to everye one of his children living at the day of my buriall xijd. to pray for my soule. Item I give to my other old trustie servante Philipp Griffiths a pece of golde of xxs. for a token of remembraunce. Item I give to everye one of my men household servantes Which hathe been in service with me one hoale yeres vli. of moneye and a blacke coote clothe. Item I give to my Woman of my kitchen xxs. and a hole quarters Wages. Item I give to Edith Coole my Cow Which I bought of Streate. Also I wille that my bargayn made with maister John Seymour and mestres Jane his wife for the somme of cccc and fiftie powndes of good and laufull money of Englande for my Mannour house of Eastlinges courte in Frampton Cotterell and the demaynes therof and for my seaven tenamentis there, shall stande in good force and strength. And the said somme of monney to be receaved by me the said Paule or by my executours or assignees and to be imployed in manner and fourme following that is to saye, one hundred poundes to discharge my brother's debtis. To Mr Jenyns my deere frende Mr Brounkers sonne in lawe. Also I give and bequeathe to my Nece Elizabeth my brothers naturall daughter an hundred poundes of the said iiijC and 1.li. so that she be ruled and ordred after thaduise and counsaill of my trustie executors touching her marriage. Item I likewise will and ordayn, that if god graunt me lif, that suche parsonnes to whom my nephew John Bushe [sic] dothe owe any money or debtis unto, yf they will come unto me or to my executors or assignees after my death, and will agree reasonable with us, uppon consideraciouns, Thenne I and myn executors or assignees shall see them paid as Wee shall thincke good hereafter or els to sett them at their libertie. Item I give to my brother in lawe Mr Hawles of Dorset shire, one pece of gold of xxs. for a token of remembraunce, and to my suster mestres Margaret his wife one dosen of diapour napkynnes. Item I geve to my veray loving friende Mr David Harris of Bristowe, one pece of golde of xxs. for a token of remembraunce. Item I geve Sir Thomas Bede of Frampton my clothe coote with buttons of silke. Item I geve towardes the reparacionnes of the Channcell of Wynterbourne, the fiftie and three shillings and foure pence Whiche Mr Robert Brodestone doth owe me as by a bille of his hande playnelie doth appeare. Item, I give to the prisonners in Newgate of Bristowe vjs. viijd. Item I give xxs. to thalmes houses off Bristowe to be divided amonge them. Item the Residewe of all my plate goods Cattell and debtis moveable and unmoveable, all kynde of Corne not before bequeathed or gevyn I wille to be imployed and distributed in manner and forme as herafter dothe followe. First, I will and ordayn that my loving Executors shall Well and truelye after my departing out of this world, by even and egall [equal] parcelles and porcions divide all my saide plate goods cattalles corne and debtis and all that is taken and reputed to be my propre goodes or substaunce into three severall partes of iuste [just] and like value. And the firste parte of the saide three partes I wille to be imployed to beare the charges and costes of my funeralles as it is above mencioned and rehersed. And the whiche remayneth of the said firste parte to pay my foresaid Legacies Which I have bequeathed amonge my freendes and others to pray for my soule. Also I give and bequeathe the seconde parte of the said three partes thus egallie [equally] divided as is beforerehersed to my nephew William Bushe, to my nevewe Edwarde Bushe my brother's naturall sonnes to my Nece Isabell my nephew John Busshes wif and to my godsonne Peter Busshe to Thomas Busshe to Robert Busshe to Dorothee Busshe and to as manny of my said nephew John Busshes children as shalbe living at the tyme and day of my departing out of this World. And likewise I give and bequeathe the last and thirde parte of theis three partes and porcionnes, thus egallie divided as is aforesaide to my deere beloved freende Mr Henry Brounker esquier of the countie of Wiltes, to my nephew John Busshe to my neview Walter Busshe and to my Nece Elizabeth Busshe my brothers naturall daughter. And I ordayne and make and appointe my said Worshipfull freende Mr Harry Brunker aforesaide and my saide nephewes John Busshe and Walter Bushe my moost true and laufull executours. And to thintent that this my laste Wille and testament may be the better fulfilled kept and perfourmed and my trustie executours better helped and assisted as occasion shall neede and require. I doo ordayn and make my Worshipfull and trustee freende Mr Archdeacon Cotterell of the Cathedrall Church of Bath and Wells, and my very assured freend Mr Thomas Silke of the Cathedrall Churche of Bristowe my moost trustie and faaithefull overseers of thexecution of this my last Will and testament. And I give and bequeathe to either of them for their paynes taking in this bihaulf three poundes six shillings and eightpence of laufull money of Englande. Thus I ende and conclude my last wille and testament subscribed with my hande and sealed with my Seale the daye and yeare above Written. And theis personnes Whose names doo here folowe I have desired to bear witnes to the same, per me Paulum Busshe Rectorem de Wynterbourne. By me John Willy of Bristow, Chamberlayn, per me Thomas Silke clericum.

Proved at London 1st December 1558. John Bushe and Walter Bushe, the executors named in the will, administrators.
[J.H. Bettey, 'Paul Bush, the first bishop of Bristol', B.G.A.S. Trans., 106, 1988, 169–72].

Many of the early canons had strong connections with Bristol and since the cathedral had limited endowments, many continued to hold other benefices or ecclesiastical offices. Roger Edgeworth, a quotation from whose sermons was used at the beginning of this volume, had been prior of the Kalendars' Guild in All Saints' church 1526–8 and thereafter amassed a string of appointments. He was a lively, popular preacher and a staunch opponent of reformers within the Church. During the fierce theological disputes between rival preachers in Bristol during the early 1530s, Edgeworth attacked 'the heretics that soweth cockle and ill seeds among the poor, settyng forth sectes and divisions'. He also alleged that the spread of Protestant views and the time spent by the laity in studying and debating the meaning of Scripture was damaging the vital commercial and trading life of Bristol.

> 'I have known manye in this towne, that studienge divinitie, hath killed a merchant and some of other occupations by their busy labours in the Scriptures, hath shut up the shoppe windows'.

Edgeworth became one of the first prebendaries of Bristol when the cathedral was founded on 4 June 1542, and the text survives of a sequence of 20 sermons which he preached in the cathedral on St Peter's First Epistle during the next few years. As well as canon of Bristol he was a canon and chancellor of Wells, and a canon of Salisbury as well as being pluralist incumbent of several parish benefices. By the end of Henry VIII's reign he was receiving an annual income of some £230, ranking him among the wealthiest of the clergy. He was totally unsympathetic to the Reformation changes of Edward VI's reign, although he suggests in one of his sermons that these were welcomed in Bristol.

> I preached ...at the Cathedrall Church there (Bristol)... in this also I was manie times and longe discontinued by the odious schisme that was now lately, and by the doers of the same'.

The Bristol cathedral <u>Computa</u> *show that he continued to receive his annual stipend of £20 as a prebend, and that he acted as sub-dean in 1550 and 1553–4, and as treasurer in 1544 and again in 1552 [B.R.O. DC/A/9/1/1, fols. 22v, 43]. Edgeworth welcomed the return of Catholicism in 1553, but refused to accept the Elizabethan Settlement in 1559, resigning his offices shortly before he died in 1560 [*<u>Oxford D.N.B.</u>*; Roger Edgeworth,* <u>Sermons very fruitful, godly and learned</u>*, ed. by Janet Wilson (1993)].*

Thomas Silke had been vicar of St Leonard's, Bristol since 1529, and as well as his Bristol canonry held the livings of Frampton Cotterell (Glos), Banwell (Som),Cheriton (Devon), and Marston St Laurence (Northants). Christopher Pacy was rector of St Werburgh's Bristol. Richard Browne had been the bishop of Worcester's representative in Bristol, and George Dogeon had been vicar of Temple and also became a canon of Wells, vicar of Chew Magna (Som), and rector of Langton Matravers (Dors).

Sale of Stone from the Cathedral 1551

In 1551 a transaction was entered into by the Dean, John Whiteare or Whythere, together with three of the canons, which reflects little credit on the probity of those involved. The canons were John Cotterell, who was the bishop's chancellor, Thomas Sylke, who had been vicar of St Leonard's, Bristol from 1529 and prior of the influential Guild of Kalendars based in All Saints' church, Bristol from 1540 until its dissolution in 1549, and Roger Edgeworth, a learned and distinguished preacher.

Without the knowledge of the bishop, Paul Bush, they entered into an agreement with Sir William Sharington, treasurer of the Bristol Mint from 1546, to sell the stone which still remained on the site of the unfinished project to rebuild the nave of the former abbey church, now the cathedral. The old nave had been demolished and work on its enlarged replacement had been started under Abbot John Newland (abbot 1481–1515). The Computa *or account rolls which survive for 1491–2 and 1511–12 show that large quantities of stone for the new nave were brought from the quarries on Dundry hill and elsewhere, and Newland's* Roll *or chronicle for 1515 records that the walls had reached 'as high as the cills of the windows on the north side and at the west end' [I.H. Jeayes, ed., Abbot Newland's Roll',* B.G.A.S. Trans., *XIV, 1889–90, 130]. The work inevitably required large quantities of stone. In 1491–2 the delivery of 40 loads of freestone from Dundry Hill quarries at 2s 6d per load is recorded, and in 1511–12 30 loads at 2s 6d are listed in the accounts. Poorer quality stone known as 'Ragges' was also obtained, and 20 loads were purchased in 1491–2 [G.Beachcroft & A. Sabin, eds.,* Two Compotus Rolls of St Augustine's Abbey, Bristol 1491–2, 1511–12, *B.R.S., IX, 1938, ix, 42, 60–1; IX, 27, 43; 287]. It was this stone which had been accumulated for the building project which was surreptitiously sold by the Dean and three canons in 1551.*

Sir William Sharington had been involved in various illegal transactions at the Mint, including the supply of under-weight coins. In 1549 he was arrested and imprisoned, but was pardoned and released after the payment of a heavy fine. He is an example of the clever, ruthless opportunists who were able to profit from the dangerous political conditions of the time. In 1540 he had been able to purchase from the Crown the former house of the Augustinian canonesses at Lacock, together with many of the estates [J.H. Bettey, The Suppression of the Monasteries in the West Country, *1989, 134–5]. Why he sought to purchase the stone from the partially-built nave of Bristol cathedral, including that already built into its walls, is unknown. The matter only became public in 1559, five years after Sharington's death , when his brother, Henry Sharington, as executor of his will and administrator of his goods, brought a suit against the then Dean, Henry Joliffe, and the three canons in the Court of Requests. Sir William Sharington had apparently paid for and carried away some of the stone, and his brother now demanded to be allowed to carry away what remained. The suit was heard in the Court of Requests in 1559 and 1562, and although the final outcome is unknown, the depositions made before the Court are informative.*

T.N.A. (P.R.O.) Court of Requests 2/271/25
5 May 1559

Henry Sharington administrator of the goods of Sir William Sharington, Knight, That whereas in 5 Edward VI one [John] Whiteheare then deane of the Cathedrall Church of Bristol with thassent of his Chapiter and of the Bishop for the time being for and in consideration of £40 paid by the said Sir William certen superfluous and ruinous walls of stone standing nigh besides the said Cathedrall Church taken and carried away by the said Sir William his assignes at his free will after which time now about 5 yeares now last past the said Sir William died intestate, after whose decease the administration of all the goods of the said Sir William was committed to your subject being the brother. So it is that your said subject hath divers tymes made request to one Henry Jolif now Dean of the said Churche and unto the Chapiter of the same Church either to permit him to take and carry away the stones and stufe according to the bargain or to repay to your said subject the said £40 but they utterly refuse etc.. Prays writ of Privy Seal.

The Answer of Henry Jolye [Joliffe]

Sayth that the Church called the Cathedrall Church of the Blessed Trinity besydes Bristowe sumtyme as a monasterye and now as a Cathedrall Church ys of a longe and ancient continuance and the same being very lytell to receive the great multitude of people commonly repayring thither for Gods service, before thys tyme mindinge to enlarge the same to theire greate costes and charges buylded certen building with free stone and other stones a littel distant from thend of the same Church meaninge to have the same convayed all under one roofe and thereby have enlarged the same and before the fynsshyinge thereof by death and other occasions the same good and godly purpose lacked fynyshinge and yet with a small charge having the furniture thereunto appointede the same was in pointe to be fynyshed and the said [John] Whytetheyer sumtyme being Dean of Bristow aforesayde not regarding his dewte whereby he was by the Ordinances and Statutes of his corporacion bounde by his othe that he should not do nor assent to do any thynge to the disheryson of the deanery or the defasynge of the Churche, did of ys owne authoritie or rather wronge take upon hym to sell the sayde buildings to the saide Sir William Sharington thereby entendinge to spoyle and deface the sayde Churche contrary to hys dewtye and he had not thereto the consent of the sayd Bishop and Chapter to the certen knowledge of the sayde Defendant nor yet any monye surmised to be payde for the same ever came in any dew order to your sayde orators knowledge apperynge by any bookes of accounts remaynyng there to be shewed amongst the records or writings of the said Dean and Chapter, and yf the same had byn by the consent of the sayd Bishop and Chapter yet onles yt had passed by sufficient writing and Chapter seale as yt did not to the sayd Defendants knowledge, the same had ben utterlye voyde to bynde the said Defendant in law, for that the same ys of the inheritance of the said Deanery etc.
Prays to be dismissed.

In reply Henry Sharington claimed that John Cotterell and another prebendary still alive had used the proceeds of the sale of stone 'about the erecting and building of certen necessarie houses for the habitacyon of the Mynysters of the said Churche'.

Continued 6 May 1561
Deposition of Thomas Shipman aged 47

Said that about 9 years ago he paid £20 out of the agreed £40 from Sir William Sharington to Thomas Sylke one of the prebendaries and that:

The takyng away the said wall and stones would not notably deface or dismember the church ther noe standding, and wold be an entere and purfect Churche although the said wall of stone were taken away.

Thomas Sylke, clerk, one of the prebendaries aged 40, deposed:

That the said Whytehere then Deane, with the consent of this deponent, Doctor Edgworth and Doctor Cotterell, not makyng the Bishopp pryvy thereunto did about 9 yeres past bargen by communication the said wall to the said Sir William Sharington in consideration of £40. The pyllar next to the Cathedrall Churche and one windowe in the east part of the newe porche and the great pylar at the west end of the said wall to the said Deane and Chapter excepted and reserved. And also that the said Sir William should not only make a strong fayre wall, but also to obtain a letter from King Edward the VI for the discharge of the said Deane and Chapter for the sale of the said wall.

The whole inconclusive episode suggests that during all the religious upheavals of the reign of Edward VI, the cathedral was not tightly controlled or carefully governed. Until he was deprived of possession by the Crown in 1551, the bishop, Paul Bush, spent much of his time at the manor house at Abbots Leigh, and evidently knew little of what was happening at the cathedral. [Joseph Bettey, 'St Augustine's Abbey and the Manor of Abbots Leigh', in Joseph Bettey, ed., Historic Churches and Church Life in Bristol, (2001), 98–108]. The sale of the stone and apparent demolition of the half-built walls of the proposed nave created a clear and unencumbered site on which during the reign of Elizabeth several domestic dwellings were erected.

REFORMATION AND COUNTER-REFORMATION
1547–1558

Administrative and Liturgical Change

Little documentary evidence survives concerning the major changes which occurred in the affairs of the cathedral and in its furnishings during all the religious upheavals which accompanied the reigns of Edward VI and Queen Mary. It is clear that during this period the original concept of a clerical community living together with a common dining room and dormitory accommodation was very quickly abandoned. The dean and canons were free to marry during Edward VI's reign, and began to reside in the benefices which they held in plurality with their prebends, coming to the cathedral in Bristol only to fulfil the statuary requirements of residence. Likewise, the minor canons and choristers soon took up employments in various Bristol churches and came to the cathedral only for the services. These were fewer, and after the publication of the Book of Common Prayer in 1549, followed by the second, more strongly Protestant version in 1552, services were far simpler and were conducted in English.

Cathedrals were exempt from the most draconian effects of the legislation passed against images, stained glass, screens and all other so-called 'relics of popery' during the years 1547–53, but were affected by the confiscations of silverware, jewels and valuables ordered by the government in 1552. Churches were permitted to keep only those items necessary for the conduct of the new and much less elaborate services. Commissioners were appointed to receive the confiscated goods and to certify the items which churches were allowed to keep. There is no account of the valuables confiscated from the cathedral, but a receipt issued on 27 May 1552 lists all that could be retained.

J. Maclean, 'Church Goods', B.G.A.S. Trans., 12, 1887–8, 81

This byll Indented the xxvij[th] daye of Maye 1553 witnessithe that the Deane and Chappitor of the Cathedrall churche of Bristoll have received of William Chester Mayor and other the Kinge ma [tes]Comissioners ij Challices the one of them gilte weyinge xvj unce qter and di quarter and thother not gilte weynge vj unce.
Itm one greate bell for the clocke

iiij other belles

Geo. Carewe [Dean deprived 1553, restored 1559]
John [Cot]herell [LL.D Preben., 31st Dec. 1543]
[Roger Ed]geworth [S.T.P. 4th June, 1542]
[Thomas] Silke [M.A., 4th June, 1546]

There had previously been nine bells in the tower, together with a sanctus bell, now only four were left. No doubt any vestments, altar cloths and hangings which may have survived from the Augustinian abbey were also seized by the government commissioners at this time.

When Catholicism was restored in 1553 the cathedral lacked vestments for the appropriate celebration of the newly-restored mass. This situation was remedied in 1555 when the cathedral received from Queen Mary and her husband King Philip a substantial gift of rich vestments.

Chapter Register 1 May 1555, Britton, 1830, 51–2

Received the first of Maye 1555 by Cloude, the carier of the gifte of the Kinge and Quenes most excellent majesties to the Catholic Church of Bristoll, the copes, vestments, etc. following:

Imprimis	iii Copes, one of Redd Satten, with streaks of gold, pst[priest], decon and sub-decon
	Another of yellow velvet, pst[priest] decon and sub-decon
	Another of blewe velvet, pst[priest] decon and sub-decon
Item	iii aulter fronts, one of yellow velvet; one red satten with streaks of gold; another of blewe velvet and yellow satten; another of violet velvet and grene satten.

In place of Paul Bush a Catholic bishop, John Holyman, was appointed. He had been a Fellow of New College, Oxford, and a monk of St Mary's abbey, Reading, and he was happy to embrace the restored Catholic regime. He was joined by a new Dean, Henry Joliffe, who replaced George Carew. Joliffe had been imprisoned during the reign of Edward for his refusal to abandon his Catholic beliefs.

Papal Confirmation of the Diocese 1555

A papal bull issued during the reign of Mary by Pope Paul IV makes it clear that even had the diocese of Bristol not been created by Henry VIII it would probably have been founded during the period of Catholic revival. The bull of Paul IV issued from Rome in 1555 empowered the papal legate in England, Cardinal Reginald Pole, to establish the see of Bristol, and confirmed John Holyman as bishop. The long Latin papal bull was addressed to John Holyman:

> Paul, Bishop and Servant of the Servants of God, to our venerable brother John, Bishop of Bristol, greetings and apostolic benediction.

The Pope proclaimed that it was now possible to found a diocese of Bristol because the health of the Church in Bristol had been restored through the suppression of heresy and pernicious schism ('pernicississimo schismate') by the pious monarchs King Philip and Queen Mary. He therefore authorised the papal legate, the new Cardinal Archbishop of Canterbury, Reginald Pole, who had recently returned from exile in Italy to establish the diocese and bishopric of Bristol [the full Latin text of the papal bull is printed in Nicholls & Taylor, II, 1881, 69–70]. *Because of the papal decree the Bristol bishopric, diocese and cathedral are remarkable for having been founded not only by Henry VIII but also by the Pope.*

THE CATHEDRAL DURING THE ELIZABETHAN PERIOD

*With the accession of Elizabeth in November 1558 and the issue of another Book of Common Prayer early in 1559, all the materials necessary for the Catholic services were once more abandoned and discarded. Evidently the rood screen and loft, surmounted by the figure of the crucified Christ, had survived all the changes of the previous decade. In 1560, the bishopric was joined to that of Gloucester, and George Carew, who had been Dean during Edward's reign was restored to his position. Canons who supported the new Elizabethan religious changes and who were appointed in 1559–60 included Christopher Pacy (canon 1560–90), who had been vicar of St Werburgh from 1544, but had gone into hiding during Mary's reign; and Arthur Saule (canon 1560–85), a Fellow of Magdalen College, Oxford, who had fled abroad to escape persecution during Mary's reign. One canon continued to hold office throughout the religious changes of four reigns. This was Thomas Sylke, who became vicar of St Leonard in 1529, and was prior of the Kalendars' Guild from 1540 until its dissolution in 1548. He was appointed as a canon of Bristol cathedral in 1546 and held the position until his death in 1575, playing a prominent part in the affairs of the cathedral and in the administration of its estates. [*B.R.O. DC/A/9/1/1; T.N.A. (P.R.O.) C1/1199; REQ 2/271/24].

The most abiding and long-serving presence during the troubled years of the mid-sixteenth century was that of John Cotterell. He became chancellor of the diocese under Bishop Paul Bush in 1543, taking a major rôle in the administration of the diocese and the conduct of the ecclesiastical court. His position became even more important during the period when the diocese was supervised by the bishop of Gloucester, Richard Cheney. Cotterell combined the office of chancellor with a canonry of Bristol from 1545 and the archdeaconry of Dorset from 1551. He was also a canon and archdeacon of Wells from 1554 until his death in 1572. [M. Skeeters, Community and Clergy, 1993, 122–48, 198–201].

In spite of the destruction of images, stained glass, vestments and other items which were regarded as 'relics of popery' during the reign of Edward VI, the rood screen, complete with its images, had evidently survived all the changes and was still in place in 1561. At that time the Privy Council wrote to the Dean and Chapter with strict instructions that the screen and its statues of the saints were to be destroyed forthwith.

John Britton, History and Antiquities of Bristol Cathedral, 1830, 52.

"After our hartie comendacions. Whereas we are credibly informed that there are divers tabernacles for images as well in the fronture of the roodeloft of the Cathedral Church of Bristol as also in the frontures, back and ends of the walles wheare the communion table standeth, for as moch as the same churche shoulde be a light and good example to the ole citie and diocese we have thought good to direct these our letteres. unto you and to require you to cause the said tabernacles to be defaced and hewen down, and afterwards to be made a playne walle wth morter, plaster or otherways, and some Scriptures to be written in the places, and, namely, that upon the walle on the east end of the quier where the communion table usually doth stande the table of the Commandments to be painted in large caracters with convenient speed and furniture according to the orders latly set forthe by virtue of the Quenes ma^{ts} comission for causes ecclesiasticall at the cost and chardges of the saide churche, whereof we require you not to faile. And so we bid you farewel ffrom London the xxi. of December, 1561"

Compared to most of the older dioceses and cathedrals, Bristol was poorly endowed. The government of Henry VIII was aware that charges of idleness and luxurious living had been made against cathedral clergy as well as against monks, and therefore ensured that the members of the new cathedral foundations were modestly rewarded. The total endowment was £679 3s 11d, of which the bishop received £383 8s 4d. One result of this was that few bishops stayed long at Bristol, and most of the cathedral clergy held other preferments. During the reign of Elizabeth there was some doubt as to whether the diocese would survive at all as a separate entity.

The diocese was for long periods (1558–62 and 1593–1603) left without a bishop, whilst at other times it was held in commendam (in trust or under protection and care) by the bishops of Gloucester. John Holyman died in 1558, the year of Queen Mary's death, and the see was vacant for four years. The Mayor and Corporation of Bristol were evidently proud of having their own cathedral, and in March 1562 wrote unsuccessfully to William Cecil 'Praying that Bristol may be continued as an independent Bishoprick, without being united to any other' [Cal. S.P. Dom. 1547–80, 196; T.N.A. (P.R.O.) SP 12/117 f 11]. Their plea was ignored and Bristol continued to be under the supervision of the bishop of Gloucester until 1589. From 1562 to 1579 Richard Cheney bishop of Gloucester held Bristol in commendam. He was a considerable scholar, but his dislike of the Puritans, alleged favour to Catholics and the emphasis which he placed on the early teachings of the Church and on traditional ceremonies brought him great unpopularity in Bristol. In August and September 1568 he preached three sermons in Bristol cathedral recommending the writings of the early Church fathers and warning the congregation against following blindly the ideas of Luther, Calvin and other Protestant writers. His sermons led to a storm of protest from Bristolians, especially mindful of the dangers of religious dissent at a time when the Catholic Mary, Queen of Scots, had sought refuge in England, and had been imprisoned; and at a time when there were constant rumours of Catholic plots against Queen Elizabeth. Cheney's warnings against reforming ideas and his explanations of the doctrine of free-will upset many of his hearers, led by John Northbrooke or Norwood, curate of St Mary Redcliffe, who was supported by other puritan clergy and laity. Cheney was aware of the discontent his sermons on the cathedral had caused. He wrote to William Cecil on 7 October 1568 telling him about his sermons and the strength of puritan feeling in Bristol. On 15 October 1568 Cheney sent a more detailed account of his sermons to Cecil, and complained about his adversaries in Bristol, led by Norwood. To ensure that Cecil was firmly on his side in any further controversy, Bishop Cheney took the precaution of granting Cecil a beneficial lease of the episcopal farm at Maismore (Glos.). His fears that the protests against his views would not easily be silenced were justified. In October 1568 a letter signed by 39 prominent citizens was sent to the Privy Council denouncing the sermons preached by Bishop Cheney and the 'very strange, perilous and corrupt doctrines, as well to the defacinge of Christes sincere gospell and God's undefiled religion, as to the no small hassardinge of the common tranquilitie wherein as we have hitherto obedientlie and quietlie lived under our Queenes Majestie'. They included with their letter some notes recording the contents of the Bishop's sermons. The following extracts from the notes show the lively style employed by the bishop and how objectionable some of his opinions must have been to Bristolians, so many of whom were fervently anti-Catholic, favoured Puritan theology and placed their whole trust in the words of the Bible.

Cal. S.P. Dom. 1547–80, 319–22

Letter to the Privy Council from 39 Citizens of Bristol 21 October 1568

**These Articles were openlye uttered and
Publyshed in Bristoll by the byshoppe of Glouc.
In three severall sermons vidzt. the 22 & 29 dayes of
August and the ffyft of September last past
Anno dni, 1568**

1. – I am come, good people, not to recant or call backe anythinge that I have heretofore said, ffor I am of that mynde now as I was then, as concernynge matters of controversye, and willbe to thende. If I had one foote in the grave and another uppon the grounde I wolld saye then as I do nowe, and therefor good people I geve you that councell that I follow myselff. Wherefor be not so swyft or hastie to credyt the newe wryters, ffor they are not yet thoroughlye tryed and approvyd as the catholycke ffathers are.

2. – Thes newe wryters in matters of controversie as Mr Calvyne and others, agree not together, but are at dyssentyon among them sellves, and are together by the eares, therefore take heede of them, yet reade them, for in openynge the text they do passe many of the old ffathers, And they are excellentlye well learned in the tonges. But in matters nowe in controversye follow them not, But followe the old ffathers and doctours, althoughe Mr Calvyn denyeth some of them. As for your newe Doctours are good to picke a Sallytt out of them now and then.

3. – Scriptures, scriptures, do you crye, be not to hastie for so the heretick allwayes cryed And had the scriptures. I wollde aske this question, I have to do with an heretycke, I bringe Scripture agaynst hym, And he will confesse yt to be scripture, But he will denye the sence that I bringe yt ffor, How now, how shall thys be tryed, marye by consent of ffathers onlie and not by others.

4. – In readynge scripture be you lycke the snaile, whiche ys agoodlie sygnee ffor when he feelythe an harde thinge against his hornes, he pullythe them in agayne. So do you: reade scriptures a god's name, But when you come to matters of controversyes, goe backe agayn, pull in yor hornes.

The Privy Council appears to have taken no action on this letter, but thereafter Cheney was involved in several other controversies. In 1571 he was excommunicated for a time for refusing to subscribe to the 39 Articles which had been issued in 1562, and the care of the Bristol diocese was committed to the bishop of Salisbury. The result was that Bristol had little effective episcopal supervision, and the future of the diocese was uncertain. Richard Cheney died in 1579 and was buried in Gloucester cathedral. His successor at Gloucester, John Bullingham, also held Bristol in commendam from 1579 to 1589. From 1589 to 1593 Bristol once more had its own bishop in the person of Richard Fletcher. He had been Dean of Peterborough and had been present at the execution of Mary Queen of Scots in 1586, when 'contrary to the dictates of humanity and of true religion, he disturbed the last moments of the unfortunate princess with unavailing entreaties to change her faith'. [British Library, Lansdowne MSS, 51, art.46]. The Corporation of Bristol was evidently pleased at the restoration of the bishopric, and when Bishop Fletcher arrived in Bristol in July 1590 he was welcomed by the Mayor and Councillors and presented with no less than 30 gallons of sack and 20 pounds of sugar. As well as being bishop of Bristol, however, Fletcher was an assiduous courtier and had obtained the office of Almoner to Queen Elizabeth, so he spent little time in Bristol. He did not come to the city again until 1592, when he received another gift of sugar from the Corporation. A year later he was translated to the much richer see of Worcester and the diocese of Bristol remained vacant for 10 years until John Thornborough was appointed in 1603. Thereafter there was a regular succession of bishops, although few of them stayed long at Bristol before securing more lucrative bishoprics [J. Latimer, Sixteenth-Century Bristol, 1900, 98].

In these circumstances there is little wonder that confusion surrounded the administration of the diocese, and that many people were left in doubt as to which diocese they owed allegiance. This was particularly true in the Dorset part of the diocese where the situation was further complicated by the large number of parishes which were 'peculiars' administered by the Dean of Salisbury. Even the Privy

Council was unsure, and in 1577 wrote to the bishop of Bath and Wells demanding a list of Catholic recusants living in Dorset. The Council's letter was then sent to the Deputy Lieutenants of Dorset who, confused by the number of 'peculiar' parishes administered by the Dean of Salisbury, replied that they were uncertain as to the diocese to which they owed allegiance [Cal. S.P. Dom. 12/117 f 21]. *As a result Catholicism remained strong in Dorset, protected by several land-owning families who adhered to the old religion, such as the Tregonwells of Milton, the Arundells of Chideock and Wardour, the Turbervilles of Bere Regis, the Martyns of Athelhampton and the Stourtons of Canford.*

Richard Hakluyt

One of the most notable and nationally-famous Elizabethan canons was Richard Hakluyt (1552–1616), the geographer and writer on exploration and discoveries in the New World. As well as being a cleric and theologian, Hakluyt's main interest was in the exciting possibilities being provided by successive voyages of discovery, and his writings did much to encourage further enterprises. His most important work The Principal Navigations, Voiages, Traffiques and Discoveries of the English Nation, *was published in 1589, and in an expanded version in 1598–1600. Because of Bristol's importance in promoting voyages of discovery, Hakluyt had visited the port on several occasions, most notably in 1582 when he successfully sought support for an expedition proposed by Humfrey Gilbert. The process whereby Hakluyt was appointed to a prebend in Bristol cathedral in 1586 illustrates the struggle among clergymen to secure such posts. His success in obtaining support for a voyage among Bristol merchants on 1582 brought him to the attention of Sir Francis Walsingham, who wrote in March 1582–3 to thank him for his efforts:*

Sir Francis Walsingham to Richard Hakluyt

E.G.R. Taylor, ed., Original Writings of the two Richard Hakluyts, Hakluyt Society, 2nd Ser., 77, 1935, II,

I understand as wel by a letter I long since received from the Mayor of Bristol, as by conference with Sir George Peckham, that you had endeavoured and give much light for the discovery of the Westerne partes yet unknowne: as your studie in these things is very commendable, so I thanke you much for the same, wishing you to continue your trouble in these and like matters which are like to turne not only to your owne good in private, but to the publike benefite of this Realme. And so I bid you farewell. From the Court the 11 of March 1582.

Your loving friend
Francis Walsingham

Encouraged by this recognition from one of the Queen's principal ministers, Hakluyt presented two volumes of his own writings to the Queen herself in 1584. These were An Analysis of Aristotle's 'Politics', *1583, and* Discourse of Western Planting, *1584.*

In return on 5 October 1584 the Queen promised to present him to a prebend in Bristol cathedral at the next vacancy. 'To Richard Hakluyt, master of arts and professor of theology, that canonry or prebend within the cathedral church of Holy Trinity, Bristol which shall be first to become vacant with all its appertaining emoluments, to hold for life'. Meanwhile in 1583, Hakluyt had secured appointment as chaplain to Sir Edward Stafford, who was the English ambassador in Paris. It was still necessary for him to fight to make good the Queen's promise of a position in Bristol, as is evident from the following letter which he addressed to Walsingham in 1585.

Letter from Richard Hakluyt to Sir F. Walsingham, 1585

E.G.R. Taylor, ed., Original Writings of the Two Richard Hakluyts, 2nd Ser., 77, 1935, II, 343–5

To the right honourable Sir Francis Walsingham, principal secretarie to her Ma[tie], give these at the Courte.

Your Honors, goodnes extended diverse ways unto mee at my being in England the last somer, [i.e. 1584] doth much encourage mee at this present to crave yo favour in a matter more than reasonable.

Yt plesed her Ma[tie] twoe dayes before my despach, uppon the sight of a couple of bookes of myne in writing, one in Latin upon Arystotles politicks, the other in English concerning Mr Rawleys voyage (the copie whereof I purpose to send yor honor immediately after Ester) to grant mee the next vacation of a prebend in Bristol, w[ch] is a thinge of very smal vallue. The words of my grant are, that I shold enjoy that next, whether that be by death, vacation, resignation, or any other waye howsoever. And yet since my cominge out of England I am advertized that one Mr Sanders, a prebend of that place, ether hath or meaneth to resigne his roome to another, w[ch] if yt be not hindered by yo[r] honors favour, my reversion wil not be worth the mony that the seales did stand mee in, for if these resignations be permitted, I may bee these sevene and sevene yeares before I shal be placed. Therefore I am humbly to beseech yo[r] honor that you wold not suffer my graunte to be frustrated by any such dealing.

This plea was successful and Hakluyt was installed as a canon at Bristol in 1586, retaining the position until his death. He could have spent only short periods in Bristol, however, for through the influence of Sir Edward Stafford, he became rector of Wetheringsett and Blockford in Suffolk in 1590, and in 1602 also became a canon of Westminster Abbey. Nonetheless, he remained active in encouraging exploration and voyages of discovery, as is evident from the following notes concerning a voyage from Bristol to Virginia in 1603.

Preparation for a Voyage to Virginia 1603

E.G.R.Taylor, ed., Original Writings of the Two Richard Hakluyts, Hakluyt Society, 2nd Ser., 77, 1935, II, 486–7

Upon many probable and reasonable inducements, used unto sundry of the chiefest merchants of Bristol by Master Richard Hakluyt, prebendary of St Augustine's, the

Cathedral Church of the said citie, after divers meetings and due consultation, they resolved to set forth a voyage for the farther discoverie of the north part of Virginia. And first they sent the said Master Hakluyt, accompanied with one Master John Angell and Master Robert Saltern (which had beene in the said discoverie the yeere before with Captain Bartholomew Gosnold) to obtain permission of Sir Walter Raleigh (which had a most ample patent for all those partes from Queen Elizabeth) to entermeddle and deale in that action. Leave being obtained of him under his hand and seale, they speedily prepared a small ship....

Hakluyt retained his canon's house in Bristol and in his will made in 1612 he included the following bequest.

E.G.R. Taylor, ed., <u>Original Writings of the Two Richard Hakluyts</u>, Hakluyt Society, 2nd Ser., 77, 1935, II, 508

Whereas I have at Bristow sundry implements, hangings and furniture there in my lodgings and chambers, I do freely give all to the only use and benefitt of the said College, to be disposed at the discretion of the right worshipfull Mr Deane'.

Richard Hakluyt died in 1616 and was buried in Westminster Abbey.

CATHEDRAL FINANCES

A detailed view of the income of the cathedral, the management of its estates, the stipends paid to clergy and members of staff and expenditure on maintenance, repairs to the buildings, charitable giving and other expenses can be gained from the <u>Computa</u> *or annual accounts which survive in an almost unbroken sequence from 1550. The following example is taken from the first volume which covers the years 1550–1556, and shows the full account for the year 1551.*

Computa 1550–1556

B.R.O. DC/A/9/1/1

Cathedral Church of the Holy Trinity Bristol

Accountt of Thomas Wright gent., receiver 1551. From all houses, manors, lands, tenments, rectories, portions, pensions and other possessions bothe temporal and spiritual due unto the Cathedral Church

Arrears	£87	19s	0½d
Rec of Walter Philips bailiff, for City of Bristol & suburbs	£90	15s	7½d
Rec of Walter Philips bailiff, for Clifton	£1	0s	8d
Rec of John Rouse farmer, for Rectory of Berkeley Hernesse	£65	6s	8d
Rec of John Thompson farmer, for Erlingham, Bradley & Wapley	£17	6s	0d
Rec of Doctor Owen bailiff, for Manor of South Cerney	£8	14s	4d

Rec of Philip Griffith bailiff, for Manor of Blacksworth	£7	9s	9d
Rec of Peter Lane Rector, for Rectory of Weare	£9	6s	8d
Rec of Thomas Player collector of rents and farmer, for Stanton Drew & Bath		17s	0d
Rec of Hugh Paulet farmer, for Manor of Halburton	£15	15s	8½d
Rec of Johanna Marwood farmer, for Rectory of Halburton	£33	0s	0d
Rec of John Berwyck bailiff, for Manor of Penmarthen	£18	19s	11½d
Rec of Rowland Morgan farmer, for Manor of Peterston	£32	11s	5d
Rec of divers farmers, for Rectory of St Oswald in the City of Gloucester	£7	5s	4d
Rec of William Jenyns farmer, for Rectory of Churchden with Hoculcylte [Hucclecote]	£11	1s	0d
Rec of Thomas Maston farmer, for Rectory of Compton Aldhall [Abdale]	£2	13s	4d
Rec of Thomas Jerich farmer, for Rectory of Worton	£7	6s	8d
Rec of [blank] collector, for Pensions and portions in the City of Gloucester	£2	3s	8d
Rec of Thomas Tasker farmer, for Rectory of Marcen	£8	0s	0d
Rec of Richard Fisher farmer, for Rectory of Hampton	£10	0s	0d
Rec of John Segar bailiff, for Rectory of Olvesden	£19	13s	4d
Rec of Robert Bradley farmer, for Rectory of Forde	£5	6s	8d
Rec of divers collectors, for Pensions and Portions in Bathwick and Newton St Low	£10	13s	4d
Rec from Thomas Blanchflower farmer, for Rectory of Kingston	£13	0s	0d
Rec from Hugh Paulet for Rectory of South Petherton	£50	0s	0d
Rec of Edith Payne farmer, for Rectory of Banwell	£38	3s	4d
Rec of several collectors, for Rectory of Tisbury	£24	0s	2d
Rec of Richard Tuchyn farmer, for Rectory of Bradford	£57	6s	8½d
Rec of Matthew Colthurst farmer, for Rectory of Broadwiger [Broadwoodwidger]	£9	10s	11d
Rec of Lady Maria Wadham farmer, for Rectory of Ile Abbots	£7	0s	0d
Rec of Thomas Speke farmer, for Rectory of Ilminister	£20	0s	0d
Rec of John[?] Pytt occupator of the said rectory of Meryett	£12	1s	0d
Rec of Thomas Speke farmer, for Rectory of Ilcombe	£2	10s	0d
Rec of Thomas Speke farmer, for Rectory of Horton	£1	5s	0d
Rec of Humphrey Worth farmer, for Rectory of Somerton	£43	13s	4d
Rec of Lady Maria Wadham farmer, for Rectory of Fyffide [Fifehead]	£4	0s	0d
Rec of Robert Cuffe farmer, for Rectory of Myddleney	£3	7s	8d
Rec of Elizabeth Dawes farmer, for Rectory of Drayton and lands in Weston	£16	0s	4d
Rec of John Seymour farmer for Lands in Great Marlow	£7	2s	5d
Total	**£781**	**16s**	**11½d**

Expenditure

Stipends	£	s	d
To Roger Edgeworth sub-dean	£1	6	8
Walter Gleson former chaplain	£1	0	0
Thomas Sylke receiver	£3	6	8
The same Thomas for the office of supervisor of all lands & tenements within the city of Bristol	£5	0	0
John Cotterell supervisus	£6	13	4
John Thess	£1	6	8
Robert Hogge precentor	£1	6	8
Richard Bette sacrist	£1	6	8
William Powell janitor within the precinct and circuit of the church	£6	13	4
Robert Welson	£6	0	0
David Watkins hospice	£6	0	0
Stephen Subcose	£3	6	8
John Boroughes sub-sacrist within the Cathedral Church	£5	16	8
William Snowe dean	£100		

John Barlowe	£20			
Roger Edgeworth	£20	canons and prebends within		
Henry Morgan	£20	the Cathedral Church		
George Dogeon	£20		£120	0	0
John Cotterell	£20			
Thomas Sylke	£20			

Richard Bettie				
Richard Phillips				
Robert Hogge	minor canons	£50	0	0
Robert Pimpton				
William Lowe				

Richard Ware deacon	£6	13	4
Rowland Dye sub deacon	£6	13	4

Nicholas Bynkes				
Edward Wawen				
John Bell	Cantators	£40	0	0
Gregory Battram				
John Palm				
Walter Gleson				

Humrey Walley ludini coristors	£10	0	0
William Cydon preceptor scole grammatice	£13	6	8
John Syssell hipodadasulin the same school	£6	13	4

Six boy choristers within the cathedral church	£20	0	0

Charities distributed for the soul of the King Henry VIII
Founder of this Cathedral

John Phillips Thomas Coles John Rutter Griffin Johns	} Paupers & almsmen	£26	13	4

Necessary Expenses for bread, wine, candles and oil used in the Cathedral church	£9	17	8
Other expenses	£6	0	0
Repairs to the cathedral church and within the circuit and precinct	£5	3	6
Expenses of divers law suits in London	£52	1	0½
To Thomas Sylke treasurer for supplussag	£130	0	0½
Payment to Sir Chidioro Paulet receiver for the King in annual settlement	£85	10	0
Sum total of payments	**£756**	**15**	**7**
& owing　　　　　　　　　43s–10½ d			

The fact that the cathedral was poorly-endowed and that many of the clergy and choir-men held other positions in addition to their cathedral office, meant that there were frequent complaints concerning absences from the cathedral services. The following warning which was inserted among the leases of cathedral property granted in 1605 provides an example of this problem. It illustrates how far the cathedral had departed from the intentions of its foundation in 1542 and from the Statutes of 1544.

Chapter Act Book (Register of Leases) 1542–1617

B.R.O. DC/E/1/1C

fol. 48　　**22 October 1605**

The Dean and Chapter capitularly decreed that every Sabbath Day morning prayer shall begin a quarter before nine and every minister and singing man of this church that shall be absent a whole service on the Sabbath in the morning shall forfeit for the first time 12d, and the second time other 12d, which shall be bestowed on the pensioners of Newgate. And if he make default the third time he shall have admunition given him according to the Statutes of this Church.

> Simon Robson (Dean)
> Robert Gullyford ⎱
> Edward Greene ⎰ canons
> Robert Temple

Former Royal Servants installed as Almsmen

The modest endowment provided for the Dean and Chapter by the arrangements approved by Henry VIII in 1542, was made even more inadequate by the requirement that the cathedral should support numerous singing men, choirboys, schoolmasters and almsmen. Moreover, at Bristol as in other cathedrals, successive monarchs used the places provided for almsmen to install former royal servants, maimed soldiers and others who could be thus rewarded and maintained at no cost to the Crown. Several examples survive in the Chapter Act Book of peremptory demands from the Crown addressed to the Dean and Chapter requiring that a place as almsman be found and accommodation provided for a royal retainer or for a man to whom the monarch felt indebted. The following is an example from late in the reign of Queen Elizabeth which was subsequently confirmed by James I.

B.R.O. DC/E/1/1(C)
from Chapter Act Book 1603–1616 fol 9v

Elizabeth Regina

Trustie and well beloved wee greet you well. Lettinge you witt wee of our especiall grace have given and graunted and by the present doe give and graunt to our wellbeloved subject Thomas Wigge the roome of an Almsman in that our Cathedrall Church of Bristoll if any such roome be voide, or the next that shallbe voide there, after the placeinge of suche as have our former licence for the like roome if anie such be. To have and to holde and enjoye the same roome of an Almsman in the saide church of Bristoll to the said Thomas Wigge duringe his natural life, togeather with all the fees, wages, dutyes, allowances and commodityes thereunto belonging, according to the foundation of the same. Where fore wee will and command you to admitte the saide Thomas Wigge to the same roome of an Almsman and place him in the same in his due course according to the tenor of these our licences. And allsoe to paye and allowe unto him from tyme to tyme after his placeinge in the same roome the wages, dutyes, and other allowances and profitts whatsoever incident to the same in as large and ample manner at all such usuall tymes as other our Almsmen there placed have and receave or of right ought to receave and have. And these our licences shallbe your sufficient warrant and discharge in this behalfe.

Given under our signett at our honor of Hampton Courte 27 day of January in the 45th yeare of our raigne 1603.

fol 10   **Confirmation by James I**

To our trustie and wellbeloved the deane and chapter of our Cathedrall church in Bristoll for the tyme beinge.
The Kinges Majestie is pleased that this poore man shall enjoye the benefitt of this graunt to all purposes as the late Queene deceased intended it unto him. 28 August 1603
signed by Julius Caesar

[Dr Julius Caesar was Judge of the Admiralty Court and a Master of the Court of Requests]

RELATIONS WITH THE MAYOR AND CORPORATION
OF BRISTOL 1542–1623

Although the cathedral was small and the diocese impossible to administer effectively, nonetheless there is some evidence that the merchant class in Bristol welcomed the new arrangement in 1542. They took pride in having their own ecclesiastical centre rather than owing allegiance to far off Worcester or even Gloucester, and were no doubt pleased by the elevation of Bristol to the rank of a city. A letter from the Mayor & Corporation in 1562 asking that the Bristol diocese should be allowed to continue as an independent entity has already been quoted. Also mentioned earlier was the evidence which comes from the will of Thomas White who was a former mayor and a prominent merchant. He had been actively engaged in buying up land and possessions which had belonged to the religious houses, including some of the goods of the Carmelite or White Friars whose friary was on the banks of the river Frome, near St Augustine's Back in Bristol. Among his acquisitions was a screen from the friary church, and in his will dated 10 September 1542 he gave this to the newly-established cathedral which significantly he refers to as 'my Cathedral Church'.

Fig. 3　Tomb of Paul Bush 1558. This was erected according to the bishop's instructions, close to the grave of his wife. It depicts the bishop as an emaciated figure, lying on a rush mat, with his head resting on a jewelled mitre, and with his pastoral staff by his side. (Photograph by Philippa Johnson).

Great Red Book, Text Part III, 130

I geve and bequethe unto my Cathedral Church called the Trynytie of Bristowe the Quere [screen] which was somtyme in the White Friers, the which Phelipp Griffyn bought of John Nelase?, and the said Quere for to be sett upp in the seid Churche at my cost and charge.

The screen was duly set up in the cathedral, and added to it were stone shields bearing the arms of Edward, Prince of Wales, and the initials of Thomas White, together with his merchant's mark. The west face of the screen was adorned with the figures of the four Evangelists and with 12 minor prophets. It was installed in what had been the monastic chancel, at the second bay to the east of the crossing; the altar and choir stalls were moved to the east end of the Lady Chapel, thus creating a circumscribed and inevitably inconvenient space for the congregation. The solid screen meant that anyone west of it had a very limited view of the chancel. The pulpit was situated in the transept and the whole congregation moved there for the sermon. The screen survived intact until the drastic restoration during the 1850s, when it was demolished, although parts of it, including the Prince's arms and Thomas White's initials and merchant's mark survive today as part of the screen on each side of the high altar. Since the cathedral had become the premier ecclesiastical establishment in Bristol, it soon became the accepted practice that the main service and sermon on Sundays should be attended by the Mayor & Corporation. They walked in solemn procession in their scarlet gowns to the cathedral from the Tolzey or Council House in Corn Street. The service did not start before they arrived and ended when they left. Relations between the city rulers, who were very conscious of their own dignity, and the Dean & Chapter were not always harmonious. During the Marian period, the Corporation refused to attend services at the cathedral unless they were ceremonially summoned and their procession was accompanied by the clergy preceded by their cross. This refusal may well have been prompted by dislike of the restored Catholic services, and by revulsion at the burning of several heretics in Bristol during Mary's reign. The government evidently took the refusal seriously, and wrote a strongly-worded letter to the Mayor & Corporation ordering them to attend the cathedral services.

Cal. S.P. Dom. VI, 1556–8, 156

24 August 1557

A lettre to the Maiour and Aldermen of Bristoll, requyring them to conforme themselfes in frequenting the sermons, processions and other publique ceremonyes at the Cathedrall Churche there to the doinges of all other cities and like corporacions within the realme, and not to absent themselfes as they have doone of late, nor loke fromhensfourthe that the Deane and Chapter shulde wayte uppon them or fetche them out of the cittie with thier crosse and procession, being the same very unsemely and farre out of ordre.

The bitter dispute over doctrine between Bishop Richard Cheney and the citizens of Bristol in 1568 was described in the previous section. Likewise the welcome by the Corporation accorded to Cheney's successor, Bishop Richard Fletcher (bishop 1589–93). After Fletcher's departure to the bishopric of Worcester in 1593, the

Fig. 4 The Tomb of Sir John and Dame Joan Young 1603. This originally occupied a prominent position at the east end of the chancel. He was a wealthy merchant and landowner who had been knighted by Queen Elizabeth during her visit to Bristol in 1574. She was the daughter of a Somerset landowner and had previously been married to Sir Giles Strangways of Melbury, Dorset. The tomb was made by Samuel Baldwin of Stroud in the typically florid style of the period.
(Photograph by Philippa Johnson).

bishopric then remained vacant until the appointment in 1603 of John Thornborough, who was also Dean of York and rector of Pickering (Yorks), so that he came to Bristol only occasionally. His episcopate witnessed another bitter dispute with the Corporation over seating arrangements in the cathedral. Because the nave had been demolished, accommodation within the remaining transepts and chancel was limited. Moreover, space was taken by screens and was further restricted by monuments, including a large monument to Bishop Paul Bush, erected soon after his death in 1558, and another ornate tomb commemorating Dame Joan Young (d 1603) and her two husbands, Sir Giles Strangways (d 1562) and Sir John Young (d 1589). During the early decades of the 17th century the Corporation of Bristol exhibited an incessant demand for sermons. The notes of Council Proceedings show that they paid for 'lecturers' or preachers in several of the city churches, and employed their own preacher to provide regular sermons in the cathedral and elsewhere in the city every Sunday afternoon and on every holy day. It was this appetite for sermons that led to their request to erect an elaborate gallery in the cathedral in 1606. Concerned that the seating provided for members of the Corporation and their wives should be appropriately grandiose, the Mayor, Aldermen and Councillors agreed in 1606 to pay for an elaborate gallery to be erected in the cathedral. This led to a fierce quarrel with the bishop. John Thornborough (1551–1641) had risen rapidly in the Church. He had been chaplain to the Earl of Pembroke and through the influence of his patron accumulated several parishes in Wiltshire and Dorset. He became a prebendary of Salisbury cathedral in 1576, chaplain to Queen Elizabeth in 1582, dean of York in 1589, and Bishop of Limerick in 1593, continuing to hold the deanery of York with his bishopric. He gained the favour of James I through his support of the King's plan for the union of England and Scotland, and he was made bishop of Bristol at the beginning of the King's reign in 1603. Thornborough never resided in Bristol, and did not visit the city until 1606, although he remained active as dean of York [Oxford D.N.B.; A.L.Rowse, 'Bishop Thornborough: A Clerical Careerist', in R. Ollard and P. Tudor Craig, eds., For Veronica Wedgewood These, (1986), 89–108]. Thomas Fuller in his Worthies of England, first published in 1662 said of Thornborough that he was of a remarkably cheerful temperament. Thornborough attributed this to a medicine which he had compounded and which he had recommended to James I as 'a great preserver of health, and a prolonger of life'. Fuller commented that:

> 'He conceived by such helps to have added to his vigorous vivacity, though I think a merry heart, whereof he had great measure, was his best elixir to that purpose.'
> [Thomas Fuller, Worthies of England, 1952 edn., 615].

Thornborough's 'merry heart' was certainly not in evidence during his dealings with Bristol Corporation, while the Mayor and Councillors obviously found him difficult, stubborn and totally unsympathetic to their concerns. This is evident from the following documentary evidence.

B.R.O. 04264/1 Council Proceedings 1598–1608 p125

7 October 1606

It is also agreed that there shalbe a Conveniente place erected and made in the Cathedrall Church at St Augustines, for the Mayor, Aldermen and Common Counsell and for their wyves to sytte in there to heare the Sermons on the Sabbathe and other Festivall dayes, and for the doing and defrayinge of the Chardges thereof It is agreed that the Mayor, Aldermen, Sheryves and every other of the Common Counsell of this City shall disburse forty shillinges a peece and that Mr Richard Smithe, Mr George Whyte, Mr Thomas Aldworth shalbe Surveyors to see the same worke performed and one of them to be Treasurer for the receypt and disbursinge of the same money and to keepe the accompt thereof.

B.R.O. 04264/1 [M/BCC/CCP/1/1] Council Proc. 1598–1608 p127–35

11 November 1606

It is agreed that yf the Deane and Chapter will not Consent to grant libertye unto the Mayor and Commattye of this Cytie by writing under their Seale to erect and sett uppe Seates in their Cathedrall church for the Mayor, Aldermen and Common Council and their wyves and officers to sitt there at Sermons then that worke shalbe geven over and noe further to proceede therein.

9 December 1606

It is agreed that the grant from the Deane and Chapter of Bristol touching the erectinge of the Seates in the Cathedrall church shalbe accepted and that xs yearlye shalbe payed to the Chamberlain of this citye to the officer that shall keape the same.

16 April 1607

It is agreed that those of the Common Counsell which have not payde his money towards the Charge of the Buildinge of the new Seates in the Cathedrall Churche at St Augustines shall forthwith paye the same to the Treasurer for that worke and that the Chamberlain shall disburse such money as shall want to even that accompte and that every one of the Common Counsell which shalbe admitted and sworne hereafter shall paye to the Chamberlain xls until the same money by him so disbursed shalbe repayde and afterwards everyone that shalbe admitted into the Common Cousell of the Cytie shall paye unto the said Chamberlain xxs for his Seate there and towards the repayringe and keepinge.

Francis F. Fox, ed., Adam's Chronicle of Bristol, compiled by William Adams, Bristol 1910

pp182–3 1606

Mr Barker (Mayor) and others of the Council this year erected and built a fair and costly gallery in the college of St Augustine over against the pulpit which stood then on the south side of the church, and the gallery on the north near the place where the pulpit now standeth; and took a lease hereof from the dean and chapter: which building cost the mayor and council £115. It was not only a fair and comely ornament to the church, but also a fit and convenient place for the Council to sit and hear the word preached, leaving the room below for gentlemen and others. They placed there our King's arms gilded, and under reserved a fair seat for the King or any nobleman that should come to this city: and under the same also fair seats for the council's and clergy's wives, and other fit places also for the bishop, dean and others of the clergy.

p184 **1608**

The gallery and fair buildings at the College was this year maliciously pulled down by Doctor Thorneborow our bishop, because his consent was not demanded therein at setting up, alleging that the College was his, and no others had authority therein without his leave. The Mayor and Aldermen demanded aid of the dean and prebends in vain, for they equivocated and joined with the bishop: at which our mayor and Council disdaining refused to go to the college at Easter and other times as they were used to do, and furnished our city with learned divines, despising the bishop and clergy: and so the college for a time grew out of request, and few of our city went thither for a time; for every Sabbath day we heard at least 6 sermons both forenoon and afternoon preached in our city by learned divines.

Another account of Bishop Thornborough's actions is given by an anonymous annalist whose notes on Bristol history cover the period 1238 to 1687. This was printed in the Bristol Memoralist *in 1823.*

1606

This Mayor, John Barber, with the rest of the Councill, took a lease of the Dean and Chapter, for to have so much room in the Cathedrall or Colledge Church as to build a fair Gallery, for the Majestrates to sitt in to hear sermon; the which was built this year, at the costs of the Mayor and Councill. It stood upon pillars, right against the pulpitt; all the fore-part being of joyner's work, curiously wrought; wherein was three seats, placed by the middle pillar, reserved for the Mayor, Dean and Councill of this city, and if occasion were, for the King, or any nobleman that should come into this city. And upon the top of the seat was the King's arms, guilded and painted. Under which gallery there was seates placed in like order, for the Majestrates' wives.

1608

This year, on the 8th of February, the Bishop of this see, named Doctor Thornborough, having been absent from the city two years, sent men to pull down the Gallery in the Colledge, which Mr Barker, in his mayoraltie, with the Councill, by the consent of the Dean and Chapter, had built for them to sitt in and hear sermon; and the reason was, because they had not his consent, neither had built a place for him. Whereupon Mr Abel Kitchen and Mr John Guy, being of the Councill of this city, were sent to London, to the Lord High Steward of Bristol; who made the case known unto the

King's Majestie, who presently appointed Commissioners to view the same, whither the Gallery did make the Church like a Playhouse, as the Bishop and other of the Colledge had reported, who had set their hands and seales to the grant of the lease for the building thereof. And an answer being sent by the Commissioners to his Majestie of the contrary, he caused the Bishop to set the gallery in its former place, at his own cost; which built it above two or three foot above the ground, and set the pulpit on the lower pillar next the Clock-house. But the King hereing of, when the Bishop came to London, he was to his great disgrace checked by the King; so that he abode at Dorchester, it being a part of his bishopprick belonging to Bristol, and would not come to Bristol for shame and disgrace......Also this year the Bishop would have forced the Mayor and all the worshipful Aldermen to come to sermon to the Colledge, as they used to do on every Sabbath and festival-day, and therefore would not suffer any bell to ring sermon in the City; but the Mayor prevented him of his purpose, and sent to the Lord Archbishop of Canterbury, who gave him authority that now they might have as many sermons in the City as they will, and where the Mayor will appoint it, and did not go to the Colledge for many years together, but went to Redcliff Church for to hear sermons on festival days.

The account of this controversy from the point of view of the Mayor & Corporation and their appeal to the Archbishop of Canterbury emerges from the following accounts of the Council Proceedings.

B.R.O. M/BCC/CCP/1/2 **Council Proceedings 1608–27**
fol 6v 30 January 1609

It is this day agreed that Mr Mayor and the Aldermen shall have Conference to morrow next with the Lord Bishoppe touchinge the Seates taken downe in the Cathedrall Church and thereupon shall move him that the same seates may be putt uppe againe as they were at the first and there to contynewe untill such tyme as the same may be viewed by indifferent Commissioners whoe maye judge whether the same be inconvenient and decent or any such deformity or Inconvenience as the same ys not to be suffered to remayne there. And yf yt shalbe adjudged by the said Commissioners that the same seates are a deformitye and not meete to stande and remayne there then the same shalbe thereupon taken downe and removed.
And yf the byshoppe shall not consent to this course then to move him that the Quire may be enlarged and drawne downe into the body of the Church and convenient Seates made there accordinge to my Lord Archbishoppes licence. And yf his lordshippe will not Consent to any of the former motions then Mr Mayor and his Brethren to request his Lordshippe that we may have our preachers permitted on the Sabaoth dayes and other festivall tymes in any Church or Churches in this Cytie untill some good order be taken touchinge seates at the Cathedrall Church.

fol 14v **14 July 1610**

It is this day agreed that there shalbe an answer made to the Byshoppe touchinge the Settinge uppe of the Seates in the Cathedrall church in the Colledge that yf it please his Lordshippe to cause the same Seates to be sette uppe againe in the same place and in such forme and heigthe in every respecte as they were at the firste and the pulpitte to be sette as yt was when the said Seates were builte Then the Mayor, Aldermen and Common Counsell will reste satisfied therewith, or otherwise they desyre that his Lordshippe will take order that they may have all theire timber waynscotte and Stuffe sent or restored unto them againe

fol 33v **10 April 1613**

It is this day agreed that yf the Seates for Mr Mayor, Aldermen and the Common Counsell of this Cytie and the pulpitte shalbe ordered by the Lord Archbishoppe of Canterbburie be putt uppe againe as yt was at the first erected in the Cathedrall Churche of the Holy and Undivided Trinitye of Bristoll by Mr Mayor and the Common Counsell accordinge to the graunt from the Deane and Chapter unto the Mayor and Commualtie, then the Mayor and Commaultie shall beare and paye the chardges of the settinge uppe of the said Seates. Provyded that the Mayor, Aldermen and Common Counsell may have a grante thereof from the Deane and Chapter to have and use the same to them selves only. And the Byshoppe and Deane to place them selves in any other seates or place where they please in the Church

fol 50 **20 October 1614**

It ys this daye agreed that Mr Mayor and the Aldermen shall use the best meanes that they maye to procure some order for the takinge awaye of the newe Seates lately erected in the Cathedrall Church of the Cytie for the Mayor, Aldermen and Counsell of this Cytie and their wyves to sytte on for the hearinge of the Sermons there on the Sabaoth dayes and holye dayes, and that the tymber and other stuffe of the same Seates may be brought from thence to the use of the Cytie

John Thornborough was translated to the much richer see of Worcester in 1617. Two successors remained at Bristol for short periods, Nicholas Felton (1617–19) and Rowland Searchfield (1619–23). Neither appears to have made any attempt to repair the rift with the Mayor and Corporation. This was finally accomplished by Robert Wright whose episcopate lasted from 1623 to 1633. He evidently made an approach to the Corporation, and as a result was warmly welcomed by them. Although the elaborate gallery was not re-erected in the cathedral, seats were found in the Quire for civic dignitaries and their wives, and peace was made between the parties. Later both Bishop Robert Wright and Dean Edward Chetwynd were admitted as freemen of the city. Evidence that seats for the Councillors were provided in the cathedral is to be found in the regular payments for cleaning them which were made by the Corporation during the 1620s to the 'keeper of the Seates in the College'.
[D.M. Livock, ed., 'City Chamberlain's Accounts', B R S, XXIV, 1966, xxiii, 112, 113]

B.R.O. M/BCC/CCP/1/2
fol 117 **8 November 1623**

This daye it was agreed that Mr Robert Aldworth and Mr George Harrington and Mr John Barker and Mr Christopher Whitson are appoynted to repayre unto the Lord

Bishoppe of Bristoll and to confere with him touchinge his Lordshippes motion made to Mr Mayor for the erectinge of convenient Seates in the Cathedrall Churche of this Cytie for Mr Mayor, the Aldermen and Common Counsell and theire wyves for the hearinge of Sermons there, and thereuppon to certifye Mr Mayor and his Brethren what shalbe thought fitte by his Lordshippe and the sayd Committee (?) to be done therein

And yt is alsoe agreed that there shalbe a good Butt of Sacke and two hoggeheddes of gascoyne wynes provided and presented to my Lorde Bishoppe as a token of the Love of this Cytie towards his Lordshippe.

BISHOP ROBERT WRIGHT AND EXPENDITURE ON THE CATHEDRAL 1630

Much work was carried out on the cathedral in 1630, during the episcopate of Bishop Robert Wright, who was bishop of Bristol from 1623 to 1633. He raised substantial sums by subscriptions from Bristolians and according to his own account was responsible for extensive work on the interior furnishings. It is not clear why Bishop Wright was so closely involved in these works, which might have been expected to be the responsibility of the Dean, Edward Chetwynd, who held the office from 1617 to his death in 1639. Chetwynd had a long involvement with Bristol, since he had been appointed as a lecturer or preacher by the Mayor & Corporation in 1606. In 1633 Bishop Robert Wright was translated to the more lucrative bishopric of Coventry and Lichfield, and it was from there that he submitted the following detailed account of the money spent on Bristol cathedral, together with a list of those who had subscribed to the work.

The work which Bishop Wright initiated included the installation of an organ. There had been an organ in the Augustinian abbey, as is clear from Abbot Newland's Roll *to which was added a note that Abbot John Newland died in 1515 and that he was 'beried in the south side of our Lady Chapell in the arch there by the dore going into the loft going to the organs' [I.H. Jeayes, ed., 'Abbot Newland's Roll', B.G.A.S. Trans., XIV, (1889–90), 124–30]. It is unknown whether this organ survived the Reformation and was still in use in 1630. The new organ was made by Thomas Dallam, a member of a leading family of organ builders. It consisted of 'a greate double organ and choir organ' and cost £258; it was installed on top of the screen or pulpitum which divided the chancel from the nave or transepts. A platform or floor for the organ to stand on had to be built, and stairs installed to provide access [L. Elvin, 'The Organs of Bristol Cathedral', The Organ, 42, (1962–3), 71–9]. Bishop Wright's work also included the setting up of figures of the four evangelists and of 12 prophets on the west side of the screen, painting the Ten Commandments at the east end of the cathedral and the installation of a clock. He also provided a finely-carved stone pulpit.*

B.R.O. DC/F/1/1

The Accompt of Robert Wright, late Lord Bishop of Bristoll and now of Coventry and Lichfield concurning all such sumes of money as came to his hands dureing his abode in that Sea by way of Free and Voluntary Contributions from some noblemen, the worthy citizens of that honorable Cittie, the right worthy the Deane and Chapter and other worthy knights and gentlemen towards the erecting of the goodly Organs in the Cathedrall Church, the greate windowe in the west end thereof, the horaloge [clock], the Beautifying of the Quire and finishing those greate and pious workes which were done in my time To the glory of God and the honour of that Cittie Anno Domini 1630.

	£	s	d
To Anselme Smarte, Glasier, for glazing the greate window in the west end of the Church as appeareth by his aquittance the sume of	20	0	0
To Edward Perfitt the Carpenter for making a floore for the Organ to stand upon and Stayers to them and bording the west windowe till it could be glazed as apperith by his acquittance	18	12	0
To Samuel Lewes the Smyth for the Iron Worke about the greate windowe as apperith by his Bill and acquittance	7	1	6
More for the Iron worke done about the new Clocke house as as appeareth by his Bills and acquittance	15	0	
To Anthony Barry for worke done by his appointment about the Clocke house as appeareth by his Bill and acquittance	5	18	9
Paid to Mr Thomas Babb for Gilding the Organs, Beautifying and guilding the Howerloge as appeareth by his Bill and acquittances	100	0	0
To Mr Thomas Dalam for making the greate Double Organ and Choire Organ and to Mr Thomas Hobson by his appointment for Tinn and for other necessary as by his Bills and acquittances appeareth	258	2	7
Given unto him, his Sonn and his Servants for their most honest paines and their Charges from London to Bristoll and backe againe	5	0	0
To William Hill the Carver for making the Canope over the Bishop's Seate and the Stuffe as appeareth by his Bill and acquittance	3	5	0
Paid to John Clarke free mason for making the greate window in the west end of the Church, finding stone and beating downe the old wall as appeareth by his acquittance the sume	40	0	0
Paid to the said John Clarke in hand for the [one?] Stone and Carvinge the foure Evangelists to have bene Sett up before the Quire doore, though worke was hindered, the sume of	5	0	0
Paid to the said John Clarke for making the Arch over the Quire Doore, new stone Stayers up to the Organ and preparing the Arches for the Twelve prophetes before the Quire dore as appeareth by Bills the sume of	7	5	0
Paid to William Tyler, Joyner, for making the Gallery where the Organs stand as by their Bills and acquittance appeareth	15	0	0
Paid to the said William Tyler for making the Table where on the Tenn Commandments are gilded at the Upper end of the Quire as by his acquittance appeareth	3	6	3

Because it was thought that the Joyners and Carver had a hard bargaine and because they did the worke exceeding well, I gave unto them over and above theire worke these sumes following (vizt)

	£	s	d
To William Tyler	2	0	0
To William Hill	2	0	0
To William Watham	1	0	0

Paid to Richard Hebditch for making the horologe and the lower end of the Cathedrall Church with divers and sundry motions in it the sume of 13 6 8

The sume totall expendeth in ready money abowt the aforesaid workes as appeareth by Severall Bills and acquittance of the workmen is 568 3 5

So the allocations excede the receipts besides Dinners and other petty things for which noe acquittance was taken 57 15 5

Robert Coventry & Lichfield
Laus Deo

The names of such Religious, Worthy and bountifull Benefactors of the honourable Cittie of Bristoll as were reall and readie Contributors towards the Erectinge of the greate and goodly Organ in the Cathedrall Church of the Holy and undivided Trinity in Bristoll aforesaid: And the new makinge of the faire and goodly window in the West end of the Church where formerly there was none: The new horologe and Clocke house, and the Beautifyinge of the Quire above and belowe, together with the severall Sumes which everie man gave to the foresaid worke, in the time of Robert Wright, then Bishop of that Sea: Anno Domini 1630.

	£	s	d		£	s	d
Mr Robert Aldworth, Alderman	20	0	0	Mr William Wyat	5	0	0
Mr Robert Rogers, Alderman	20	0	0	Mr William Heyman	4	0	0
Mr George Harrington, Alderm	5	0	0	Mr Charles Driver	3	0	0
Mr John Doughtie, Alderman	5	0	0	Mr Thomas Cole	5	0	0
Mr William Pitt, Alderman	5	0	0	Mr Thomas Heathcott	5	0	0
Mr John Barker, Alderman	20	0	0	Mr John Pearce	2	10	0
Mr George Gibbs, Alderman	5	0	0	Mr George Gibbs	2	0	0
Mr John Gunninge, Alderman	5	0	0	Mr Sage	1	0	0
Mr John Langton, Alderman	5	0	0	Mr Anthony Pruett	1	0	0
Mr Humfry Hooke, Alderman	10	0	0	Mr John Prigg	1	0	0
Mr John Tomlinson, Alderman	5	0	0	Mr Phillip Ellis	1	0	0
Mr Henry Yate, Alderman	2	0	0	Mrs Clifton, Widdow	1	0	0
Mr Henry Hobson, Alderman	4	0	0	Mr Ralph Farmer	1	0	0
Mr Matthew Warren	5	0	0	Mr Murwent	1	0	0

	£	s	d
Captaine Humfry Browne	10	0	0
Mr Thomas Wright	6	13	4
Mr Andrew Charlton	6	0	0
Mr Richard Hallworthy	10	0	0
Mr Richard Longe	11	0	0
Captaine John Tayler	5	0	0
Captaine Giles Elbridge	10	0	0
Captaine Richard Aldworth, the Curtaines for the Organs	[Blank]		

	£	s	d
Mr William Jones, Three Bells for the Horologe and in money	2	0	0
Mr Thomas Colston	10	0	0
Mr Francis Creswicke	10	0	0
Mr Nathaniell Butcher by will	5	0	0
Mr Ellexander James	5	0	0
Mr Thomas Clement	2	0	0
Mr John Locke	1	10	0
Mr Walter Ellis	5	0	0
Mr Oliver Snell	1	0	0
Mr Derricke Poplie	10	0	0
Mr John Gunninge	5	0	0
Mr Thomas Floyde	2	0	0
Mr William Hobson	1	2	0
Mr Robert Elliot	1	0	0
Mr Edward Peeters	5	0	0
Mr Abraham Edwards	1	0	0

	£	s	d
Mr William Willett	10	0	0
Mr William Colston	2	10	0
Mr Francis Derricke	10	0	0
Mrs Whitson, Widdow	5	0	0
Widdow Butcher, the Elder	5	0	0
Mr Edward Pitt	2	0	0
Mr Marten Elin	2	0	0
Mr William Yeomans, Atturny	2	0	0
Mr Robert Redwood, Gent	2	4	0
Mr Thomas Hobson	1	0	0
Captaine Hull	3	0	0

	£	s	d
Mrs Gulliford, Widdow	1	0	0
Mr Richard Garson, Singing man	3	0	0
Mr William Hughes, Vintner	5	10	0
Mr Edward Dakers	1	0	0
Mr Humphry Andrewes	1	0	0
Mr William Dale	1	0	0
Mr John Beven, the makinge of the Curtaines	2	0	0
TOTAL	**363**	**19**	**4**

Noble Men and Gentlemen

	£	s	d
Lord Digby, Earle of Bristoll	10	0	0
Lord Viscount Sleago	5	0	0
Sir Edward Seabright, Bart	5	0	0
Doctor Jones, Chancilor of Bristoll	10	0	0
Thomas Smith, Esquire	5	0	0
John Dowle, Senior, Esqr	3	0	0
Nicholas Heale, Esqr	5	0	0
Francis Browne, Esqr	5	0	0
Arthur Norton, Esqr	10	0	0
Mr Hodges	4	0	0
Mr John Cottrell	2	0	0
Mr Bridges, parson of Winterborne	4	0	0
Mr Andrew Whittington	2	0	0
Mr John Price, Barrister	5	0	0
Mr Anthony Hodges	1	0	0
The Summe is	**76**	**0**	**0**

From the Rt Worshipfull the Deane and Chapter of the Cathedrall Church of Bristoll:

	£	s	d
Imprimis: for their old Organs sould to St Steevens the summe of	30	0	0
It. Given more in money at severall times	40	0	0
The Summe is	**70**	**0**	**0**

	£	s	d
It. Received for the Remainder of Boords bought upon Perfitts account and left when the worke was done, the summe		2	6	8
Summe Totall received is	510	6	0

Robert Coventry & Lichfield
Laus Deo

Bishop Wright's work on the cathedral included the installation of a finely-carved stone pulpit and a large organ. The organ consisted of 'a greate double organ and choir organ'; it was made by Thomas Dallam and cost £258. His episcopate in Bristol was evidently popular and successful, but not all observers viewed him with favour. The author and antiquarian, Anthony Wood (1632–95), wrote that Robert Wright was grasping and covetous, and alleged that the bishop had enriched himself by selling long and beneficial leases of episcopal lands. The wealth he acquired enabled him to purchase an estate of his own at Newnham Courtney (Oxon) for £18,000. This suggestion also appears in Archbishop Laud's writings. [Anthony Wood, Athenae Oxonienses, *(1813–20 edn.), IV, 800–2; William Laud,* Works, *(1853 edn.), V (ii), 346].*

It was no doubt in order to defend himself against such allegations that Bishop Wright wrote to Archbishop Laud on 29 March 1637 a long letter entitled:

A true relation of things that I, Bishop Wright of Lichfield and Coventry have done in every place (for the benefit of posterity) where God blest me with any means, since I let [left] University, as my soul shall answer at the last day.

The letter includes an account of his work at Bristol cathedral as follows:

I caused to be sett up as goodly a pair of organs and as richly gilded as any be in this Kingdom, and made a goodly window in the west end of the Church where before was a plaine stone wall and noe light. I richly beautified the east end of the quire and the entrance thereto. I sett up one of the finest stone pullpits in this Kingdom. Whereas the clock stood upon pillars of wood in the face of the Church, I made a new clock-house of stone in the interior of the Church, with the fairest and most artificial horologe in these parts.

Archbishop Laud endorsed this letter with the words 'Not for ostentation but to affront malice' [Cal. S.P. Dom. 1636–7, 531].

Fig. 5 The pulpit provided by Bishop Thomas Wright in 1630. With its elaborate tester or sounding-board and the colourful heraldic panels, it overlooked the transepts where the congregation assembled to hear the sermons.

(By Thomas Rowbotham 1826. © Bristol's Museums, Galleries & Archives)

DESCRIPTIONS OF THE CATHEDRAL IN 1634

ARCHBISHOP LAUD'S VISITATION 1634

William Laud became Archbishop of Canterbury in August 1633. He was strongly opposed to Puritanism within the Church and concerned to do all he could to promote a spirit of reverence, decency and beauty within cathedrals and parish churches, and a suitable dignity in the conduct of the services. To further this aim he began a series of visitations of cathedrals during 1634. They were conducted by his vicar-general, Sir Nathaniel Brent, who was Warden of Merton College, Oxford. Brent was assisted by Laud's secretary, William Dell. Both Brent and Dell made marginal notes against the replies to their enquiries made by the Dean and Chapter of Bristol cathedral.

The answers to the detailed questions reveal that since the communal life, as originally conceived, had been totally abandoned, very different arrangements now prevailed within the cathedral. The dean and canons all held other benefices and most of them spent only their obligatory terms of residence in Bristol. Some of their houses within the precinct, together with the library room and communal hall, were leased to laymen. The minor canons also held other appointments and officiated in other Bristol churches, attending the cathedral only for the daily services. Their number had been reduced from six to four, so that the stipends from the two vacant posts could be shared among the rest. Functions such as that of' gospeller' and 'epistoler' were now carried out by others, and the stipends shared. The vicars choral or lay clerks served as organists or parish clerks in other churches, and in consequence some were unable to attend both of the Sunday services in the cathedral. The almsmen were non-resident and posts such as that of cook, caterer and butler survived as sinecures. The original intention of a schoolmaster and an usher or under-master to teach the choirboys and others had been abandoned, and the two posts were amalgamated. The aged organist, Elway Bevin, although formerly of high reputation, was now incapable of fulfilling his office. On weekdays the transepts of the cathedral provided a convenient short cut to the bishop's residence and other houses in the Lower Green. College Green was cut up by the passage of horses and carts and was used for all sorts of secular traffic. The chapel dedicated to St Jordan, which stood on the Green, was used as a schoolroom. The reference to tennis being played there possibly refers to the game of fives which was very popular throughout the west country, and was often played against the outside walls of church buildings. The large edifice erected within the cathedral to provide appropriately grandiose seating for the mayor and corporation, as well as for their wives, meant that space for other members of the congregation was cramped and unsatisfactory. There is little indication of passion or fervour in the conduct of the services or of anything other than the perfunctory performance of statutory duties. The full text of the visitation is as follows:

Historical Manuscripts Commission, IV, 1890, Appendix 124 to 126, 141 to 144

Bristol 1634

I. Articles for the Cathedrall Church of Bristoll to be enquired of in the Metropoliticall Visitation of the Most Reverend Father in God, William, by God's providence, Lord Archbishop of Canterbury his Grace, Primate of all England and Metropolitane, In this present yeare of our Lord God one thousand six hundred and thirty four.

1. Imprimis, whether every member of this church att his first admission doth sweare to observe such statutes as have beene hitherto used as statutes a[nd not] contrary to the lawes of the realme of England?

2. Item, what other benefices ecclesiasticall the deane, archdeacon, preb[endaries], or other eccl'icall persons of this church, have besides their roomes and places in [the] said church?

3. Item, howe the xlij., xliij. and xliiij. chapters of the constitutions made in the convocation, Anno 1604, and confirmed by his Matie, under the greate seale of England, for the residencyes of your deane and other prebendaryes, as well upon their prebends, as upon their other benefices are observed?

4. Item, whether the number of those that serve the quire, and all other ministers of this church, be kept full, and the quire sufficiently furnished with able singers, and daylie service there song according to the foundation of this church?

5. Item, whether your divine service be used, and ye sacraments administered in due tyme, and according to the booke of comon prayer, and by singing and note according to the statutes of this church?

6. Item, whether all the members of yor church, especially the prebendaryes and [ecclesiasticall] persons, doe use seemely garments and attyres, as namely, all graduates their surp[lice and] hood for their degree of schoole, and other inferiours their surplice and cap, according to the canons and constitutions sett forth by his Matie in the convocation, in Anno 1604?

7. Item, whether ye prebendaryes and preachers of your church doe preach yearly the full number of sermons appointed by the statutes and ordinances of ye said church, and the late constitutions eccl'icall in their owne persons or by others, and who doth [most] usually preach them, and how often have you sermons or lectures in the weeke in [the] cathedrall church, and by whome and what be the statutes of this church in that behalfe. And if you have any certaine lecturer, what hath he for his paines?

8. Item, whether the muniments and evidences of this church be safely kept, and in such manner as is required by ye statutes thereof, of what persons is the foundacon of [your] cathedrall church, namely, of how many prebendaryes, cannons, petticannons, vicars chorall, choristers, virgerers, gramer schoole master, and schollers or [other] like, and who is bound to mainetaine and finde them, and are they att this present full and serve the church in their owne persons, as by the law they ought to doe. And [are] they elected as the statutes of this realme and of this church doe require?

9. Item, whether the choristers be well ordered and the number of them furnished, and who hath the charge of catechising and instructing of them in the principles of religion, and whether are they soe brought up?

10. Item, whether the officers of this church, namely, steward, tresurers,

bow[sers], receavers, accomptants, and such like, doe yearly make a true accompt of their receipts and pay such money as is due to the church upon their accompts, and whether any such person be now indebted unto the church, and in how much?

11. Item, whether the cathedrall church be sufficiently repaired both in the body, chancell, and all other iles and places belonging to the church, and by whose default is it unrepaired? And are the houses and edifices belonging to the Deane and Prebendaryes and to others who are allowed by the s[tatutes] of this church to have houses kept in sufficient and good repaire, as by y^e [statute] is required, and are they used as they ought to be, and are there any incr[ochments] made by any in any kinde whatsoever. And is yr churchyard kept in decent manner without any prophanation?

12. Item, whether the prebendaryes and other the preachers of this church [in] their sermons doe use to pray for the Kinges Matie, the Queene, Prince, and all [his] highnes issue, and doe give unto his highnes in their prayer according to the five [and] fiftieth constitution his whole stile, and soe doe pursue the particulars in the [said] constitution appointed for that end to be observed?

13. Item, whether there be within this church or ye precincts and limitts [thereof] any usurers contrarie to the statutes in that behalfe made, drunkards, adulterers, fornicators, incestuous persons, Symonists, open recusants of [either] sect, or such as neglect to repair to the church to service, or doe not receive [the] comunion thrice yearly, or are vehemently suspected of any of the crymes aforesaid, or any that be familiarly and daylie conversant with re[cusants], or notorious papists, or harborers and receavers of any such into their houses?

14. Item, whether are your capitular meetings duly and orderly kept [as by] statute is required?

15. Item, what new buildings are there within the precincts of your church, and by whome and by whose license or connivance they were soe built? What lay dwellers and inmates are there within the same precinct, and who they are; and what inclosures and incrochments are made by any or upon your church or churchyard, and by whome and what or wherein are they?

16. Item, whether is your church and close made a comon throughfare, and what posterne dores are there made to private houses and by whome? and whether be the offices of your church sold or granted in reversion? and whether doe any of your church officers live in the towne?

17. Item, what is the yearly allowance of your schoolemaster and usher of your free schoole (if you have any), and whether is the same or any part thereof wth held from them or any of them, and by whome, and whether are they diligent in performing thir duty, and is not the same schoole neglected or abused in any kind.

The articles added by Brent are as follows:

18. Item, whether are anye advowsons of benefices have bin graunted to any p'sons before hand contrarie to the lawes of this realme or of this church,

19. And whether any contracts have byn made for anye resignacon of their former livinges before or after their institucons into those benefices whereof they had advowsons?

20. Item, what vestmentes, utensills, and ornaments have you belonging to yor churche, and whether have anie of them byn made awaye or aliened, and by whome?

II. The answere of the Deane and Chapter of the Cathedrall Church of Bristoll, to the Articles of the moste Revend Father in God, William (by God's providence) Lord Archbishop of Canterbury his Grace, Primate of all England and Metropolitane, given to them in his Metropoliticall visitacon, in the yeare of o^r Lord God one thowsand six hundred thirtye and foure.

Ad 1^m. They answere, that every member of the church doth (for ought they knowe), at his firste admission, sweare to observe the founder's statutes, such as have beene usually propounded unto them, and hitherto used as statutes, and not contrary to the lawes of this realme.

Ad 2^m. They answere, that the deane hath the viccaridge of Berkeley in Gloucestershire; the archdeacon the p'sonages of Cucklington and Bayford in Som[er]setshire. Doctor Greene the p'sonages of Stockden, in Wiltes, and of Avington in Hampshire, and the donative of Littlebury in Essex. Mr Marcks the viccaridges of South Petherton and Merriott in Som[er]setshire. Mr Norris the viccaridge of Stonehouse in Gloucestershire. Mr Cuthbert the p'sonage of Stocklinch Attersay [Ottersey] and the donative of Weste Dolishe [Dowlish] in Som[er]setshire. Mr Tucker the p'sonage of Portishead and viccaridge of Longe Ashton in Som[er]setshire, and Mr Weeks the p'sonage of Sherwell in Devonshire.

Ad 3^m. They answere (every one for his owne p'ticuler) that they are carefull for the keeping of their residence both in this cathedrall church, and upon their benefices soe farre as they conceive themselves to bee bound by the mentioned constitucons of the church. And if in any yeare there bee any delinquency in this behalfe, that they have heretofore presented the same, and shalbe readye likewise soe to doe unto the bishopps at their visitacons.

Ad 4^m. They answere, that there are but foure petty canons who have the stipend of the other two vacant places by the direccon of the late bishop in his visitacon, only untill provision can bee made to fill up the number. And these said foure pettie cannons (one of them being only deacon, and the other three preistes) undertaking to discharge the office of the gospeller, by the direccon aforesaid, the stipend of that place is conferred uppon the singingmen and organist for their incouragement untill thinges may bee better setled. The place of the epistoler hath been for many yeares executed by one of the vicars chorall, who receiveth the stipend for the same. And for the organist , hee is a verie olde man, who, having done good service in the church is not now able to discharge the place, but that hee is holpen by some other of the quier. As for the singing men their number is full, and for the moste pte verie able men (onlie one excepted); by all which the dailye service is ordinarily well performed according to the foundacon of this church.

Know yt[which] one is &c.

Ad 5^m. They answeare affirmitively, only the Letany beeing said every Sunday and holieday morning at six a clocke praiers, is not usually sung againe at ten a clocke praiers for wante of a full quier, some of the singing men being clercks of parrishes or organistes in the cittye.

*Require it to
be constant, &c.
Ad 6^m. They answere affirmatively, saving that they doe not constantlie and continually weare square cappes.

Ad 7^m. They answere, that they for the moste pte preach their turnes required by the statutes and the orders of their bishop, upon the Sundayes and solemne festivalls themselves, or by other sufficyent and allowed preachers procured by them, in their absence, to supply the same. As for the lectures in the weeke daies, they have not any, neither have they anie statute to that effecte.

Ad 8^m. They answere firste, touching the evidences, &c., That as they found them, they are safely kepte, and in that manner as is required by the statutes. (Their letters of foundacon and donacon, together with the box wherein their seale is, and counterptes of leases in beeing, and other thinges of greater moment, being kepte in their sealing cheste). The booke of statutes and other recordes in the custodie of the deane, or in his absence of the subdeane, treasurer or senior prebendary present. As for other auncient wrytinges, which have come unto their handes, they are kepte where they found them in their sealing house. The audit house wherein formerlie they were kepte (as they have heard) together with another roome, which some affirm was heretofore a library, beeing before their tyme suffered to fall into decay and turned into a dwelling house, and leased out by their predecessors. Secondly, for the persons of which the foundacon of their church consisteth; they are p'ticulerlie menconed in the first of the statutes: de numero eorum quae in ecclesia cathedrali Bristoli sustentantur, whereunto for answere they referre themselves. All which p'sons (besides some other officers, as auditor and chapter clercke) have their severall mainteynance from their church allotted by the statutes, and some of them with augmentacon, and they are chosen and admitted according to the direccon of their letters of foundacon and statutes of their church, and (for ought they knowe) as the statuts of the realme require. And for their fulnesse at the present and serving of the church in their owne p'sons, it hath beene in parte already answered to the fourth article, and shalbe farther in the nexte and seaventeenth articles.

*Enquire this of
the almesmen
Onlie the almesmen live absent with some wrong unto their church, yet yeelding some allowance to the sexton for doing their service. As for the under officers of cater, cooks, and butler, appointed by statutes to attend the comons table, that table beeing (as they conceive) for want of mainteynance, by

*Order will be taken
in the statutes, &c.
order, long since dissolved, their pay is continued and (their places graunted by pattent, as heretofore) they are enioyned their service as occasion may require.

Ad 9^m. They answere concerning the choristers, that insteed of six appointed by the foundacon with the allowance of five marckes a peece, they found only foure with the allowance of foure poundes a peece, the other foure powndes being taken (as they conceive) towardes the increase of the master's stipend, from ten pounds to twenty marckes, and of the six singing men from twenty nobles to eight poundes a peece p'annu. But they have of late yeares made full againe the number of six boyes

*Here is noe mencon
of theyr being
catechised
by giving that foure poundes to two more, who serve in their surplisses as the other foure, in the quier, expecting to bee preferred when the. others remoove. But the weakness, through age of their M^r causeth that they bee not soe well ordered or

instructed as they otherwise should, but for helpe hereof are comitted to the care of some others of the quier, and some of them alsoe goe to the gramar schoole.

Ad 10^m. They answere, that their predecessours having before theeir tymes leased out their manno^{rs} to the farmers and appointed their rentes to be paied within the p'cinctes of the church to the treasurer, hee only is the officer that receiveth and paieth all dues, giving an yearly account at their audit.

Ad 11^m. They answere, that their predecesso^{rs} having much neglected the care of their fabricke, there hath of late yeares beene great charge by them bestowed upon the same; soe that for the present, the chancell body and iles of the church are in good repaire (for ought they knowe): and further provision is made for the p'fecting thereof. And as for the deane and prebendaries houses they are in good repaire,

* Who is that prebend? except one prebendaries house, which before their tymes was utterlie ruined; but the prebendary hath another allotted him in leiu of the same, and hath beene formerly presented at severall visitacons. And as for incroachmentes, in their tyme they know not of any. For their churchyardes they have one within their cloyster, w ^{ch} is well fenced, and is not (for ought they knowe) prophaned. And as for their great greene, ancientlie called Magnum Coemiterium, it being soe open bewixt them, and those that dwell on the other side, there bee many

*Consider of those disorders disorders,which they rather wish then well knowe how to remedye.

Ad 12^m. They answere affirmatively to all the p'ticulers of it.

Ad 13^m. They answeare negatively for any thing they knowe.

Ad 14^m. They answere, that they now doe keepe their solemne meetinges at Midsomer and their audit, as is required by statute; as alsoe two other solemne chapters, according to the order of their laste bishop, and at other tymes as they have occasion for the business of their church. And as for the inferior chapters for their quier, though they bee not exactlie kept every fortnight, yet bee they called, and the quier is called upon at tymes as they conceive needfull, and the p'ditions kepte by the chanter are inquired after.

Ad 15^m. They answere, that they knowe no new buildings erected within the precinctes of the church, except one house at the weste end of the church, and let out as a tenement by their predecessors before their tyme; but their are divers lay persons, both men and women, which inhabite among them, as the bishop's chauncellor and register, and the late deane's wife, and some others; some dwelling in their owne houses, and some in pte of the houses of some of the prebendaries. As

*Take care y ^{t} this whipping post be removed. for incroachmentes, they know of none, only a post of correction in their great greene or coemiterium magnum, lately set up by the cittye, whereat there is offence taken by them as a thing done in predjudice of their liberties and imunities. And (as some of their

*And consid^r of these buildings companie conceive) they are likewise p'judiced in some new buildings, as namely, a house at the foot of Brandon hill; another house on the waste at St Augustine's backe, and some other like

incroachmentes by the citty pretending the grownd to bee their waste. And some of the Company doe conceive, that some seates set up in the bodye of the church come within the compasse of this article.

Ad 16ᵐ. If by the close bee meant the greene called Magnum Coemiterium, it is the comon way from the citty to their church and their dwelling houses, and other places lying beyond; but it is made too comon by ryding of horses, and halliers drayes and *Consider of theyr* other passages, if it may bee remedied. The church alsoe is a *riding of horses, &c.* passage to the Bishop's pallace and other dwellinge houses in the cloysters; but they forbid and restraine any offensive carriages that way. They knowe of no offices in their church solde by them, neither any reversion, but of such as are joyned in pattent with them, who have the actuall possession of the places. If by officers bee meant such as attend the service of the church, as ministers and singing men they live many of them nere the church, but some others in the towne; and their auditor and chapter clercke live in the towne alsoe.

Ad 17ᵐ. They answere, that the yearly allowance of the schoolemaster is by statute only twenty marckes, and for an usher twenty nobles, both which stipendes have beene conferred upon the schooolemaster heretofore undertaking the whole charge of the schoole, and receiveth the whole twenty powndes; and they conceive hee is diligent in his place.

Ad 18ᵐ. They answere, that they knowe no crime or offence soe comitted, which they conceive worthy to bee presented.

Ad 19ᵐ. They answere, that there have beene some advowsons of benefices of late ** this granting of* yeares graunted in this church; but whether such grauntes are *advowsons is directly* contrary either to the lawes of this realme or of this church they *agˢᵗ theyr statutes.* leave it to the determinacon of the Lord Archbishop's Grace of Canterbury their present visitor. And as for such contractes as are enquired of they knowe not any.

Ad 20ᵐ. They answeare, that they knowe not of any vestments or utensils that have beene in their tyme made away or aliened; neither have they any vestments; **they must thinke* As for utensils, both for the comunion table and pulpitt, they have *of providing some.* some which are kepte safe, and what is wanting, as the state of their poore church will afford, shalbe provided wᵗʰ their beste speed and conveniencye.

> Edward Chetwind, Decan
> Christopher Greene, Sub-dec.
> Rob. Markes, Receptor
> William Norris
> George Cuthbert
> Tho. Tucker, Thesaurar
> Joh. Weekes

III. The answers of the petticanons and vicars chorall to the articles exhibited in the Metropolotoicall visitacon of the most Reverend father in God

William Laud by God's providence Lord Archbishopp of Canterbury, holden in the cathedrall church of Bristoll in the yeare of our Lord God 1634.

1. To the first article, wee know nothing to the contrary.

2. To the second, wee answere, that Mr Deane hath the vicarage of Barkley, in the in the countie of Gloucester. As for the archdeacon, wee know not what liveinges he hath. Doctour Greene hath two liveings, the one is called Stockton in Wiltshire, and the other in Hamampshire, Mr Markes hath Southpetherton, and Merriott in Som[er]setshire, Mr Norris hath Stonehouse in Gloucestershire, Mr Cuthbert hath Stocklinch, Mr Tucker hath Portished and Long Ashton in Som[er]setshire, and Mr Weelkes hath one liveing in the countie of Devon, Mr. Almon hath St Maryport, and Mr. Reade hath Little St Augustines in Bristoll.

3. To the third wee answere, that all have kept their annuall residence, but what they have done uppon their benefices wee know not.

4. To the fowerth we answer, the quire is supplyed by tenn, where there should be twelve, that is, 4 petticanons, 6 laymen, an organist, 4 choristers 2 secondaries, and dayly service duly p'formed.

*Why are two wanting?

5. To the fiveth wee answere they are duly p'formed.

6. To the sixth wee answere they doe.

7. To the seaventh wee answere, that the deane and prebendes doe preach themselves, or some others for them when their turnes is. For lectures there are none.

8. To the eight wee aunswere, that the munimentes are kept safe for ought wee knowe. For the number there is a deane and six prebendes, fower petticanons, where there ought to be six; six viccars chorall, an organist, six choristers, one virgerer, one schoolemaster, one usher, one gospeller, one epistoler, one sexton, fower almsmen, an audito^r, a cater, a butler, a cooke, an under cooke, a porter, what other officers we know not, because wee knowe neither the foundation nor the statutes. The gospeler's place is p'formed by one Richard Jackson, one of the viccars chorall, being a layman. The schoolmaster doth p'forme his owne place, and the ushers. The cato^r, butler, and cookes have their pay, but they doe no service.

*That is not fitt

9. To the nynth, concerning the choristers, they are taught and instructed, but not by the organist, by reason of his age, but by some others of the quire, of theire owne freewill.

10. To the tenth article, wee know nothing to the contrary.

11. To the eleaventh, the church and church yeard, and other ediffices are all in repayre.

12. To the twelveth article wee answere, it is p'formed.

13. To thirteenth wee answere wee know none.

14. To the fowerteenth wee answere, they are orderly kept.

*Consider of these lay-dwellers, &c.

15. To the fiveteenth, wee know that there are lay dwellers in fower of the prebendes houses. And some other lay dwellers within the presinkes of the church.

[16.] To the sixteenth wee answere, that the church is not made a thorowe fare, and for posterne doores wee know none, and whether the offices of the church be solde or graunted in reversion, wee know that some of them are.

*Let that be enquired.

17. To the seaventeenth article wee answere, that the yearly allowance of the schoolemaster is 13^{li} 13^s 4^d , and for the usher 6^{li} 6^s 8^d . And in regard ther is no usher, the schoolemaster hath the whole paye, and doth dischardge both places.

18. To the eighteenth wee answere, wee know nothing. As for the two last articles underwritten, wee answere that wee heare of certaine advowsons of benifices, but to whome, they have bine graunted or in what manner wee know not, and for the vestmentes wee know none.

Edw. Almond.	Richard Jacksone.	James Blowar.
John Mason.	Thomas Prince.	John Lukins.
James Reade.	William Cooper.	John Ham.
Robert Perry.		

IV. The answeare of the Schoolemaster of the Cathedrall Church of Bristoll, to certayne articles enquired of in the Metropoliticall Visitation of the most Reverend Father in god, William , by god's providence Lord Archbishoppe of Canterbury his Grace, Primate of all England and Metropolitan for this present yeare of our Lord God 1634.

1. To the first, hee answeareth affirmatively, for ought hee knoweth

2. To the second, that the deane, archdeacon, all the prebendaryes, and two of the petty canons have benefices, some one, some two; but what the severall names of those benefices are, hee knoweth not.

3. To the third, that hee takes no notice of the residencye of the deane and prebendaryes either at the cathedrall church or on theyr benefices.

4. To the fourth, that hee hath knowne sixe petty canons to serve the quire, but now there are but foure, who performe the service and receive the pay of the other two. The singers are able, and the organist skillfull, but is disabled by age to execute his place. Mr Jackson, one of the singers, hath had the epistler's place many yeares, and the pay due to the gospeler is divided amongst the quire, who daily sing service in this church.

5. To the fift, hee answeareth affirmatively.

6. To the sixt, likewise affirmatively, save that the cappe is not constantly used.

7. To the seventh, likewise affirmatvely. There is no constant man that preacheth for the deane or prebends, but sometymes one, sometymes another; and wee have no lecture at all.

8. To the eighth, hee answeareth that hee is unacquainted with the muniments, evidences, statutes, and foundation of this cathedrall church, & therefore can say nothing heereunto.

9. To the ninth, that there are foure quiristers and two secondaryes; the catechizing and instructing of them belongs to the organist, but hee performeth it not, by reason of his age. Two of them are sent to the grammar schoole, and the rest have others to looke unto them.

10. To the tenth, hee answeareth affirmatively, for ought hee knoweth.

11. To the eleventh, likewise affirmatively, for matter of reparations; neither knoweth hee of any encrochments or profanation of that place wch is bounded and now used as a churchyard, lying within the cloysters.

12. To the twelveth likewise affirmatively, saving that the praysing of God for all those which are departed out of this life in the fayth of Christ, is not generally used.

*Call for the use of it.

13. To the thirteenth, hee answeareth negatively, for ought hee knoweth.

14. To the fourteenth, affirmatively.

15. To the fifteenth, that hee knoweth of no new buildings since his tyme; but there are divers lay dwellers within the precincts of the church, and some of them in foure of the prebendaryes howses: hee knoweth of no inclosures or encrochments on the church or churchyard.

16. To the sixteenth hee answeareth, that the church is a passage to the bishop's house, and other howses in the cloysters, but all carriages are forbidden to passe that way: hee knoweth of no posterne doores to private howses: the auditorship was some yeares since granted to Mr Thomas Browne for his life, and to his sonne in reversion. No church-officer that I remember but the chapter-clerks liveth in the towne.

17. To the seventeenth hee answeareth, that the yearly allowance of the schoolemaster is 13^l 6^s 8^d and of the usher 6^l 13s 4^d. But the whole 20^l hath beene enjoyed by two or three schoole-masters, his immediate predecessours, and likewise by himselfe for these fifteene yeares by the consent of the bishop, deane, and chapter.

18. To the eighteenth hee answeareth, that he knoweth not of any other offences or crimes committed by any of this church that are presentable.

19. To the nineteenth, that some advowsons of benefices have beene graunted before hand, but whether unlawfully or no hee knoweth not; neither knoweth hee of any contracts made for resignations.

20. To the twentieth, that what vestments, utensils, & ornaments belong to the church hee knoweth not; neither knoweth hee of any that have beene made away or aliened by any body.

Henry James.

V.   An explanation of certaine darke answeres exhibited by the Deane and Chapter of the cathedrall church of Bristoll to the most reverend Father in God, William by the divine providence Lord Archbishop of Canterbury, &c. in his visitacon there the last of May, anno Dni. 1634.

In resp. ad. 2. Whilst every man answers for his owne particuler, the generall fault of Non Residence, according to statute (somwhat moderately interpreted in the decrees of our first bishop, confirmed by o^r first deane & chapter), whereof most are

*This may be reg- ulated if there be the need by the statutes.

guilty, is concealled, viz. A new found residence of 28 dayes in one yere is deemed to be sufficient, and they that p'forme onely such residency are p'takers of all profittes & beneficiall offices as far forth, yea & before him that shalbe resident 6, 5,

or 4 monethes according to the menconed mitigacon in o^r first bishop his decrees.

In resp. ad 4 et 5. Our places allotted by the foundacon are not full. There is great want of an usher, the master being an ordinary preacher and chaplyn to the Lord Bishop. The schollers who of ould were wont alwaies to repair to the morning

*It were well y^t boyes came to church

service in the cathdedrall church half an hower after six doe wholly absent the themselves therefrom, & are not culpable.

* If Jackson be soe rich another man were fitter to have y^t benefit, &c.

Mr Jackson, the singing man, reputed to be able to dispend 200^{li} p'ann. hath the epistoler's place annexed to his singing man's. the stipend of the gospeller's place ys diverted to other, not so necessary uses. Two pettycanons places are voyd, and the yerely pencon of x^{li} each, divided amongst the other four, at w^{ch}

time most of them were beneficed persons, the rest were allowed to officiat other cures, not without some hindrance to o^r church service, and were well contented with this onely favo^r.

Our singing men are, some clerks of parishes in the city, some organists, whereby their ordinary attendance in our church is much hindred, especially on Sunday mornings.

*Let that be remedyed. We very seldome or never have the Letany sung on Sunday morninges cathedraliter.

It hath long been a comon practice, if Mr Mayor come before our *I divine service is ended, abruptly to breake off service, if the service chaunce to be ended before his comyng, all the congragacon stay, & expect his comyng before the sermon begin.

I like neyther of These two, and require that both be remedyed.

Ad 4 et 11. The prebend whose house is utterly decayed, hath the house auntiently the schoolmaster's. The schoolm' the house of a petty canon, without any care for restitution thereof to that poore place. The rome auntiently the library (wch being remanent might bee reverted to the first use, is converted to a chamber in a private dwellinghowse, and leased out as a part thereof. The house of comons (auntiently for the use of the quire) is alienated from them, and let out by lease to a straunger, soe are other houses within our precincts set out to straungers. Our quiremen wanting houses convenient for their service in our church, and oftimes neglecting their dutie by reason of their remote dwelling in the citie.

*Let there be care taken of all these abuses, &c.

Our great chuchyard is thus prophaned.

1. The most pleasant middle walke thereof (the most used of old by such as expected the service in our church) is now made by the halliers of the city, a comon highway for drayes to carry clothes in great basketts to Brandon hill to dry, by meanes whereof the walke is as it were plowed up. The same is made a comon highway for other horse passengers, whereas the auntient way for both, was through the lane comonly called Frog lane, a neerer and fitter passage.

2. This whole churchyard is made a receptacle for all ydle persons to spend their time in stopball, and such lyke recreacons, even oftimes from morning to night, the time of divine service not excepted, no not oft tymes on Sundayes and holydaies.

3. The schoolhouse standing on this site, is made at all times as a comon tennis court, and ys in a manner fitted for that use.

4. In the churchyard the city hath of late set up a whipping post, & tooke upon them awthority to arrest here, and in the very cloysters adjoyning to our church.

Ad 15. Our prebends for the most part lett out their houses to lay persons, sometimes dangerous by prying into the state of our church, sometimes disrespective, at all times burthensome to such as live and reside there.

There is in the opinion of many of sound judgment a graund enclosure in our church by reason of certaine seates set up in our sermon place by the citezens by vertue of a long lease from the deane & chapter (scilz. For ever), conteyning 29 foote & a half in length & 11 foote in breadth on the south side of the said church for the maior, aldermen, & comon councell wth 20 foot in length on the north side & 11 foot in breadth for their wives, wch seates are appropriated to them, so that neither knight nor esquire, lady nor gentlewoman have any proper place where to heare the sermon.

*His Ma^{ty} hath com'anded to have moveable seates in ye body of the church, and the standing ones to be taken downe, &c.

Thies seates for the manner of site, stand soe remote from the pulpit that they betray the cheefest place of audience, where the maior &c. were wont to sit on benches with backes, moveable, to the more vulgar and meaner auditory.

2. By reason of the height of the first seat from the ground (the bottome thereof being welnigh two foot from the pavement) wth an higher rising by degrees of the seates succeeding, to the last, together with the altitude of men sitting & standing in the last seat wth their heads covered, doe hinder the hearing of the greatest part of those that are behind, and of such as were wont to heare in a little chappell backwards, called by the name of Sr Theodore Newton's chappell.

Ad 16^m .There being noe article directly concerning the ymployment of money given in pious uses, neither is the last article enquiring after offences & crymes p'sonall, deemed to comprehend the same, by wch meanes this grand abuse is lyke to escape without

*Let this be considered of.

Notice, viz., The xx l. to be bestowed yerely on highways, is not rightly & truly ymployed according to the statute and auntient presidentes.

Soe likewise is a contrary practice, of having a lecture (at Little St. Augustine's

*Examine how this belonges to ye cathedrall, &c.

every Sonday in the afternoone in the place of catechising), the resort to wch especially with contribucon, is made a marke of cognizance of the holy from the p'phane as they terme them.

Endorsed by Dell:-
Farther advertisem^{ts} concerning ye church of Bristoll.

The organist mentioned in the answers given to the Archbishop's visitation articles, and who is described as 'disabled by age to execute his place', was Elway Bevin, one of the most distinguished of the musicians to be engaged at Bristol. He was born about 1550, and is thought to have been educated in London where he was taught music and composition by the greatest of the Elizabethan church musicians, Thomas Tallis. By 1580 he had moved to Wells as a vicar choral, and by 1585 he was installed as master of the choristers at Bristol cathedral. Soon afterwards he was also being paid as organist. During his long tenure at Bristol he composed many pieces of church music and wrote a text book on composition entitled Briefe and Short Instruction of the Art of Musicke. *His reputation as a musician and composer was recognised in 1605 when he was appointed to the honorary position of Gentleman Extraordinary of the Chapel Royal. His 'Dorian service', which comprised settings of various parts of the Communion service together with the Magnificat and Nunc Dimittis, was later printed in several books on church music. By the time of Laud's visitation in 1634 Bevin must have been nearly 80 years of age, and incapable of performing all the duties of his office. In 1637 he was finally dismissed by the Chapter.*

B.R.O. DC/A/8/1

fol. 6v

14 February 1637 the Dean and Chapter capitularly ordered and decreed that Elway Bevin be removed, expelled and dismissed from his office of Organist and Master of the Choristers'.

It is not clear why Bevin was so precipitately dismissed from his offices at the cathedral. It has been suggested that throughout his life he was a secret Catholic, but concealed his true opinions in order to pursue his career as a professional church musician. It may be that in his extreme old age he became more outspoken about his beliefs, so that the Dean and Chapter felt obliged to dismiss him; or it may be that they were no longer prepared to tolerate the fact that through age and infirmity he was no longer able to perform his duties. He died in 1638 and was buried in the churchyard of St Augustine the Less.
[Oxford DNB; J.G. Hooper, Elway Bevin,(Bristol 1971); Graham Hooper, 'Organists and Masters of the Choristers of Bristol Cathedral' in Elizabeth Ralph & John Rogan, eds., Essays in Cathedral History, Bristol, 1991, 85–6].

Description by Three Soldiers in 1634

In the same year that Archbishop Laud's Visitation was taking place, the cathedral was visited by three soldiers from Norwich, who were making a journey through England, noting all the places they visited. Their seven-week walk began on 11 August 1634. Little is known of these three soldiers except that they were a Captain, a Lieutenant, and an 'Ancient' or Ensign. From internal evidence it appears that the actual writer was the Lieutenant whose name was Hammond. The three men evidently enjoyed their visit to Bristol and were impressed by the busy harbour and the number of ships, as well as by the churches and public buildings, and by the splendour of the Avon Gorge. As soldiers, they were interested in the defences of the city, and witnessed the exercises of the Trained Bands, consisting of three companies of infantry. Their description of the cathedral and its precincts was as follows:

L.G. Wickham Legg, ed., A Relation of a Short Survey of 26 Counties, 1904, 94–6. (The original manuscript is in the British Library, Lansdowne MSS 213).

In a neat and pleasant Ascent is seated the Cathedral Church * which is unfinished, and so much as is, was begun, and intended only for the Quire, and High Altar, and may (as much is of it) compare for strength and beauty with any other; neere it is a fayre and large Colledge yard, beautify'd with many shady Trees, and most delightful walkes, about which stands many stately Buildings (besides the Bishops Palace, the Deanes, the Chancellors, and the Prebends Houses) wherein many Gentlemen and Gentlewomen of note and ranke doe live; In her are rich Organs, lately beautify'd and indifferent good Quiristers.

Many fayre Monuments amongst the rest are there: On the south side of the Church in Newtons Chapell is the Monument of Sir Henry Newton in Alabaster in Armour, with his Lady, and 2 Sons and 4 Daughters. This knight tooke the King of Morocco and brought him Captive into England, who knealeth in his Mauritanian Royall habit with his Crowne of his head, holding the point of his Sword, and offring it up as a Trophee to his Conqueror.

On the other side of the church is Berkeleys Chapell, where the Lord Berkeley, and his Lady, lieth plaine under free stone.

On the south side of the Quire, is another plaine Monument of Freestone of the Lord Berkeleys, in his Coat of Maile, Armour and Targett.

Also the Severall Monuments of Sir Charles Vaughan, and Sir Robert Young, in

Armour, with their Helmetts and Gauntletts.

In the Chancell is the Monument of a naked Bishop in Alabaster; and 3 Abbots, that were good Benefactors to the Church.

And for the rest, wee refer you to our Table Bookes.

In the Cloysters is a fayre Conduit of Freestone, and leads with many Spouts, which continually runs, and waters all the Colledge with that sweet Rockwater.

* Bristow Cathedrall. Bishop Cooke, Dr Chetwin, Deane.
 Dr Green Sub-Deane and 5 Prebends more
 Dr Jones Chancellor
 10 singing Men, whereof 4 in Orders, and 6 Boyes

CIVIL WAR AND COMMONWEALTH

Although the cathedral building and furnishings escaped major destruction and desecration during the Civil War and the subsequent Commonwealth, the clergy, liturgy and cathedral precincts were greatly affected. As a major port and 'the metropolis of the west of England', Bristol was a prize greatly to be desired by both sides in the conflict. At first the Parliamentary side was in the ascendant, but on 27 July 1643 the city was taken by the royalist forces commanded by Prince Rupert. In August 1643 Charles I attended a service of thanksgiving in the cathedral, amid scenes of great rejoicing. In 1643 Parliament had agreed that, in return for military assistance from Scotland, The Solemn League and Covenant should be imposed on all Englishmen. This involved accepting the form of church government and worship which had been adopted in Scotland. The Covenant included an agreement to:

> Endeavour the extirpation of popery, prelacy (that is Church government by archbishops, bishops, their chancellors and commissaries,deans, deans and chapters, archdeacons, and all other ecclesiastical officers depending on that hierarchy), superstition, heresy, schism, profaneness, and whatsoever shall be found to be contrary to sound doctrine and the power of godliness, least we partake in other mens' sins, and thereby be in danger to receive of their plagues; and that the Lord may be one, and His name one in the three kingdoms.

While Bristol remained under the control of the royalists, however, the bishop and cathedral clergy continued as before. Similarly when in 1645 Parliament declared that the Book of Common Prayer should be replaced by a Directory of Public Worship, church services remained unchanged in Bristol. Even in November 1645, three months after Prince Rupert had surrendered Bristol to the Parliamentarians, the Directory of Public Worship was not being used in the city. On 13 November 1645 two members of the Parliamentary force in Bristol, Colonel Martin Pyndar and Harcourt Leighton wrote to the Speaker of the House of Commons, William Lenthall, informing him of the situation in Bristol and complaining of lack of resources, numerous wounded soldiers requiring medical aid and payment, and telling him of the unhelpfulness of various Bristol merchants. They ended their long letter with the following:

We shall only adde that for want of able ministers, <u>Directories</u>, and orders for the use of the same, the people here sitt in darkness and the collegiate men still chaunt out the Common Prayer Booke to the wonted height and in private parishes they thinke of noe other discipline, there being hardly three sermons in the whole citty on the Lord's day, and but one upon the last fast, the late holly-dayes [holidays] being more solemnly observed than the Sabbath.

[<u>Historical Manuscripts Commission</u>, 13th Report, Appendix, Vol. I, (1891), MSS of the Duke of Portland, I, 310].

Following the royalist defeat at Naseby on 14 June 1645 the parliamentary forces began gradually to control the west-country, culminating in the capture of Bristol on 10 September 1645. Before his surrender of Bristol, Prince Rupert had agreed terms with the parliamentary forces under Fairfax and Cromwell, and these included the pledge not to interfere with the cathedral and its clergy. Once Bristol fell to parliament, however, the cathedral could not escape the general confiscations of Church property and the alterations to the liturgy which soon followed. In 1647 parliament again ordered the abolition of the whole ecclesiastical hierarchy of bishops, deans and canons, and decreed that cathedral revenues should be devoted to the enhancing of parish clergy and other causes. The lead was stripped from the roof of the bishop's palace, but Bishop Thomas Howell refused to move, although his wife was heavily pregnant. She died not long afterwards and was soon followed to the grave by the bishop himself, leaving several children. Thomas Fuller, who would have known the bishop personally, described him as a meek man and an excellent preacher.

'His sermons, like the water of Siloah, did run softly, gliding on a smooth stream; so that his matter by a lawful and laudable felony did steal secretly into the hearts of his hearers'[Thomas Fuller, <u>Worthies</u>, (1840 edn.), III, 515–6]

According to William Barrett, who from the mid-18th century devoted himself to collecting historical information on the city, parliamentary soldiers 'made the palace a malthouse and there they grouned at a mill erected there as well as made their malt for several years'. [William Barrett, <u>History & Antiquities of the City of Bristol</u>, 1789, 330]. *The lands and property of the cathedral were sold to numerous different purchasers. Services within the cathedral were no longer conducted according to the Book of Common Prayer, but preaching continued, and in September 1648 the Corporation of Bristol ordered the burgesses who were serving as the city's MPs to present a petition to Parliament:*

B.R.O. M/BCC/CCP/1/4 1642–49 fol 183 5 September 1648 Petition presented to Parliament by the Corporation

Touching allowance out of the deane and chapters lands towards the maintenance of preaching in the Cathedrall within this Cittie and other uses ...... And the burgesses of this Cittie in Parliament are desired to pursue it with effect

B.R.O. M/BCC/CCP/1/4 fol 197 23 July 1649, Council Proceedings

Alderman Aldworth requested to invest £3000 on behalf of the city in the purchase of lands formerly belonging to the Dean and Chapter of the Cathedral

Lands were accordingly purchased in Somerset and south Gloucestershire, only to be recovered by the Church at the Restoration in 1660. More lead was stripped from the roofs of cathedral buildings by the Corporation in 1655. This was probably taken from the cloisters, since the main part of the cathedral continued throughout the Commonwealth period to be used for sermons. Evidently the Corporation soon reconsidered their decision and early in 1656 they ordered that the lead should be sold to pay for repairs to the cathedral.

B.R.O. M/BCC/CCP/1/5 fol 99, Council Proceedings 1649–59 8 January 1656

It is ordered and agreed that Mr Chamberlin doe forth with sell such lead as he hath in his keeping and lately was taken of some part of the Cathedrall or Cloysters next adjoining and that the monie made on sale thereof he lay out in necessary reparacons of the said Cathedrall

The Parliamentary Survey 1649

The major documentary source produced by all the upheavals of the Civil War and its aftermath was a major, detailed and accurate survey of all the properties belonging to the cathedral. This was part of a nationwide survey ordered by Parliament of all the lands, buildings and income which had belonged either to the Crown or to the Church and which had been confiscated by the Commonwealth. The Surveys were intended to provide a complete description and record of all the royal or ecclesiastical possessions prior to their sale. This authoritative and detailed survey and valuation of all the cathedral properties in Bristol, Gloucestershire, Somerset, Wiltshire and elsewhere is naturally very long, covering 214 manuscript folios. It is far too long to be included in this volume, and in any case most of the lands, tenements and other possessions were leased by the Dean and Chapter whose only involvement with them was as a source of income. The following extracts are taken from the section describing the properties within the immediate precinct of the cathedral. These surveys give a good indication of the way in which houses for the bishop, dean, canons and cathedral staff had been built on the site of the former nave and were tightly packed into Lower College Green and in the area to the east of the cathedral which was known as the 'Masonrie'. The 1649 Survey was conducted under the supervision of William Webb and was carried out by several surveyors, including John Pegg, John Grange, John Griffith, James Hibbins and David Offley.

B.R.O. DC/E/3/2
Parliamentary Survey June 1649

By virtue of a commission to us graunted, grounded upon an Act of the Commons of England assembled in Parliament for the abolishing of Deanes, Deanes and Chapters, Canons, Prebends and other officers and titles belonging to any Cathedrall or Collegiate Church within England and Wales

fols 16–22

The Dean's House

Consisting of a kitching, three larders, a Pantrie, a bakehouse, a little seller, a coale house and foure other roomes in the first storie; one dineing roome, one hall and a studdy adjoining and seaven chambers and one closet adjoining in the second storie; and over that one small gallerie and a cockloft over the hall; one house and two little gardens, the one on the west side of the house and the other in the corner of the little greene aforesaid adjoyning to the schoolmasters house.
The premises are now in the possession of the state and are worth to be let £10 per annum.
The materials of the said house besides the charge of taking downe are worth £100.
Length: North to South 100 feet 9 inches;
Breadth: East to West 61½ feet.

Dr Weekes house

Abutting eastward on the Deans House, in the little green westward on the Bishops barn.
Consisting of one kitching, a Parler, a hall, a small butterie in the first storie; five chambers, a studdy, a closett over the said hall, parler and kitching in the second storie; a garrett and a cockloft over the said chambers in the third storie; a little garden under the window of the said house and a stable in the little Colledge greene adjoyning to the Bishopps stable.
Yearly rent £5 10s 0d.
Worth to be sold in respect the premises are in good repair £60.
Length: East to West 61 feet.
Breadth: 24 feet.

Mr Tuckers house

Late one of the Prebends of the church of Bristol.
In College Green, abutting westward on the Chancellors House and eastward on a little common yard that leads to the cloisters. Consisting of a little seller, a hall, a butterie, a kitching in the first storie; three lodging chambers in the second storie; a cockloft in the third storie.
Yearly rent £3 10s 0d.
Worth to be sold £30.
Length: East to West 40 feet.
Breadth: 24 feet.

Chancellors house

Known by the name of the gatehouse, late possession of Dr Jones late chancellor, being between the Colledge Greene of the Cathedrall Church of Bristol and a greene called the little greene, abutting westward on the deanes house and eastward on a house called Mr Tuckers house. Consisting of one kitching, a larder and a butterie in the first storie; a dineing roome, two little chambers in the second storie; one lodging chamber with a closet in the third storie, covered with leade; one stable with a hayloft, a garden and a little garden house.
Yearly rent £6.
Worth to be sold in regard of the leade and other materials £100.
Length: East to West 68 feet.
Breadth: 21 feet.

Dr Greenes house

Late one of the Prebends of the Cathedrall, consisting of two sellers lyeing under the great hall called the Bishopps hall, one kitching with a loft over it, a little butterie nere the kitching, a little hall, a Parler wainscoated in the first storie; two chambers and a studdy in the second storie; a garret over the aforesaid chamber in the third storie; one little garden walled about lyeing east uppon the Cloysters and west on the little greene.
Yearly rent £3 10s 0d.
Worth to be sold £30.
Length: East to West 64 feet.
Breadth: 20 feet.

Dr Markes house

Late one of the Prebends, situate lyeing and being in the Colledge little greene abutting eastward on the Bishopps Cort Wall and westward on the greene called the little greene, with two gardens lyeing on the south side of the said house conteyning by estimation half an acre more or lesse. And the house consists of one kitching, a seller, a hall, a buttery in the first storie; five chambers over the aforesaid roomes in the second storie. The premises are in the present possession of the state; but not tenentable, but worth to be sold £25.
Length: East to West 99 feet.
Breadth: 66 feet.

Dr Robsons house

Late one of the Prebends, in the little greene abutting northward on the said Church, and southward on the late Bishopps house. And consists of one kitching and a larder in the first storie; a hall, a buttery and foure chambers in the second storie and covered with lead; one garden lyeing within the Cathedrall Church yard.
Worth to be lett £4 per annum.
Worth to be sold in regard it is covered with lead £100.
Length: North to South 60 feet.
Breadth: 32 feet.

Mr Williamsons house

In a greene called little Colledge greene, abutting eastward on the late Bishopps house, and westward on the Registers house. And consisting of a little roome called the Porters Lodge, a Coale house, a wood house, a kitching, a hall, a Parler, and two small roomes between the hall and the Parler in the first storie; three faire chambers and a Closett over the aforesaid roomes covered with leade in the second storie.
Worth to be sold £105 because not tenantable.
Length: East to West 82 feet.
Breadth: 28 feet.

Mr Cuthberts house

Late one of the Prebends, in a greene there called the little Colledge greene, abutting eastward on the Chancellors garden and westward on the schoolemasters house. And consisting of a kitching, a butterie, a seller, a hall and one other roome and a wood house in the first storie; five lodgeing Chambers over the aforesaid roomes in the second storie; and a little cockloft over one of the Chambers in the third storie; and a little garden on the south side of the said house.
Worth to be let £4.
Worth to be sold £35.
Length: East to West 55 feet.
Breadth: 20 feet.

The Organists house

In the little greene, abutting North on a house called the Sextons house and South on the deanes garden. And consists of two small sellers and a large seller called a store house in the first storie; five chambers and two closetts in the second storie; and a little garden lying west of the said house.
Yearly rent £3.
Worth to be sold £35.
Length: North to South 70 feet.
Breadth: 22 feet.

The Sextons house

In the occupation of Richard Barry, sexton of the said Church, in the little greene abutting south on a house called the Organists house and northward on the deanes stable. And consists of two small roomes in the first storie; and a garret over the said roomes in the second storie. The said Barrie now inhabits in it as hee did formerly as being sexton to the said Cathedrall.
Worth to be let 20 s per annum.
Worth to be sold £10.
Length: East to West 20 feet.
Breadth: 11 feet.

The Schoolmaster house

In the little green abutting eastward on the house late of Mr Cuthbert and westward on the deans garden. And consists of a kitching, hall, a Parler, a butterie in the first storie; three chambers and a Closett in the second storie; with a little garden on the south side of the said house. Now in the tenure of one Mr Addams, schoolmaster, now inhabited by the said schoolmaster by order of the Committee of Bristol without paying Rent.
Worth to be let £4 per annum.
Worth to be sold £35.
Length: East to West 70 feet.
Breadth: 22 feet.

fols 24–26

The Masonrie

Survey of houses, lands and tenements called the Masonrie and Covent Orchard in the possession of John Peirce, draper, belonging to the late deane and chapter of Bristoll, July 1649.

Messuage or tenement in the occupation of one Mr Yeomans and called or knowne by the name of the Masonrie or Covent Orchard abutting East uppon St Austins Back, West uppon the Cathedrall Church yard and south uppon the Bishopps garden, consisting of a kitching, a little larder, a hall, a parler and a seller in the first storie; a dyneing roome and two chambers in the second storie; and two chambers in the third storie.
Length: East to West 33 feet and 9 inches.
Breadth: North to South 24 feet and six inches.
With one acre of pasture and a garden contayning half an acre of grounde more or lesse unto the said house adjoyning and walled about with a stone wall, as alsoe a small stable and still house standing in the said parcell of grounde.
Worth to be sold £16.

One other messuage or tenement in the occupation of Mrs Drake abutting westward uppon the Cathedrall Church and Eastward on a little tenement now in the occupation of Charles Warde, consisting of a little kitchin, a butterie, a hall, a little parler, and a small seller in the first storie; five small lodginge chambers in the second storie; one other small chamber and a garrett in the third storie; with a garden conteyning halfe an acre more or lesse incompassed with a stone wall.
Length: East to West 61½ feet.
Breadth: 24 feet.
Worth to be sold £8 10s 0d.

Alsoe one other small tenement in the occupation of William Hall abutting west uppon the foresaid tenement of Mrs Drake and East uppon a little tenement in the occupation of Charles Warde, consisting of one Roome in the first storie; and two chambers in the second storie.

Length: East to West 16 feet.
Breadth: 14 feet.
Worth £2 9s 4d.

Alsoe one other small tenement in the occupation of Charles Warde abutting East on St Austins church yarde and West uppon a tenement of the aforesaid William Hall, consisting of one small roome in the first storie; and one small roome in the second storie.

Length: East to West 14 feet.
Breadth: 12 feet.
Worth £1 10s 0d.

Alsoe one other little tenement in the Masonrie yarde in the occupation of Alexander Caroe abutting South on the said Mr Yeomans garden and North on a little tenement in the occupation of George Watson, consisting of two roomes in the first storie; and two roomes more in the second storie.

Length: North to South 20 feet.
Breadth: 12 feet.
Worth £4 0s 0d.

Alsoe one other small tenement in the occupation of George Watson, abutting South uppon Alexander Caroes house and North uppon Mr Denhams house, consisting of a kitchin and a hall in the first storie; and two chambers in the second storie.

Length: North to South 20 feet.
Breadth: 12 feet.
Worth £4 0s 0d.

Alsoe one other small messuage or tenement in the occupation of Goodman Denham, abutting North uppon a little tenement of Charles Warde and South uppon a little tenement of George Watsons, consisting of a hall and a kitchin in the first storie; and two chambers in the second storie.

Length: North to South 20 feet.
Breadth: East to West 12 feet.
Worth £4 0s 0d.

Memorandum

That the aforesaid John Peirce by Indenture of lease date the 13th of February in the first year of King Charles graunted to him by the late deane and chapter of Bristoll holdeth all the last mentioned premises with the appurtenances for the term of fourty yeares from the day of the date aforesaid under the reserve and yearly rent of Three pounds tenn shillings and Eight pence payable at the Lady Day and Michaelmas by equal portions, but they are worth upon improvement fourty pounds nyne shillings and fower pence over and above the yearly rent reserved as appeareth by the particulars before mentioned.

Memorandum

There were seaventeen yeares of the aforesaid terme to come on the thirteenth day of February last.

The Lessee is to keepe the premises in repaire and att the end of the terme soe to leave them.

With aforesaid lease and all the premises therein conteyned by the meane assignment and conveyance were assigned and sett over unto Jeremiah Martin of the Citty of Bristoll Doctor in Physicke as was made appeare to us by the sight of the deede.

Other Properties around the Precinct

Alsoe one other parcell or plott of ground called or known by the name of the Innward Greene situate lyeing and beinge in the County of the Citty of Bristoll betweene a place called the Bishopps Walke on the North side and a meadow called Canons Marsh on the South side and Abutts Eastward on a place called St Augustines Back and Westward on a stable and garden and fenced about with a stone wall, with two old buildings within it called the Prebends stables, and contains by estimation two acres two roods.
Worth per annum £3 10s 0d.

Alsoe one other parcell of pasture ground called or knowne by the name of the East Heyes, situate and lieing and being under Brandion Hill nere the Citty of Bristoll, and fenced about with a stone wall and now in the occupation of one Mr Young, contains by estimation two acres two roods.
Worth per annum £3 0s 0d.

Alsoe one other Close or parcell of ground called or knowne by the name of the West Heyes, with a little house and garden within it, situate lieing and being nere Brandion Hill aforesaid, bound with Canons Marsh on the South side and the highway on the North side, and Abutts Eastward on the Bishopps Parke and Westward on the lyme kills, and now in the occupation of one Mr Hollister and contains by estimation two acres two roods.
Worth per annum £6 0s 0d.

Alsoe one other parcell of ground called or knowne by the name of the Colledge Close or the Greate Greene lyeing and adjoining on the North side of the Cathedrall Church and containes by estimation two acres two roods.
Worth per annum £1 16s 8d.

Alsoe one other parcell of ground called the Butts, Abutting North upon St Augustines Church and South on the maine river, and conteynes by estimation one rood.
Worth 3s 4d.

Alsoe one other parcell of pasture called Culver Close situate and lyeing nere the Citty of Bristoll now in the occupation of William Speering, Abutting East upon

Stonyhill and West uppon a Close called the Citty land and conteines by estimation one acre one rood.
Worth £1 10s 0d.

fol 102

All that Messuage or Tenement Scituate lyeing and being in the Colledge Greene of Bristoll joining to the West side of the Cathedrall Church, in the tenure or occupation of Ann Spalldon, widdow, with a small garden thereunto adjoyning, Conteyning in length 33 foot and in breadth 30 foot.
Let on lease for 40 years from 23 June 3 Charles I (1627).
Rent £1 6s 8d, but worth per annum £4 0s 0d.

Services in the Cathedral 1649–60

Evidence for the continuation of Services and preaching in the Cathedral during the Commonwealth period is provided by the orders issued by the Trustees for the Maintenance of Ministers who were appointed by Parliament to oversee the arrangements for public worship following the abolition of the Church of England and the suppression of the Book of Common Prayer.

Lambeth Palace MSS 969 fol. 11 9 January 1651

Order that £159 per annum shall be paid to such godly and able Minister as shall be approved to officiate in the Cathedrall Church of Bristol. The money to be taken out of the rents and revenues of the late Dean and Chapter of Bristol.
The £20 per annum for the poor and £20 per annum for the highways, and payments to the almsmen and schoolmaster to be maintained.

22 February 1653

Mr John Knowles, a godly and painful preacher to receive £150 per annum for officiating in the Cathedrall.
[This order was renewed each year from 1654 to 1659].

Tenure on the Chapter Estates

The fact that the tenements which had been built to the east of the cathedral, in the area known as the Masonrie, were all leased to one man for a long period of years and at a low annual rent illustrates the general policy of the Dean and Chapter at this time. Urban properties were let on long leases for low rents and heavy entry fines.

As with most contemporary landed estates in the west country the widespread rural possessions of the Dean and Chapter were let to tenants by copyhold tenure, generally for three lives. The three named persons held successively, having as evidence of their title a copy of the entry in the court book or roll. Annual rents were low or even nominal, and the income was derived from the fines or fees charged for the insertion of new lives into the leases. The consequence of this policy of tenure was that the Dean and Chapter had only occasional contact with their tenants and played little part in the community life of those upon whom they depended for their income.

A few leases continued to include payment of part of the annual rent in kind, and, for example, as late as 1676 the Dean & Chapter granted a lease of a house in Clifton for £3 per annum 'and a Couple of Capons as in the old lease' [B.R.O. DC/A/8/1 fol 35].

An important feature of copyhold tenure was that it was subject to the customary law of each manor, and since these customs differed considerably, even between neighbouring manors, there was great variety in the rights enjoyed by copyholders and in the obligations laid upon them. Manorial customs differed over matters such as heriots or dues payable to the lord at a tenant's death , over the right of widows to retain possession of the property during her lifetime or widowhood, the ability to nominate a successor, and over rights of grazing on commons, access to stone, wood, chalk, marl and other natural resources. Because of the importance and variation in these manorial customs, the surveyors in 1649 were careful to record the customs of each of the manors they surveyed. Such surveys did not entirely eliminate disputes, however, since manorial custom depended upon long use as defined by the testimony under oath of the oldest tenants. An example of such a dispute occurred during the later 17th century on the estates of the Dean and Chapter at Bradford-on-Avon and Tisbury. These were two of the most important and lucrative properties belonging to the Dean and Chapter. Both had belonged to the Benedictine nunnery of Shaftesbury, which had been founded by King Alfred and was the richest religious house for women in England. Both were made part of the endowment of the newly-created cathedral at Bristol in 1542. The rectory and parsonage lands of Bradford-on-Avon, together with the associated chapelries ,had been leased in 1581 for 99 years to Anthony Webb at an annual rent of £221 6s 10d. In addition, there was considerable income from the rents of farms, mills, houses and other properties in and around the town [B.R.O. DC/E/27/2–5]. *At Tisbury in 1649 the copyhold tenements were leased for £47 2s 7d per annum and the tithes were worth £140 per annum* [B.R.O. DC/E/3/2]. *The dispute over the manorial customs of both places illustrates both the importance of such customs for tenants and also the long-continuance of these ancient rights, many of which were medieval in origin. It shows the complexity of copyhold tenure, and the way in which custom beneficial to tenants over such matters as widows' estate could deprive the landlord of a fine on a tenement for many years. The dispute was not finally settled until 1721 when the Chapter clerk, George Roberts, copied a list of the customs from 'an old Register of Shaftesbury abbey' which both sides in the argument accepted as authoritative* [B.R.O. DC/E/26/3; DC/E/27/37].

CHAPTER BUSINESS 1663–1719

The series of volumes recording business conducted at the regular meetings of the dean and chapter of Bristol are known as 'Chapter Minutes', but at other cathedrals they are usually called 'Chapter Act Books'. They are not the minutes of meetings in the modern sense, but simply a brief record of decisions taken relating mainly to the granting of leases, the management of cathedral properties and endowments, arrangements for periods of residence by the various members of Chapter, and appointment of minor canons, singing-men, a schoolmaster and other members of the cathedral community. The Minutes also record the formal business of the election of each new bishop by the dean and chapter, which merely involved the acceptance of the person named in 'the King's Writ of Congé d'Elire'. Occasionally other matters of concern to the cathedral are included, but generally the entries are brief, with few indications of how decisions were reached. The series begins with a volume covering the years 1663 to 1751 [B.R.O. DC/A/8/1], and continues to the present, although there are a few gaps and some pages are illegible. The earlier volumes do not survive, but a dispute between Dean Thomas Chamberlayne and some of the canons during the years 1749 -52 over the dean's right to make appointments to minor offices, led to extracts concerning such appointments to be copied from the earlier volumes, starting in 1542. These extracts were bound into the front of the first surviving volume. Another copy of the same extracts also exists [B.R.O. DC/A/12/1]. The dispute is also referred to at the end of the volume of Chapter Minutes 1663–1751 [B.R.O. DC/A/8/1]. The entry refers to the dispute:

> 'Touching the right of naming Minor Canons, Schoolmaster, Lay Clerks or Singing Men, Sub-Sacrist or Sexton and other Officers and Ministers of this Church. The Dean asserting this right was solely vested in him.'.

It was agreed to submit the dispute to the arbitration of 'Right Reverend Fathers of the Church'. It was in connection with this dispute that the entries concerning early appointments were made and later bound into the volume of Chapter Minutes. The entries are not all in strict chronological order. The following selection of extracts provides an indication of the business conducted, particularly concerning the minor offices. Minor canons and singing-men were evidently only admitted after the agreement of the choir concerning their qualifications, and the records of their appointments are generally followed by the words 'having first interrogated the Choir touching his Qualifications and being answered that he was a fit person'. It is clear from many of the entries that there were frequent problems over the behaviour of the holders of the minor offices.

B.R.O. DC/A/8/1

Extracts from the Register Books of the Dean and Chapter of the Cathedrall Church of the Holy and Undivided Trinity in Bristol 1545–1624

October 37 Henry VIII (1545)
Letters Patent from the Dean and Chapter of the Office of the Master of the Choristers to Humphrey Walley.

10 March 35 Henry VIII (1544)
Letters Patent from the Dean and Chapter of the Office of Subsacrist to John Borrow.

10 October 4 Edward VI (1550)
Letters Patent from the Dean and Chapter of the Office of Manciple to Richard Cottrell.

1 July 3 Edward VI (1551)
Letters Patent from the Dean and Chapter of the Office of Butler to Richard Windsor.

13 December 38 Henry VIII (1546)
Letters Patent from the Dean and Chapter of the Offices of Minor Canon and Subsacrist to Richard Bettie.

10 October 1 Edward VI (1547)
Letters Patent from the Dean and Chapter of the Office of One of the Six Clerks to Walter Gleesson formerly a Lay Clerk.

Same date
Letters Patent from the Dean and Chapter of the like Office to William Bell formerly also a Lay Clerk.

31 August 2 Edward VI (1548)
Letters Patent from the Dean and Chapter of the Office of Cook to David Watkins.

1 July 2 Edward VI (1548)
Letters Patent from the Dean and Chapter to Robert Pingston of the Office of Minor Canon.

1 March 4 Edward VI (1549)
A like Grant to Robert Hogge of the Office of Minor Canon.

1 August 5 Edward VI (1551)
A like Grant to John Phillips of the Office of Minor Canon.

10 October 4 Edward VI (1550)
A like Grant to George Colly of the Office of Janitor.

1 July 5 Edward VI (1551)
A like Grant of the Revertion of the said Office to Roger Hatton.

31 July 5 Edward VI (1551)
A like Grant of the Office of the Master of the Choristers to Walter Glesson.

25 January 6 Edward VI (1552)
A like Grant of the Office of Butler to Thomas James.

fol. 9 **A visitation of the Dean and Chapter 6 August 1589**

Present the Vice-Dean, 3 Prebends, the Schoolmaster, 3 Minor Canons, the Organist, 7 Singing-Men, 4 Choristers, and 3 Paupers [almsmen] who were sworn to give faithful answers.

Griffin Hughes, Schoolmaster was admonished to be more diligent, and if he appeared to be so at Michaelmas then next, he should receive of the Treasurer 33s 4d.

John Atkins was presented as not Sufficiently Instructed in Musick to be one of the Minor Canons, and he had notice given him that if he did not better qualify himself by Michaelmas then next he should give up his place.

Robert Stewart a Minor Canon for his unskillfulness in Musick had Notice to Provide himself elsewhere by Michaelmas then next.

William Blomer and John Hunt were admonished to improve themselves in Musick by Ladyday or they should lose their Places.

fol. 14 January 1620

The Dean and Chapter suspend Toby Brooking from his office of Singing-man for diverse misdemeanors.

fol 13 4 March 1623

The Dean and Chapter suspend Edward Almond from his office of Minor Canon

5 March 1623

The Dean and Chapter restore the said Edward Almond to his office of Minor Canon

10 June 1623

The Dean and Chapter suspend Mr Norton, Mr Almond and Mr Prince from their sallaries for diverse offences. The same day in the afternoon the said Mr Almond appeared in the Chapter House before the said Dean and Chapter and submitted himself, confessing his offence. Whereupon the Dean admonishing him, released him from his Suspension.

fol 13v 1 October 1623

The Dean and Chapter restore Thomas Prince to his stipend

30 October 1623

Mr Edward Almond is charged with being guilty of sundry offences. At the same time Mr Mason is accused of sundry offences for which the Dean suspends him from his stipend.

10 November 1623

Mr Almond is remitted his Offence, Mr Norton and Mr Mason are restored to their Stipends.

3 November 1624

John Bartlett for a very great Offence is Suspended from his office as a Minor Canon.

12 November 1624

John Bartlett is by the Dean and Chapter restored to his office and sallary and received an admonition [*In 1626 Edward Almond was admitted to the office of Precentor with the agreement of the choir*].

The Cathedral and Corporation

B.R.O. M/BCC/CCP/1/6 **Extract from Council Proceedings 1659 -75**

In spite of continuing controversy between the cathedral and the corporation over rights on College Green and other matters, the corporation still assembled at the cathedral to hear sermons on all important occasions. They came in procession from the Tolsey or Council House, preceded by their ceremonial sword, and in their scarlet gowns or 'formallities'. The following example from the Council Proceedings shows an agreement to meet for thanksgiving at the end of the Civil War and for the Restoration of the Monarchy. The merchants who made up a high proportion of the members of corporation had suffered badly during the upheavals of the previous decade and warmly welcomed the Restoration of Charles II.

fol. 21 **20 June 1660**

Whereas Thursday next is appointed to be observed a publique day of Thanksgiving it is agreed that the Colledge be the Church whereunto the Mayor, Aldermen and Common Council will goe in their formallities to heare a sermon on the saide Thanksgiving day.

The Chamberlain and Waterbailiffe are hereby ordered to take care that the great gunns be prepared and charged to be shott of on the said day.

The Mayor is desired by his officers to give notice to the Masters and Wardens of the Companyes within this Citty that themselves and their Societies doe attend in their formallities by 9 of the clock in the morning the said day of thanksgiving to waite on the Mayor and Common Counsell to sermon and that none of them doe faile therein.

Problems and Controversies 1660–1677

With the restoration of the monarchy in 1660 the Church of England was reinstated, together with the hierarchy of bishops, deans and canons, and their endowments were returned. Many of the appointments were made as a reward for loyalty to the

Crown or for suffering endured during all the upheavals of the previous two decades. At first it was difficult to find a bishop for the poorly-endowed see of Bristol, but at length Gilbert Ironside (1588–1671) agreed to take the position. He was a wealthy man, with an estate at Long Bredy in west Dorset where his father had been the incumbent. He himself was rector of the nearby parishes of Winterbourne Abbas and Winterbourne Steepleton. As a royalist his lands were sequestered during the Commonwealth and he was badly treated, but his properties were restored in 1660 and he was created bishop of Bristol in January 1661. It was remarked that although he had never held any senior position in the Church, nor any chaplaincy to a nobleman or prince, that 'being wealthy he was looked upon as the fittest person to enter upon that mean bishopric' [Oxford D.N.B.; White Kennett, A Register and Chronicle Ecclesiastical and Civil, (1728), 295; Anthony Wood, Athenae Oxonienses,II, 939–40]. *Gilbert Ironside remained as bishop until his death in 1671 when he was buried without any memorial near the steps to the bishop's throne in the cathedral. He seems to have made no major impact either upon the diocese or the cathedral. The only exception occurred in 1668 when he made an unsuccessful claim against the Dean and Chapter for possession of the land and property on the south and west sides of the cloister* [B.R.O. DC/A/5/1].

Also rewarded for his loyalty was Henry Glemham, a courtier and brother of a well-known royalist soldier, who was made dean in 1660. He is chiefly remembered in Bristol for two fine stained-glass windows which were installed at the east end and of the north and south choir aisles. The window in the north choir aisle survives. It is not certain how these windows were acquired, nor who paid for them. There appears to be no truth in the persistent legend that the windows were a gift from Nell Gwyn, one of the mistresses of Charles II. Along with the bishop and dean, the cathedral chapter was restored with a full complement of six canons, together with the various holders of the minor offices. Some of the new canons had been staunch royalists and had suffered in consequence. They included Richard Towgood, who had been ejected from the parish of St Nicholas, and Richard Standfast, who had similarly been deprived at Christ Church. Both now returned as canons of the cathedral.

Ironside's successor as bishop was Guy Carleton (1605–85: bishop of Bristol 1672–9); he had been dean of Carlisle. He was a very different character from Ironside. Carleton had been a fervent royalist during the Civil War, and had fought in the royalist army and had been sentenced to death by Parliament. He escaped from prison and fled abroad with Prince Charles and the remnant of the court. At the Restoration Carleton became a royal chaplain, and was appointed dean of Carlisle and a prebendary of Durham. He became bishop of Bristol in 1672, but because of the poverty of the see he was permitted to retain his profitable prebend at Durham. He was uninhibited and out-spoken, quick to engage in controversy and single-minded in pursuing his objectives. He was energetic in the persecution of the growing number of dissenters in Bristol. His episcopate witnessed a massive persecution of dissenters, and a vigorous enforcement of the succession of laws which had been passed against them. The bishop also plunged with enthusiasm into what seems from a later perspective to have been a totally unnecessary quarrel with the mayor and corporation of Bristol. The mayor, aldermen and councillors took their formal attendance at the cathedral sermons very seriously, with solemn procession in fur-trimmed scarlet gowns and with special seats provided for them.

Clearly Bishop Carleton found their pretensions unbearable, and relations broke down soon after his arrival in Bristol. It had been the custom to start the service with a Bidding prayer for the corporation, followed by prayers for the King, archbishops, bishops and ecclesiastical dignitaries. The bishop objected to giving precedence to a group whom he dismissed as 'a parcel of coopers and heelmakers', a phrase hardly likely to endear him to the corporation. Not all members of the cathedral chapter supported the bishop. Canon Samuel Crossman, who was a distinguished writer of hymns, was particularly unhappy over the bishop's objections and sought peace with the corporation by continuing the customary order of the service. In return the bishop sought unsuccessfully to have Crossman suspended from his office as canon. For their part, the councillors revived a claim to have their ceremonial sword carried erect before them in their procession and through the cathedral, into the quire. In 1678 they spent £21 9s 0d on a gilded unicorn to be placed in the cathedral to hold their sword. To this the bishop objected and was supported by the dean and chapter. The disputes and ill-feeling continued throughout Carleton's episcopate, only ending when he was translated to the more lucrative see of Chichester in 1679, where he also became involved in feuds with members of the Chapter and with Chichester corporation [Oxford D.N.B.; John Latimer, <u>Annals of Bristol in the Seventeenth Century</u>, (Bristol 1900), 360, 369, 378, 385, 389].

The following extracts provide more details of the controversies and ill-feeling engendered during Carleton's episcopate at Bristol. The first extract shows that Carleton, like so many other bishops of Bristol, was desperate to improve the income of his see, in spite of the fact that by the King's special permission, he continued to hold a prebend at Durham 'on account of the smallness of his bishopric'.

Cal. S.P. Dom. 1673–5, 359

Dr Guy Carleton, Bishop of Bristol, to Sir Joseph Williamson, newly-appointed Clerk to the Privy Council 16 September 1674

Greater men, I believe, you have many ambitious of the title, but none I am sure more friend, or that more cordially congratulate you than myself. I am well assured you are a son so truly affected to the Church of England, that you will look on a piece of service done to God and His church in the first place as the first fruits of your new employment, as the best omen of good success in all your other future addresses in that place. The revenue of the bishopric of Bristol is so small that the King, I have been told, said it was scandalous, and that, if he were put in mind, when anything convenient for an addition to it fell in his gift, he would annex it for the better support of that dignity. A fair opportunity is now offered. Dr. Compton is now to be Bishop of Oxford, and parts with a parsonage near Chambridge (Cambridge), and, if his Majesty will bestow the presentation to it on me, I am offered in exchange for it £400 per annum to be annexed to the see of Bristol in *perpetuum*, by a gentleman that has a love for Church. His Majesty cannot have a fairer opportunity to endow this very poor bishopric, and, if it be lost, I must not expect the like in my time, nor, I fear, those that succeed me. I hear Lord North's son, that is to be, as reported, Clerk of the Closet, puts in for it, but the King will have a thousand opportunities to gratify him as well or better in some other way, but a thing so convenient as this by way of augmentation will scarce be met with in an age. I doubt not but your interest and zeal for the Church may speedily effect this good work, in which you will be no less than a second founder, I am sure, a grand benefactor, to this bishopric.

Cal. S.P. Dom. 1675–6, 6

Letter from Thomas Cole to Sir Joseph Williamson 6 March 1675

Our bishop has been very vigorous in his proceedings against the conventiclers and with a probable good success the principals of the Independent, Presbyterian and Anbabaptist factions being legally convicted and committed to custody, but not without some riotous and insolent carriages even in the Council House and at the Tolzey. But within these two days Thompson, a very eminent Independent, fell sick of a fever and died in prison, which has opened the mouths of all the dissenting party so wide, that they complain of the severity of the civil and tyranny of the ecclesiastical laws in so much that yesterday night, shortly after Thompson's burial, a libel was found in the Mayor's house with these threatening expressions or to this purpose, that, if they must be subject to these persecutions, as they term it, there were many eminent and sufficient men, and numbers of apprentices and inferior rank would venture their lives and fortunes for their freedom, and 'tis probable that of this city two parts of three may be that way inclined. Such is the constitution of this place, and now, what the consequences of this may be I leave to your wisdom to judge.

John Thompson, referred to in the above letter, was a prominent nonconformist minister in Bristol. He was imprisoned in Newgate gaol as part of the Bishop's campaign against Dissenters. In gaol he contracted a fever from which he died. His death caused a scandal in Bristol, and greatly increased the unpopularity of the Bishop.

Cal. S.P. Dom. 1677–8, 320

Letter from Henry Coventry, Secretary of State, to Bishop Carleton 23 August 1677

The Bishop of London has reported on your Lordship's complaint that the Corporation of Bristol will have their preachers, in the prayer for sermon, to pray for the Mayor and every member of that Corporation before they pray for the bishop, dean, and canons, and that even in the cathedral, and threatened their ministers that, if in obedience to their bishop they do otherwise, they should not have a penny maintenance from the city. I desire you to inform me whether the Bristol magistrates require their ministers to pray for them before archbishops and bishops in general, or only before the bishop and clergy of the city; and that the ministers give me an account what orders they received and from whom. When fully informed, I will represent the matter to the King, and there shall be no want of zeal in me, to do the Church all right.

Not all members of the Cathedral Chapter were in agreement with Bishop Carleton's views. Prominent among those who deplored the disputes which were provoked with the mayor and councillors was Samuel Crossman (1625–84). He had been a supporter of Parliament and from 1647 had served as a minister in Suffolk. Following the Restoration of Charles II in 1660, he was ejected and imprisoned for a time. Having decided to conform to the Church of England, Crossman was episcopally ordained in 1665. In 1667 he became a prebendary of Bristol cathedral and vicar of St Nicholas in the centre of the city. Later, he served as Treasurer to the Chapter, and in the final year of his life was appointed Dean (1683–4). He died on 4 February 1684 and was buried in the cathedral.

During his ministry in Bristol, Crossman published several devotional works and religious poetry. One of his poems 'My song is Love Unknown' was set to music and became a popular hymn which still finds a place in modern hymn-books. Being resident in Bristol, Crossman was better placed than many of his fellow-prebendaries to assess the feelings of the corporation, and was acutely aware of the number of nonconformists in the city. Consequently he deplored the controversies stirred up by the belligerent Bishop Carleton, and in published sermons such as 'A Humble Plea for the Quiet Rest of God's Ark' Crossman strove to promote religious unity and concord in Bristol. For his part the Bishop was not slow to condemn Crossman and to threaten him with various measures of ecclesiastical discipline. So bitter did the conflict become that in 1677 Crossman was provoked into producing a vigorous protest and a statement of the treatment which he had received. The following is the summary of this statement:

Cal. S.P. Dom. 1677–8, 351–4

Statement by Samuel Crossman DD 12 September 1677

The Bishop of Bristol forbids a layman living within the precincts of the cathedral to pay any rates to the poor, which till then had been usually paid. The person refusing is prosecuted by the City, for which prosecution the Mayor himself is arrested on the Church's account. The Bishop requires the Dean and Chapter to bear the charges and to indemnify this man in the whole suit. While these discontents lay unhappily broiling in men's minds, our Bishop in his visitation speech last July gave a quick reflection on such as prayed for coopers and heelmakers before the most dignified persons in the Church. Now it has been the custom of this city, as the Dean and some others relate, to pray for the magistracy and in the close for the clergy, through the succession of eight or nine bishops without any offence taken at it. On this and some other passages in the Bishop's speech, delivered in a mixed audience, the city became further distasted, some in magistracy proverbially laughed at, the general talk in the streets, Who said his prayers right or wrong? and the ministers at an utter loss what to do, not without some indecencies in their proceedings hereupon. The Bishop being offended, I sought access to him at his house, but could not be admitted. He told me afterwards in open court, that he would not have such things taken up in private. Accordingly he sends his apparitor to cite me to appear next day at court to answer articles, and to show cause, if any, why I should not be suspended for not obeying his monition (that is, how I prayed). I appeared, no articles were exhibited, but the Bishop tells me in open court, I was a perjured person, deserved to have my gown pulled off my back and the like. I was amazed, and hope I have given no just cause for such severe language. He appointed me, after these heats were over, to certify my observing his said monition the Saturday following. I certified I prayed as I conceived I lawfully might. Now it was thus: Having prayed for the King by all his titles, I prayed for the Queen, the Duke of York and all the royal family, His Majesty's most honourable Privy Council and all that are put in authority under him, the ministers of God's holy Word and Sacraments as well as Archbishops and Bishops as other pastors and curates in these very words, without mentioning either Mayor or Corporation here, for avoiding offence to the Bishop, because he told me, I serve my Mammon to humour a company of schismatics, who had excommunicated themselves out of the Church of God. But this satisfies him not. He cites me afresh on pain of suspension and tells me, I was a saucy proud fellow of a Presbyterian hypocritical heart, upbraiding my preaching, praying, speech, face and whole ministry very opprobriously before all the people at which uncomfortable posture my case now lies. After four court days of appearing in person and divers others by a proctor I cannot obtain to be dismissed, but am at length, as I am informed decreed to be suspended. I have many times preached before the Bishop; he never expressed any offence at my order in prayer till now. He singles out me alone for prosecution in this unhappy difference, though he knows most of the ministers of the city still pray for the Mayor and Corporation here *in terminis* before they mention any of the clergy, yet none of them are cited by him. If my offence be, as his Chancellor tells me, that I pray not for the clergy before the Privy Council, I answer to the Dean, the Surrogate, and probably others also have so prayed at the cathedral in the Bishop's audience even since his admonition without any blame from him, and how frequently the method is used at Whitehall and elsewhere is known to all observing persons. I acknowledge I have feared such an alteration thus violently set on foot at this juncture in our city might rather *conflare invidium* than promote the real concerns of the Church. I neither did nor do intend any obstinacy in it, if greater wisdom shall see it needful. The real truth is, many serious persons grow even distressed at the great increase of disobligements amongst us. The Mayor and magistrates have already left off coming at their usual times to the cathedral with other like evidences of very high disrespect. I can no way justify many renitencies of the city in these heats, but could on some experiences say mild steady practice mixed with some personal condescensions, as it best becomes the Church, so it soonest wins that people. I lay myself and case at the feet of my superiors. Our Bishop is pleased to pursue me even to ruin, because I cannot keep pace with all his actings, and some of them, which I forbear to mention, I freely confess I cannot. I have assured both him and the chief of the city that I will animate no faction, whatever displeasure he may take against me. I have had no hand in fomenting these differences between the Church and the city. How far and how faithfully I have laboured to allay them, persons of repute and integrity both in the Church and the city will, if need be, attest. As to my ministerial carriage, I have, since my first coming hither, now near ten years, constantly officiated the whole Liturgy every Lord's day myself, I have used the vestments appointed and read Common Prayer thrice a week in my parish church. I have not neglected nor scrupled any ceremony or appeared in the city at any time but in a clergyman's habit. In the cathedral, being Treasurer, whereas I found that church in debt and confused in their accounts ever since the restoration, I not only adjusted all accounts and cleared off their debts, but brought in also a church stock and a dividend, both in ready money, and have since given to the cathedral two <u>Bibles</u> and two large <u>Common Prayer Books</u>, all very fairly bound, the only books of ornament at this day there. I am become a fool in mentioning these things, but my present joyless circumstances constrain me to it. My dilemma is hard; returning to Bristol, I am likely to be suspended, staying here, I am far from my family, at expenses here, at charges there, to provide supply for my cure, and not without some sad apprehensions how little benefit the Church is like to reap by any such unhappy jars in the bosom of it. If I be, as our Bishop openly says both to me and of me, unworthy to be any longer of the clergy, I will betake myself to some honest secular employment, but, if I have consisted with my duty and uprightly served the Church, I crave my person and ministry might not be thus exposed and vilified before the people, but encouraged either for the better continuing my service where I am or some more quiet disposal elsewhere as to greater wisdom shall seem meet.

Cal. S.P. Dom. 1677–8, 382–3

Extract from a letter from Sir John Knight, Bristol MP to Sir Joseph Williamson, Clerk to the Privy Council 29 September 1677

The Bishop has very much abused the Mayor and the rest of the Justices here. Sometime since by his means the Mayor was arrested for legally proceeding against a person for not paying to the poor rate, pretending the land was within the precincts of the Church, which the Bishop would fain exempt with the Dean and Chapter from paying to the poor and make their precincts a kind of sanctuary and free from the course of his Majesty's laws, and he has also forbidden the same person, though legally made, to be an overseer and collector of the poor or to be churchwarden, pretending themselves to be out of any parish, and since also he has upheld him from collecting the money for the ships, so that by his means here is a failure of justice.

At a visitation lately he commanded all the clergy under their canonical obedience to pray for himself and the bishops before the Lords of the Council and the Mayor of this city, that is his Majesty's lieutenant here, and before the rest of the Justices out of malice to them, a thing never done for 60 years before in the time of seven bishops before him saying that they prayed for coopers and heelmakers before him, rendering by it as much as in him lay, the government contemptible and, to trample them underfoot, even in a manner to make them come to hear it, or not go to church at all, which sort of penance they think they ought not to be enjoined to bear. He has since questioned some of his clergy for not obeying his illegal commands, and actually passed a decree of suspension, not as yet published, against one, to bring the rest to obey. This affront put the magistrates to choose some of the clergy to preach before them lately at their solemn occasions, but the Bishop, by several letters I have by me, forbad them to preach before us, so that he will not let us have a chaplain to preach on solemn occasions, which by law every private gentleman may have in his chapel. This he puts on his clergy under canonical obedience, which if admitted for law, as I am sure it is not, he may at any time silence all such as will not preach what doctrine he pleases, and so ruin the established religion, a point never pretended to before. I could tell you of so many imprudent acts he has lately done that are of so ill a consequence to the government in Church and State that it ought not to be borne with or passed by. He went away last Tuesday to Newmarket to complain to his Majesty against us, but, I presume, he is so well known that his complaints will find small or no credit there against us. I may safely say, it had been good for the Church of England he had never been born, he executing such an arbitrary power that he would by his actings put the mitre above the crown and himself above the reach of his Majesty's laws and government. Such a supremacy was never set on foot in England under colour of a canonical obedience that he claims, that must not be yielded to. I therefore in behalf of this city who are now all in peace [ask you] not to give credit to his complaints nor to countenance him that he has done so much wrong to Church and State. If thought fit, some of us will attend whenever his Majesty and Council shall appoint, to answer his clamours and to make good what I have set down.

The opposite view was expressed by Richard Ellsworth, a Bristol merchant, in a letter to Sir Joseph Williamson on 27 October 1677 [Cal. S.P. Dom. 1677–8, 423–7]. He complained that the mayor, Sir Robert Cann showed undue favour to dissenters and slighted the Bishop. In particular Ellsworth praised the Bishop's strenuous efforts against 'the practices of Dissenters and the Fanatic interest'.

It is remarkable that these fierce quarrels are not mentioned in the Chapter Minutes. Instead, the Minutes provide details of the revival of a separate, long-running argument between the chapter and the corporation over the cathedral precinct, the parochial status of houses erected there, and rights to College Green, Brandon Hill and Canons' Marsh. There had been disputes between the Church and corporation of Bristol about the control and management of this area since the later Middle Ages. The cathedral authorities wished it to be a 'Liberty', entirely under their jurisdiction, as was the case with the surroundings of some other cathedrals. This was just the sort of issue in which Bishop Carleton delighted, and in 1677 he encouraged the dean and chapter to pursue this claim once more. The details are found in letters from the mayor and corporation, copies of which are included at the back of the Quarter Sessions Minute Book covering the years 1671–81. The first letter reveals that the Bishop had attempted unsuccessfully to insert a clause into a Parliamentary bill for improving the income of poor clergy. This would have declared that Bristol cathedral precinct to be exempt from the authority of the city council. Further details are provided by the two letters which follow:

B.R.O. JQS/M/5
fol. 249

From the Mayor and Council to Sir Robert Attkyns, one of the justices of his Majesty's Court of Common Pleas, 12 May 1677

My Lord,
Wee have desired Sir John Knight to deliver you a Copy of a paper given into us by the Deane and Prebendarys of the Church of Bristoll, the purpose and ayme whereof is to exempt themselves not only from the jurisdiction of the Citty butt in truth from all temporal jurisdictions whatsoever which in our opinion will not only be a great infringement of the liberties and privileges of this Citty butt allsoe of very ill

consequence and pernicious to the government, the particular transaction whereof wee referr to the relation of Sir John Knight. In a case of this moment and difficulty wee make itt our request to you that you will be pleased to afford us your advice and assistance with Sir John Knight to support our rights and undoubted Immunitys, and the frequent experience wee have of your readiness to promote all good acts for the weale and preservation of this Citty assures us of granting the request of

> My Lord your Lordshipp's most
> humble servants
> William Crabb, Mayor
> Robert Cann
> John Lawford
> Richard Streat
> Thomas Stevens

fol. 248v

The Honourable Sir Robert Attkyns   18 June 1677

Wee make bold to acquaint your Lordshippe that the Deane and Chapter doe persevere in the Contest with the Citty with unbeseeming Rigor and Severity as by arresting of the Mayor by endeavoring to obteyne Commission of Charitable Uses In which they nominate none but Creatures of their own to be Commissioners. Wee humbly begg your Lordshipps opinion whether wee are not exempted by that Statute from the Inquisition of Such Commission and if your Lordshipp happen to see my Lord Chancellor that you would please to acquaint his Lordshippe with the proceedings of theirs and then wee are sure they will receive very slender encouragement from his Lordshippe to proceed in his severe manner and to make soe great a breach betweene the Church in this Citty and the Government.

> William Crabb, Mayor
> Robert Cann
> John Knight
> John Lawford
> Richard Crampe

The Renatus Harris Organ 1682–3

Apart from the installation of the so-called 'Glemham windows' in the cathedral in the years following the Restoration in 1660, the most remarkable addition to the building during the years dominated by controversy with the corporation, was the installation in 1682–3 of a large new organ. The instrument was made by the distinguished organ-maker, Renatus Harris (circa 1652–1724), who was a Catholic recusant, but who built or worked on organs in more than 60 cathedrals or major churches. The new Bristol organ was installed on top of the screen which had originally come from the Carmelite friary and now divided the chancel from the transepts which constituted the nave within the cathedral. It replaced the organ installed in 1630, during the episcopate of Bishop Robert Wright. The work also included the making of a finely-carved case for the organ. The cost of the organ and the case are given in the extracts from the Computa *which are shown later in this volume. The extracts from the Chapter Minutes show that a subscription was raised in Bristol to help pay for the organ, but no details of subscribers are given. Neither does the name of the highly-talented carver who produced the organ case appear in the Minutes. The large organ had three manuals and consisted of a great organ with 12 stops, an echo organ with seven stops and a choir organ [L. Elvin, 'The Organs of Bristol Cathedral',* The Organ, *42, (1962–3), 71–9]. Additional work on the organ is also detailed in the entry of 1719 which is shown below. This was also carried out by Renatus Harris who had moved to Bristol in c1719. He died in 1724 and was buried in St Nicholas church [Oxford D.N.B.].*

B.R.O. DC/A/8/1

Further Entries in the Chapter Minutes 1669–1719

The following extracts are selected from the main series of Chapter Minutes starting in 1663. Some of the entries consist of brief notes with only the year and no other date given.

An Order from King Charles II 26 August 1669

Charles Rex

Trusty and welbeloved Wee greete you well Letting you meete That we attending the releife of our poore Subject Christopher Knight who served us at sea in the late warrs against the Dutch and in an engagement in July 1666 lost his right Arme as appears by certificate under the hands of Captain John Read and John Hawes Chirurgion. In consideration whereof wee have given and granted And by these presents for us and our heires and successors doe give and grante unto the said Christopher Knight the roome and place of one of our Almesmen belonging to our Cathedrall Church of Bristoll if any such place be there now void or the next shalbecome void there after the placeing of such as have our former graunte for the like place there for and dureing his naturall life. Wherefore wee will and command you not only to admitt and place the said Christopher Knight in the said Almesmans place belonging to our Cathedrall Church aforesaid But also to pay and allow unto him from tyme to tyme after his admittance All such wages, fees, duties and other allowances as shalbe due and incident to the same place in as large ample and beneficiall manner as any other our Almesmen there have receive and enjoye or of right ought to have, receive and enjoye by the Foundation thereof. Provided allwayes that if the said Christopher Knight have any Almesmans place elsewhere then this our present graunte unto him to be void and of none effect. And these our letters shalbe your sufficient warrant. Given under our Signet at our Pallace of Westminster the twenty sixth day of August in the one and twentieth yeare of our raigne.

To our Trusty welbeloved the deane and chapter of the Cathedrall Church of Bristoll now and for the tyme being and to any others whome it shall or may concerne.

Your Majesties pleasure signifyed by Sir Charles Cottrell, Master of Requests.

W Trumball

Controversy with the Mayor and Corporation over the Cathedral Precinct 1676–7

fol 23v **1676**

Mr Crossman appointed with others to discours the Mayor about the wrongs done to the Church by the Citty concerning the waterworks under Brandon Hill and concerning the pound and pales in the Higher Greene.

fols. 25–25v **3 February 1677**

With an earnest willingnesse to live peaceably and still enjoy peace and friendshipp with the Right Worthy the Mayor and the Worthy the Aldermen of the City of Bristoll, the Dean and Chapter of the same City doe present unto them these grievances in writing according to their owne directions humbly desireing their worships therein to doe them right:

1st They doe conceave that your Tenants on the Colledge Greene have incouragement from you not to pay them any rent for their pales before their houses, forasmuch as you have lately graunted to Mr Northen the lease of a house on the Greene in which you have given him liberty to sett up two posts foure foote or thereabouts from the wall on their grownd which they can make appeare to be a manifest Injury, their predecessors having heretofore graunted leases of the pales and receaved rent for them.

2ndly That upon them and their Tenants and Inhabitants dwelling within the precincts of the Church there have bin severall taxes and offices imposed with a dessigne as they conceive to make the Cathedrall with the houses belonging to the precincts thereof to be parish to Little St Augustines which is contrary to the Foundation of King Henry the 8th which they shall make appeare when thereunto called.

3rdly That the Gates of the Lower Greene are required by the Constables and Watch to be opened at all houres in the Night without leave of the Dean and Chapter. Whereas by the Statutes of the Founder which they are bound by oath to observe and keepe there is a sworne porter appointed who upon his oath is to open and shutt them only at their Command.

Besides all this, wee make it our humble desire that if you have any record for rideing through Cannons Marsh when you ride the Shire Stones before these late troubles, that you will be pleased to acquaint us with it and if in this or any other of the things formerly mentioned you willbe pleased to lett whether you have sufficient authority for the doeing of what has bin done, that you appear unto us wee shall thankfully acknowledge it and humbly acquiesce in such satisfaction.

fol. 27v **25 June 1677**

At a Chapter then held being present Deane Mr Standfast subdeane, Mr Quinton, Mr Crossman, Mr Horne at which Chapter Mr Heath, organist had his first admonition for debauching of the choiremen in keeping of some of them all night at Cards.

fol. 36 **12 April 1679**

Christopher Knight was admitted and sworne an Almesman in the roome and place of old Kinchin

fol. 41 **7 April 1681**

Att a Chapter then held in the Chapter house between the howres of five and six in the afternoone of the same day being present the Reverend the Deane Mr Chetwind sub-deane, Mr Standfast and Mr Crossman Prebendaryes. Att which Chapter Nathaniell Hawkins for his often neglect in comeing to Church, and for his disorderly behaviour then when he does come the Deane and Chapter gave him his first admonition according to the Statute.

fol. 42 **26 May 1681**

John Bromley was by the Deane and Chapter (for good causes and considerations them moveing) dismissed of his place in the Cathedrall and Thomas Callow was admitted a secondary in his place.

fol. 43v **30 May 1682**

Att a Chapter held between the howers of two and five it was ordered that the Petty Canons constantly attend the service of the Church, and that Mr Wallis and Hawkins be carefull in teaching the Choiristers to sing and Mr Heath inspect the method of teaching them, and that noe person belonging to the Quier shall depart the Church on Sundayes until Divine Service and Sermon be ended without a Sufficient excuse to be approved on by the Deane and the Prebends, and that Mr Wallis doe give Choiresters moderate Correction as they shall deserve it.

fol. 44 **23 June 1682**

Itt was ordered by the Chapter that the names of the Benefactors who Contributed to an Organ erected before the late unhappy troubles, and the names of those who Contribute to the present Organ now preparing, with the sums they give to the same, be fairly written in our Chapter Book and alsoe in the Table in the Church for that purpose preparing.

fol.49 **26 October 1682**

The Deane and Chapter give order and decree that Mr Crossman, present Treasurer to the Deane and Chapter, shall give his owne Security for a hundred pounds which was borrowed of Mr Brookhouse for present use till money could be raised to defray the charges of erecting a fair, great Organ in the Colledge Church and other ornaments of the Church, and will give him their Security for the same.

The Organist Dismissed 13 December 1682

fols 51–51v

Att which Chapter it appearing to the said Deane and Chapter that Paule Heath Organist Master of the Choristers have had severall admonitions for keeping a Disorderly Alehouse Debauching the Choir men and other Disorders there and neglecting the Service of the Church and beeing now Credibly Informed that the said Paule Heath doth still keep ill order in his house and hath suffered one Routh, a Barber, to trimme in his house on the Lords day commonly called Sunday to avoyde the penaltys agreed by the Company of Barbers to be inflicted on such offenders and alsoe an act of Parliament made on 9 Car. 2 ^{D} against such offenders and the penalties therein mentioned, and beeing alsoe Credibly Informed that the said Paul Heath did on the – day of this instant month of December with severall of the neighbourhood and town dwellers sitt Tippling in his house until some of them were drunk or very much over gone with liquors. One of which said Company was found dead the next morning in his said house, and hath often times suffered unlawfull games to be used in or about his house and great Disorder to be committed. The said Deane and Chapter takeing into Consideration the Scandall and danger that may accrew to this Cathedrall Church by Suffering the said Paul Heath to remaine still (the premises notwithstanding) a member of the same, did therefore with a unanimous and joynt consent, order and decree to remove, expell and dismisse the said Paul Heath from his said office and place of Organist and Master of the Choristers, as also from all the benefitts advantages and profitts whatsoever belonging to the same; and accordingly did and doe by the present act utterly and forever soe remove, expell and dismisse him from the same.

Following Paul Heath's dismissal a new organist, Joseph Gibson, was appointed. He was paid £20 per annum, and was joined by David Edwards as assistant organist who was paid £2 per annum. David Edwards was one of the almsmen, so his salary was in addition to the £6 13s 4d he already received.

fol. 52 **3 February 1683 Evidence of Civil War Damage**

Whereas the Stable formerly belonging to the Prebendary wherein Mr Samuel Crossman one of the prebends of this Cathedrall Church [lives] beeing Altogether Demolished in the late rebellious times and the ground whereon the Same stood beeing now granted unto Robert Bound of the Citty of Bristoll, Shipwright, and the same prebendary haveing now noe Stable belonging unto itt doe unanimously consent, order and decree that the Stable and Chamber or hay loft over the same lying neare adjoyning unto the Organist his house in the Lower Green late in the possession of Doctor Baron be granted and it is hereby granted unto the said Mr Samuel Crossman and his successors to be from henceforth used, taken and enjoyed as a Stable belonging to his prebendary for the use and benefitt of his successors.

fol. 57 **29 June 1683**

An agreement in Chapter not to grant any more leases of the area called the Masonrie, east of the cathedral, but this is to be used for dwelling houses for the Choir.

fol. 59 **22 October 1683**

An agreement in Chapter to grant a lease to five men of 'all that peice of waste or voyd ground lying on the North West side of the upper Green for the term of forty yeares to build five severall fair houses thereon'.
Fine thirty guineas, annual rent £5.

fol. 60v **21 November 1683 The Great Organ**

An agreement in Chapter to pay the sum of £100 owed for 'the Great Organ and other ornaments in this Cathedrall Church'.

During the early 1680s the Chapter, having met in the Chapter House according to the Statute, adjourned the meetings to the dean's house or the house of one of the prebends 'the Chapter House being out of repaire'. *There are no entries in the Chapter Act Book between 1684 and 1714.*

fol 102 **23 January 1718 Arrangements for the Residence of Members of the Chapter**

The Dean and Chapter did Capitularly meet according to the Statutes of this Church

Residences for the year ensuing are as follows:
Mr Waterman October and halfe November
Dr Lye halfe November and all December
Mr Lucye January and halfe February
Mr Catberd halfe February and all March
Dr Harcourt April and halfe May
The Honourable Mr Dean halfe May and all June, all July and halfe August
Dr Baron halfe August and all September

fol. 107v **13 June 1719**

The dean and chapter agreed to pay Mr Renatus Harris £140 'for the Trumpett Stopp and the Eccho Trumpett and the addition of the C fol and the Key in the Organ of the Cathedrall Church and for all other work and repaires by him done to the same Organ, and in full for all other Moneys due to him'.

EXPENDITURE 1660–1670

B.R.O. DC/A/9/1/7 Extracts from the Annual <u>Computa</u> or Accounts of the Cathedral

The <u>Computa</u> record in formal Latin the income from the widely-scattered estates, properties and endowments of the cathedral. They also record stipends of the clergy and officials and other expenditure. They were carefully compiled and neatly written out each year. The task of supervising the production of these detailed annual accounts fell upon the Treasurer. He was one of the prebendaries and was chosen by his colleagues each year. Treasurers generally served for three or four years, and received a small annual sum in recognition of the difficulty and time-consuming nature of the task. The figures they produced were evidently carefully checked by other members of the Chapter. An example of this occurs in the accounts for 1686. At the end of the long and detailed entries the following note in English was inserted:

Memorandum, that upon the re-examining of these accounts wee whose names are subscribed doe find them to bee miscast, and that there is really due from Mr John Rainstorp, Treasurer to the Church, the summe of £99 10s 5 1/2d.

> William Levett, Dean
> Thomas Horne, Vice Dean
> John Chetwynd
> Richard Towgood

Expenditure in 1665

The Latin text of the accounts has been translated.

Allocations for the Church by George Williamson, Treasurer for the year 1665 for stipends, fees and charities

	£	s	d	
First, the sum of £85 for our Lord the King taxes and tenths	85	10	0	
Item, the stipend of the Dean this year	100	0	0	
Item, stipends of the six prebendaries				
Dr John Weekes	20	0	0	
Mr George Williamson	20	0	0	
Mr Richard Towgood	20	0	0	£110
Mr John Dashfield	10	0	0	
Mr Richard Standfast	20	0	0	
Mr Samuel Wood	20	0	0	

	£	s	d
Item, the stipend of the Schoolmaster (Informatoris Scholae)	20	0	0
Item, the stipend of the three Minor Canons (the 4th -[post being vacant])			
Jacob Read	16	0	0
George Willington	16	0	0
John Massy	16	0	0

£48 (for the three Minor Canons)

	£	s	d
Item, the stipend of the Precentor	2	0	0
Item, the stipend of the six Lay Singers			
Henry Worgan	12	0	0
Derrick Almond (absent)	0	0	0
Peter Chambers	12	0	0
John Gibson	10	0	0
Roger Adams	12	0	0
Richard Wrentmore	12	0	0

£58 (for the six Lay Singers)

	£	s	d
Item, the stipend of the two Secondary Lay Singers			
Robert Lewis	9	11	8
Daniel Williams	7	3	4

£16–15s (for the two Secondary Lay Singers)

	£	s	d
Item, the stipend of Thomas Deane, Organist	17	0	0
Item, the stipends of the four Choristers			
John Ash	4	0	0
Nathaniel Hawkins	4	15	10
(who took the place of a secondary singer for the last term)			
John Massy	4	0	0
John Holcomb	4	0	0

£16–15–10 (for the four Choristers)

	£	s	d
Item, the stipends of the secondary Choristers			
Richard Smith	2	0	0
Benjamin Moon	2	0	0

£4–0–0d (for the secondary Choristers)

	£	s	d
Item, the stipends of four Almsmen			
Leonard Stallard and his successor Henry Kinchin	6	13	4
John Gething	6	13	4
David Jones	6	13	4
John Belsher	6	13	4

£26–13–4d (for the four Almsmen)

	£	s	d
Total of all payments allocated this year	**504**	**14**	**2**

Allocated for fees and stipends of the officials serving the Church this year

	£	s	d
First, Subdeacon, Mr Richard Towgood	3	6	8
Item, Receiver, Mr Richard Standfast	3	6	8
Item, Treasurer, Mr George Williamson	3	6	8

	£	s	d
Item, Auditor, Rowland Tucker	3	13	4
Item, Under-Cook, Edward Bisse	3	6	8
Item, Subsacrists, Hercules Williams and John Rice,			
his assistant	10	0	0
Item, John Meredith, Janitor and Verger	8	0	0
Item, Thomas Townsend, Sub-Janitor	1	0	0
Item, Richard Williamson, Chapter Clerk	4	0	0
Item, the Illustrious Lord Marquis of Dorchester,			
Steward	5	0	0
Item, the Most Distinguished Lord John Churchill,			
Councillor	2	0	0
Item, Robert Redwood, Plumber	5	0	0
Item, the Collector of the Church Rents	2	0	0
Total fees paid this year	**57**	**0**	**0**

To Sir John Paulet for the manor of Halberton and			
the rectory	5	0	0
of Southpetherton	5	0	0
To Sir Richard Trevillian for the rectory of Middleney		3	4
To Sir Christopher Guise, for Berkeley Herons	1	16	10
To Maria Ellis, widow, for Bathford [deducted]		7	1
To Sir George Speak, for the rectory of Ilminster			
[deducted]		7	6
To Sir Robert Cross, for the vicarage of Chew Magna			
[deducted]		18	0
Total payments for the royal taxes	**8**	**12**	**9**

Other necessary payments this year, divers sums for Charity, repairs etc.

First, for Charity for ordinary paupers distributed each			
Sunday after Evening prayers	20	0	0
Item, extraordinary Charity for the destitute and beggars			
given out following occasional demands	10	15	4
Allocations for the repair of the public roads	20	0	0
Divers sums for necessary repairs of the church	43	14	7
Item, other sums for ordinary expenses this year	128	8	6
For other expenses, ordinary and extraordinary omitted,			
which sums appear in the detailed book	47	17	9
Total of all the payments for Charity, repairs, and expenses			
	270	**16**	**11½**

Total of all the receipts this year	**934**	**16**	**3½**

Sum of all payments this year	**899**	**7**	**0**

So it appears from these accounts that the church has			
a surplus of	**35**	**9**	**3**

Examined by us: Henry Glemham, Dean
                  Richard Towgood, Sub-dean
                  Richard Standfast
                  Samuel Wood

Each year the Computa *record substantial sums spent on repairs to the cathedral, and it seems clear that considerable trouble was taken to maintain the building. For example, in 1666 the* Computa *record that £128 3s 3d was spent on 'Expensis Extraordiniis' and a further £208 1s 2d 'pro Necessarius Reparationis'. To these accounts a note was added in English:*

Memorandum that this laid Accompt hath been allowed this year, viz. Twenty pounds laid out this year upon the highwaies, which twentie pounds hath not been laid out but is reserved in his hands towards the rebuilding of the Cloisters, which twentie pounds being added to the Sixtie two pounds seaven shillings three pence halfpennie makes in the whole Fowerscore and two pounds seaven shillings and threepence halfpennie there is fourty pounds resting in his hands towards the rebuilding of the Cloisters, and other fourty two pounds seaven shillings and threepence halfpennie to be a dividend for this yeare 1666.

                  Henry Glemham, Deane
                  Richard Standfast, Sub deane
                  George Williamson, Receiver
                  Richard Towgood

This expenditure was no doubt necessary to repair damage done during the Civil War and Commonwealth. During the next few years similar large sums were spent on work which is generally unspecified. For example, in 1667 £227 3s 0d was spent on building work and a further £40 on rebuilding the water conduit in the centre of the cloisters. In 1670 there is a reference to the sum of £741 5s 6d spent on repairs to the cathedral 'since his Majesty's happy return' [B.R.O. DC/A/6/6]. *Details are given below.*

During the 1660s and 1670s money continued to be allocated for the repairs to the cloisters and other unspecified work on the cathedral and surrounding buildings. For example, in 1672 £22 10s 3d was spent on repairs (pro necessariis Ecclesiae et ecclesiae domnum reparationibus) *and a further £111 18s 3d for extraordinary expenses which are said to be shown in the Book of Particulars (pro* Expensis extraordinariis ut patet ex libro Particularium). *Unfortunately, only one of the Books of Particulars, from which the* Computa *were compiled, has survived; this is for the years 1699–1745* [B.R.O., DC/A/9/2/1]. *Details of this Book of Particulars are included later in this volume. In 1679 ordinary expenses on repairs amounted to £40 10s 8d and extraordinary expenses accounted for £103 0s 3d. In 1680 the sums were £101 0s 0d and £197 0s 6d respectively. A small additional expense during these years was the sum of £2 per annum allocated to Thomas Moon for attending to the cathedral clock (*observantis et reparantis Horologium).

Expenditure on the Cathedral in 1670

This account comes from a small manuscript volume by G. Pugh, entitled 'Historical Memoirs of the City of Bristol'. This appears to have been written in the late 17th century and is bound in a contemporary agreement by the dean and chapter for the appointment of a chapter clerk from which the right-hand edge has been cut off. The short book consists almost entirely of an historical account of the Augustinian abbey and its abbots, but also includes the following brief description of expenditure in the 1670s. The identity of the author is unknown, and it is not clear from where he derived these figures, but they do illustrate the large sums which had to be spent to repair the damage and make good the losses which occurred during the Commonwealth.

B.R.O. DC/A/6/6

A True Account of What hath been extraordinarily expended by the Dean and Chapter of Bristol since his Majesty's Happy restauration.

Bristol, October the 17th 1670

	£	s	d
Imprimis, In and upon the repairation of the Church, the Ornaments and Utensils thereof	741	5	6
Item, in repairing theyr own houses and other buildings belonging to the Church	570	0	0
Item, In an humble present and benevolence to his Majesty	400	0	0
Item, Towards the redemption of Captives formerly given £50 and now £10, total	60	0	0
Item, In Augmentation to poor Curates and the Inferior Members and Officers of the Cathedrall	503	13	4
Item, In Abatiment of fines, some upon the score of Purchasing in the late ill times, some upon the Account of Loyaltie, and some in order to contenting and gain upon the love of their Tenants	1470	0	0
Item, In Charitible uses beyond what their statutes doe require	110	0	0
Item, In what losses they have sustained by what they have forgiven to bad Tenants	500	0	0
Total Sum	**4354**	**18**	**10**

All which we are ready to make good in particulars, if at any time we shall be thereunto required. In witness thereof we, the said Dean and Chapter, have hereto affixed our Common Chapter Seal, dated the Day and Year above written.

BISHOP JONATHAN TRELAWNY

The diocese of Bristol was brought to the forefront of national affairs during the episcopate of Jonathan Trelawny (1685–9) when he, with six of his fellow bishops, was imprisoned for refusing to order the reading in their diocesan parish churches of the Declaration of Indulgence issued by James II in 1688, which gave rights of public worship to nonconformists, both Catholic and Protestant. Among the bishops who joined Trelawny in his refusal were Archbishop William Sancroft, Thomas Ken of Bath and Wells and the previous bishop of Bristol, John Lake, who had been translated to Chichester in 1685. The bishops were all imprisoned in the Tower of London and put on trial for seditious libel. They were finally acquitted amid scenes of great rejoicing throughout the country.

Jonathan Trelawny was born at Trelawne, a couple of miles inland from the fishing port of Looe in south-east Cornwall. His family had been prominent in the service of the Crown in Cornwall since at least the early 15ᵗʰ century, and loyalty to the Crown and attachment to the Protestant faith of the Church of England were guiding principles throughout his life. During the Civil War his grandfather had raised one of the regiments of the Cornish army that fought so valiantly against superior Parliamentary forces at the battle of Lansdown, near Bath in 1645, and his father and brothers all served in the royal army. Jonathan Trelawny himself, notwithstanding his clerical status, had served as vice-admiral for the Cornish coast during the 1670s. This makes the stand which he felt compelled to take against the commands of James II in 1685 all the more remarkable.

Trelawny was born in 1650 and was ordained deacon in 1673 and priest in 1676. He became rector of St Ive near Trelawne in 1677, combining it with the nearby Trelawny family living of South Hill, although he resided in neither parish, but at Trelawne. In spite of his family connections, his elevation to a bishopric was unexpected. His biographer wrote of him

> 'Trelawny was unlikely to commend himself for higher ecclesiastical office on grounds of piety, pastoral care or academic distinction. Trelawny was what a later age would call 'a hearty Christian'. He enjoyed good wine, good tobacco and boisterous company. He was a frequent and dedicated user of bad language'.

[M.G. Smith, 'Fighting Joshua' A Study of the Career of Sir Jonathan Trelawny 1650–1721, (1985), 17].

It was Trelawny's part in ensuring that Cornwall, and in particular the Cornish militia, remained steadfast in their attachment to James II in June 1685 when the Duke of Monmouth landed at Lyme Regis and attracted the support of large numbers of men from Devon, Dorset and Somerset before leading them to defeat and its horrendous aftermath at Sedgemoor, that ensured his promotion. The King demonstrated his gratitude by appointing Trelawny as the new bishop of Bristol in July 1685. This was in spite of the misgivings of the archbishop, William Sancroft. Trelawny's initial reaction on hearing that the King proposed to appoint him to the bishopric of Bristol was of dismay. His father, Sir John Trelawny, had died in 1681,

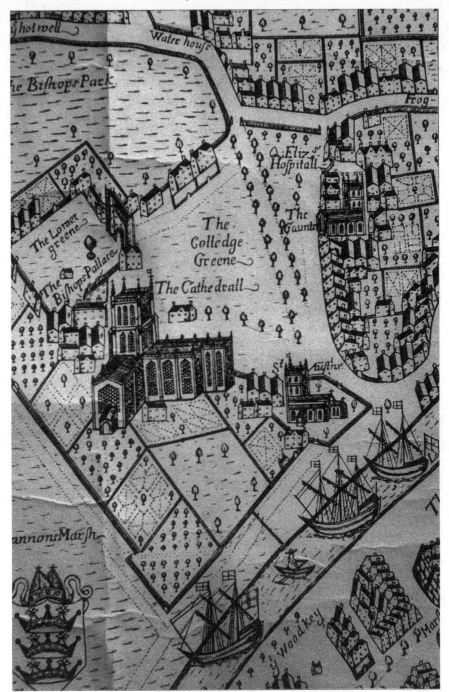

Fig 6 Jacob Millerd's Plan of the Cathedral Precinct 1673. This shows the former chapel of St Jordan on College Green, the deanery and other houses west of the cathedral, the bishop's palace, St Augustine the Less, St Mark's chapel or the Gaunts, and the shipping in the river Frome. Canons' Marsh and the slopes of Brandon Hill remain free of building development.

leaving large debts. As ardent royalists throughout the Civil War, the family had suffered badly during the Commonwealth period, and their fortunes had still not recovered. The meagre income of the Bristol bishopric, coupled with the heavy expenses that the position entailed, would do little to relieve the burden. Jonathan Trelawny immediately wrote to Lawrence Hyde, earl of Rochester, who was the King's brother- in-law, pleading for a more lucrative see, such as Exeter, Peterborough or Chichester. His appeal was unsuccessful, but the letter is interesting for the way in which he emphasised his loyalty to the Crown, and for the details it gives of the income and expenses he expected from the Bristol bishopric.

Clarendon Papers
10 July 1685

My Lord,——Give me leave to throw myself at your lordship's feet, humbly imploring your patronage, if the Bishop of Exeter cannot be obliged to accept of that now vacant see which he seemed to incline to when his removal to Peterborough was purposed; and I am assured from those about him that if the king should be pleased to tell him he is resolved on his translation to Chichester he will readily close with it; and let me beseech your lordship to fix him there and to advance *your creature* to Exeter where I can serve the king and your lordship.

I hear his majesty designed me for Bristol, which I should not decline, was I not already under such pressure by my father's debts, as must necessarily break my estate in pieces, if I find no better prop than the income of Bristol, not greater than £300 per annum, and the expense in first fruits, consecration and settlement will require £2000. If Peterborough and Chichester be both refused me I shall not deny Bristol, though mine own ruin goes with it, if it be the king's pleasure or any way for his majesty's service that I should accept of it, but I hope the king will have more compassion on his *slave*, and that your lordship will vouchsafe a better lot to

My Lord,
Your most humble and devoted servant,
J. TRELAWNY.

Trelawny's plea was unsuccessful, and he was formally appointed to Bristol on 17 October, and was consecrated bishop on 8 November 1685. As a bishop Trelawny proved to be energetic and forceful. At 35 years of age he was younger and more vigorous than many newly-appointed bishops, and he entered upon the duties of his diocese with enthusiasm. Soon after arriving in Bristol he conducted visitations of the diocese and the cathedral, and although this produced no startling results, he carefully recorded the names and duties of all the cathedral clergy and lay staff. This list is reproduced below:

B.R.O. EP/J/1/34
A visitation of the Cathedral in 1686

A primary visitation of the cathedral was conducted in the Chapter House by Bishop Jonathan Trelawny 19th January 1686, in the presence of Joseph Eaglestone, notary public.

Dr William Levett, Dean

Mr John Chetwind, Sub Dean	
Mr Thomas Horne, Receiver	
Mr John Rainstorpe, Treasurer	Prebendaries
Mr Stephen Crispian	
Mr Walter Hart	
Mr Richard Twogood	

Mr John Fielding, Arch Deacon of Dorsett
Mr James Taylor, Schoolemaster etc.

Roger Adams	
Daniel Williams	
John Holcomb	Singing men
Nathaniel Hawkins	
John Gittoes	
Walter Massey	

Thomas Callow	Secondaries
Thomas Noakes	

Samuel Ball	
John Jones	
John Bosden	Choristers
Samuel Turky	
Thomas Nicholson	
Edward Hardie	

Samuel Davies	
Christopher Knight	Almsmen
John Belcher	
Joseph Cox	

Edward Goodyard, Verger etc.
Roland Tucker, Auditor
John Cobb, Chapter Clark

Relations between the previous bishop, John Lake, and the dean, Richard Thomson, had not been cordial. Thomson had been appointed in 1685 through the influence of the Duke of Beaufort, and in spite of the opposition of Bishop Lake and members of the Bristol Corporation. Although dean for less than a year, Thomson had proved difficult and obstructive. In particular he had strongly opposed Bishop Lake's proposals for improvements in the cathedral services, including weekly celebrations of Holy Communion. Thomson had also objected to the bishop's visitation of the cathedral, in spite of complaints to the archbishop, William Sancroft. In a letter of thanks to the archbishop for his translation to Chichester, Lake expressed his relief 'to be freed from the impertinence and insolence of our Dean' [M.G. Smith, op. cit., citing Bodleian Library, Tanner MSS, CXXIX, fol. 148]. *Fortunately for Trelawny, Dean Thomson died shortly before his arrival in Bristol, and he was able to establish good relations with the new dean, William Levett, who was appointed in 1686. In a letter to the archbishop in 1687 Levett praised the work of his bishop and declared his appreciation for the help and support he had received. He wrote 'There have of late alsoe in this place beene very undutifull misbehaviours towards former Bishops. I hope we shall now all contain ourselves in due Bounds'. Much of the credit for the improved relationship between bishop and cathedral was evidently due to Trelawny's more emollient style and character* [M.G. Smith, op. cit., 27–30, quoting from Bodleian Library, Tanner MSS CXXIX, CXXX Letters to Archbishop Sancroft (1685–7)].

During the first two of his three years as bishop of Bristol, Trelawny had remained true to his own and his family's strongly royalist principles, and had respected the King's catholicism by not persecuting catholic recusants in his diocese. During his visitation of Dorset he had dismissed a case brought against a dozen recusants at Cerne Abbas, and in Bristol he had declined to proceed against a catholic priest who attempted to establish a Mass-house at the Hotwells. In his visitation charge to the diocesan clergy in 1686 he urged them to avoid preaching anti-papal and anti-catholic sermons or inflaming popular feeling against catholics. Trelawny's concern to obey the King's desire that there should be no persecution of catholics brought him great unpopularity in Bristol, where most of the ruling elite and almost the entire population of the city were fervently anti-catholic and suspected the Pope of fostering all sorts of unspecified ills amongst them. In June 1686 Sir John Knight, one of the Bristol MPs, a former mayor and a leading figure in the city, wrote to the Earl of Sunderland, Lord President of the Privy Council, accusing Trelawny of being a crypto-catholic and seeking to impose catholicism in his diocese. Knight's suspicions were increased by the fact that a contingent of the royal army consisting of the Queen's Regiment was stationed in Bristol and was commanded by the bishop's brother, Charles Trelawny. The bishop's long and impassioned response to Knight's suggestions indicates how seriously he took the matter, and the fact that he was already being torn between what he perceived as his duty to the King and his episcopal duty to uphold the interests of the Church of England.

Cal. S.P. Dom. (1686–7) 184–6

Letter of Bishop Jonathan Trelawny to the Earl of Sunderland written from Trelawne 25 June 1686

I was exceeding troubled when I found from the letter addressed by Sir John Knight to your Lordship, that after the whole tenure of my life before, and my particular care at Bristol to recommend obedience and his Majesty's service to all persons I there conversed with, and that after the injunctions I lately made requiring all the clergy of my diocese upon their canonical obedience strictly to observe his Majesty's commands directed by your Lordship to the Archbishops, I should at last fall under the suspicion of being in any way disrespectful in my behaviour to his Majesty either in regard of his religion or government; but when I saw from whom this charge came, I expected no better, considering how I disrespected him at Bristol upon the accompt of his carriage to the King, and forbade the clergy of the Cathedral the conversing with a man so dangerous as he was.

My Lord, if it would not seem too long, I would give you an account of what I did before I went down, and afterwards at Bristol.

In order to the getting some knowledge of the people I waited on my Lord Chancellor for his character, and of those persons, if any such there were, on whose honesty I could depend; among others his Lordship gave me a true account of the nature of this person, and that the chief man I could rely on there was Mr Rumsey the town-clerk. Acordingly when I came there I made my inquiries of him, showed him public civilities, made him the first visit before the Mayor, which very much incensed the town. Being further info[r]med of Sir John Knight, I publicly, whereon I could, slighted him, and hearing how busy he was in promoting ill apprehensions of the government, I employed some persons to watch him narrowly, who bringing me an account of some dangerous things said and done by him, I sent them to my brother Colonel Trelawny to be showed to the King, which Mr Hellier my receiver at Bristol will produce, and I desire he may be commanded to do so. Having thus used him all the while I was there, I so far disobliged him that if his objections can be of any weight there will be enough of them, though your Lordship will easily find they proceed from malice and revenge.

As to things he objects [to] in my directions to the clergy, I exactly followed his Majesty's orders to me, and only enjoined them in relation to the Roman Catholics a strictness of life to outdo them, of which if the King requires further assurance my papers which are now by me shall be sent up.

Whilst I was there I preached but once, and that the sermon I had the honour to preach before his late Majesty, enforcing of a good life and loyal behaviour to the Government, which I purposely chose to make a pattern to the rest of my clergy, and to prevent what stories I since find and then feared.

The persons who were constant at my table were the officers of her Majesty's regiment commanded by my brother, for which the town said I was a Papist.

As to the commands he says I laid on the Mayor to prevent the celebrating of Mass in the city, the whole truth is as it follows.

Being well informed that before I went down the character of my being a Papist went before me, and from persons who were there believed, I was jealous of myself that something of that nature would be offered me at my first coming as a trial of me, and accordingly it happened; for the next day after I came, which was Sunday, I had an information brought me that at a particular house mass was then saying, upon which I replied it being not my business I would talk with the Mayor, and so looking on this thing brought to try me, I told Mr Mayor that he ought to look into it, and bring me an account of it, which the Mayor afterwards upon inquiry finding to be false, I was the more convinced that this report was laid as a snare for me, but however had it proved true I had an intention to have sent an account to the King (which for that purpose I demanded of the Mayor) to have known his Majesty's royal pleasure, and to have stopped all things till that was known.

This is the naked truth of the business, and unless this be commanding Sir J. Knight to do what he did, he might as well have charged me with falsifying the Duke of Beaufort's letter, or directing him to the postscript of which I had no other notice but from the public news.

If the King shall distrust my comportment at Bristol, I humbly beseech his Majesty to take it from Mr Ramsey, Sir William Pool, or any person of known and approved loyalty. If his Majesty shall suspect my behaviour as to the interest of the Roman Catholics, my Chancellor can satisfy him when and how many I commanded him not to take notice of when presented on purpose for the hardest severities of the ecclesiastical censures. Let Sir Winstone Churchil be heard as to what I did and said in my visitation of Dorsetshire; and Sir John Arundel how I protected the Roman Catholics of this country in the late King's reign, when some of the justices had resolved to have punished them with all and the most rigorous laws against them.

And now having given this accompt, I hope it will fully satisfy the King, for since it hath been the blood and pride of our family to be in all times true to the King, your Lordship may easily believe that as this suspicion of disrespect to the King is a trouble to me, so if it should not be removed it would increase, for I should be sorry if I was the only man of the family that ever fell under the displeasure of his prince.

This staunch royalist feeling makes the stand he took over the Declaration of Indulgence in 1688 all the more remarkable. The King's first Declaration of Indulgence was issued in April 1687, granting full liberty of worship in public. Bishops were invited to sign an 'Address of Thanks for the King's Declaration' and to commend it to their clergy. On 26 April 1687 the Earl of Sunderland, who was President of the Privy Council, wrote to Bishop Trelawny asking that he should sign it himself and recommend it to his clergy.

Camden Society, 1ˢᵗ Ser., 55, (1853), 17–20

My Lord   Whitehall, 26 April 1687

The King commands me to send your lordship the enclosed, being the copy of an Addresse which the Bishops of Durham, Rochester, Oxford, and Chester have signed and sent to the clergy of their respective dioceses, recommending to them to joine in it. His Majestie does not doubt but your lordship will do the same, and not only promote the signing of it in your diocesse, but also amongst the clergy of your acquaintance.

I am, my lord,
Your most humble servant,
SUNDERLAND P.

Bishop of Bristol

In the event, only two of the clergy in the diocese of Bristol, both in Dorset, agreed to sign, and Trelawny duly returned the document with the two signatures. In April 1688 James II issued a second Declaration of Indulgence, ordering that bishops were to distribute it throughout their dioceses and that it should be read on two successive Sundays in every church in the kingdom. The archbishop of Canterbury, William Sancroft, and six other bishops including Trelawny, petitioned the King, requesting him to withdraw the order. The King's response was to arrest the bishops, imprison them in the Tower of London, and order their trial for publishing a seditious libel against him. After a lengthy trial in June 1688, they were finally acquitted on 30 June. The news of their release brought great national rejoicing. Trelawny's determined stand against what was perceived as a catholic threat brought him great popularity in Bristol. On the news of his release from prison the church bells were rung, bonfires were lit and any previous doubts about the bishop's attachment to the Church were silenced. In Cornwall Trelawny achieved a popularity which is still remembered in the song which has become virtually the Cornish national anthem:

Trelawny he's in keep and hold
Trelawny he may die
Here's twenty-thousand Cornish men
Will know the reason why.

The next few months witnessed a totally unexpected transformation in Trelawny's career. Support for the King waned rapidly, although he remained determined to implement his policy of toleration for catholics. The policy was already facing ruin and determined opposition in the country when William of Orange landed with an army at Torbay on 5 November 1688. Amazingly, with this threat poised to drive him from the country, James II summoned Trelawny to an audience in London and bestowed on him the ancient and wealthy bishopric of Exeter, a diocese which included the whole of Devon and Cornwall. This lucrative appointment later enabled Trelawny to settle his substantial debts. In December as William III and his army moved towards London, James II finally fled to France. By this time Trelawny had already accepted the new monarch and transferred his allegiance to him. On 5 December 1688 a part of the army assembled by William marched into Bristol under the command of the Earl of Shrewsbury. The Earl brought with him a letter for the bishop from William of Orange. The bishop's immediate reply shows his complete transfer of support to the new monarch.

[J.Dalrymple, <u>Memoirs of Great Britain and Ireland</u>, (1771–3), II, 335].

May it please your Highness
I received the great honour of your Highness's letter, and beg leave to return you my most humble thanks for those kind opinions you have been pleased to conceive of me, which I shall endeavor still to preserve.
My Lord Shrewsbury (with whose conduct we are all extremely pleased) will give you a full account of what hath been done here, which if your Highness shall approve of, it will be great satisfaction to me, that I have borne some part in the work which your Highness has undertaken with the hazard of your life, for the preservation of the Protestant religion, the laws, and the liberties of this kingdom.
I desire Almighty God to preserve you as the means of continuing to us the exercise of our holy religion and our laws, and humbly beseech your Highness to believe me very ready to promote so good a work, and on all occasions to approve myself your Highness's

Most obedient, faithful, humble servant,

Bristol, Dec. 5, 1688   J. BRISTOL

THE CATHEDRAL INCOME AND EXPENDITURE 1699–1742

As noted earlier in this volume, the carefully compiled annual <u>Computa</u> *provide a detailed account in Latin of the rents received from each individual property belonging to the cathedral. The following example, taken from the account for 1699, shows the widely scattered nature of these properties, and the total income derived from each county. In addition, details are given from the entries relating to the rents received from land and buildings within the cathedral precinct, showing some of the houses which were crowded onto the site of the former nave and around College Green and Lower Green, some of which had been converted to tenements and were in multiple occupation. Many other houses in this area were occupied by cathedral clergy and staff who paid no rent and are therefore not listed. The account also shows the stipends paid to the clergy and lay staff and gives a brief outline of other expenditure during the year.*

BRO, DC/A/9/1/8 **Computa 1682–1715. From the entries for 1699**

Rental from properties in:	**£**	**s**	**d**
Wiltshire	85	13	3½
Devon	119	10	0
Gloucestershire	149	9	1
Somerset	306	9	8
Bristol	146	6	6½
Total rental income	**807**	**8**	**7**

	£	**s**	**d**
Properties in the Cathedral Precinct (*'intra et prope princta Ecclesia'*)			
Imprimis, John Smith for a Tenement formerly the widow Martin's			
John Pearce the Covant Orchard and buildings with the Store House near the church of St Augustine the Less	3	10	0
Item, William Abbotts for a building near the cathedral church on the west side, now converted into several tenements	£2	0s	0d
Item, the executors of Edward Chetwind for a newly-built house on the great cemetery (*'supra magna camiterium'*), now converted, to three Tenements formerly in the occupation of Richard Noakes		6	8
Item, John Jones for one garden and house and stable in the place called the Lower green or the Inner green		3	6
Item, John Jones, verger for the herbage of the great cemetery or Green	1	0	0
Item, Susanna Arundell for a Tenement on the Green formerly Smarts Tenement		6	0
Item, John Phelps for a Tenement on the Green formerly Hurnes		6	0
Item, Richard Towgood for a Tenement on the Green 5s 0d, for a garden in a place called the Little Marsh 1s 0d, and for a piece of land adjoining the garden 6d (*'pro fragmenta terra eidem horto adjacenie 6d'*)		6	6

Item, the Widow Nicholas for a piece of land in the Lower Green	1	0
Item, Henry Lloyd for a Tenement in the Lower Green formerly Powells	10	0
Item, Saince[?] Bayly formerly Bussell for one entry	2	6
Item, Hamond Wytherly for a Tenement on the Green built by Thomas Wilcockes	1 0	0
Item, Alice Edwards for a Tenement and Stable on the Green built by the same Wilcockes	10	0
Item, Thomas Holworthy for a Tenement on the Green built by the same Wilcockes	10	0
Item, Elizabeth Rolestone for a Tenement on the Green built by Samuel Rolestone	10	0
Item, Anthony Varder for a Tenement on the Green built by the same Rolestone	10	0
Item, Geffrey Pinnell for a Tenement built at the same time on the Green by John Avery, plumber	1 0	0
Item, Anthony Varder for two Tenements on the Green built by the same Rolestone	1 0	0
Item, Susanna Northen for pales (*'pro le pailes'*) on the Green	0	6
Item, Daniel Williams for pales and two postes on the Green (*'pro le pailes et 2 posts supra le Green'*)	2	0
Item, John Price for walls on the Green	2	0
Item, Robert Bound for a Tenement and pales at a place called the Deans Marsh or the Lower Grounds	2 10	0
Item, Jonathan New for a Tenement and pales at a place called the Deans Marsh or the Lower Grounds	2 10	0
Item, the same Jonathan New for other pales on the Deans Marsh or the Lower Grounds	2 0	0
Item, Susanna Arundell for a piece of land on the Green near the Tenement of the said Susanna Arundell	1	0

Total Rental for the Cathedral Precinct	**20**	**18**	**4**

Payments (*'Allocationes'*) in the Cathedral Church of Bristol made by Thomas Cary, Treasurer this year 1699

	£	s	d
Translated from the Latin			
Allocation of divers sums for stipends, fees, etc.			
Imprimis, for royal taxes to Sir Thomas Bridges paid	85	10	0
Item, stipend of the Dean 100	100	0	0
Item, stipends of six prebendaries:			
Mr Stephen Crespion £20			
Mr Richard Towgood £20			
Dr Nathaniel Lye £20	120	0	0
Mr Charles Livesay £20			
Mr Thomas Cary £20			
Mr Richard Smith £20			

	£	s	d
Item, stipend of John Yates, schoolmaster ('informatoris scholae')	20	0	0
Item, stipend of James Taylor, precentor	2	0	0

Item, stipends of four Minor Canons:

		£	s	d
Mr James Taylor	£16			
Mr Thomas Paradis	£16	64	0	0
Mr Samuel Paine	£16			
Mr Benjamin Bayly	£16			

Item, stipends of six lay singing-men:

		£	s	d
Walter Massey	£12			
John Gittoes	£12			
Thomas Callow	£12	68	0	0
William Coles	£12			
Arthur Wood	£12			
Joseph Pope	£ 8			

Item, stipends of four choristers:

		£	s	d
Thomas Dixon	£ 4			
John Elliott	£ 4	16	0	0
James Jones	£ 4			
Edward Elliott	£ 4			

Item, stipends of two secondary choristers:

		£	s	d
John Wood	£ 2			
Stephen Perryman	£ 2	4	0	0
Item, stipend of Joseph Gibson, organist		20	0	0
Item, stipend of William Coles, singing-master		2	0	0

Item, stipends of four almsmen:

		£	s	d
John Belcher	£ 6 13s 4d			
Christopher Knight	£ 6 13s 4d	26	13	4
David Edwards	£ 6 13s 4d			
Thomas Grafton	£ 6 13s 4d			
Total		**528**	**3**	**4**

	£	s	d

Fees and Stipends of Officials serving the Church this year 1699

	£	s	d
Imprimis, the Sub-Dean, Doctor Nathaniel Lye	3	6	8
Item, the Treasurer, Thomas Cary	3	6	8
Item, the Receiver, Thomas Cary	6	13	4
Item, the Auditor, John Cobbe	8	0	0
Item, the Sub-Sacrist, Edward Goodyard	8	0	0
Item, the Janitor and Verger, John Jones	8	0	0
Item, the Chapter Clerk, John Cobbe	8	0	0
Item, the Keeper of the Clock, Edward Goodyard	2	0	0

Item, the Assistant Organist, David Edwards	2	0	0
Item, the Plumber, John Avery	5	0	0
Total	**49**	**13**	**4**

Other Payment this year 1699

Imprimis, Charity to the Poor distributed this year	20	0	0
Item, Contribution for the Repair of the Public Roads	20	0	0
Item, for Repair and Maintenance of the Church	151	18	0
Total	**191**	**18**	**0**

Total Income received this year	**807**	**8**	**7**
Total Expenses this year	**769**	**15**	**2**
Remaining in the Church Account	**37**	**13**	**5**

Examined and approved by us 8 June 1700

George Royse, Dean
Nathaniel Lye, Sub-dean
Stephen Crespion

THE BOOK OF PARTICULARS 1699–1745

Although the successive volumes of the Computa *are an invaluable source of information concerning the income derived by the cathedral from its various estates and properties, as well as listing the stipends and wages of the cathedral clergy, staff and pensioners, they provide no more than brief headings of other expenditure. A much more thorough and detailed description of expenditure especially concerning the maintenance of the cathedral, is provided by* The Book of Particulars *covering the years from 1699 to 1745. The* Particulars *were the detailed accounts of expenditure from which the summaries in the* Computa *were compiled. In many ways this is the most informative of all the financial accounts relating to the cathedral, but unfortunately only one volume survives. Inevitably many of the entries for successive years are repetitive, but nonetheless the volume shows more clearly than any other source the workings of the cathedral organisation, the way in which the building was used, maintained and decorated, and the various people who were involved in its day-to-day running. Above all, the* Particulars *show that in spite of the fact that the Dean and some Canons were non-resident, appearing in Bristol only for their periods of residence, the cathedral building was well maintained and carefully looked after. This evident concern reinforces the remarks of successive visitors which are quoted in this volume, stating that the cathedral structure and furnishings were in good condition. The* Particulars *show regular payments to masons, plumbers, carpenters, tilers and glaziers as well as careful maintenance of the organ, bells, clock, cloisters and furnishings. There was regular expenditure on the precincts, including College Green. The fact that the senior clergy were non-resident involved constant payments for correspondence with them, but the regular services in the cathedral continued, accompanied by the choir and the organ, and the school continued to function. Four pensioners were supported, although they no longer lived within the precinct. These were men nominated by the Crown who had grown old in royal service or had spent long years in the army or navy. As well as their pensions, some of them were paid additional sums for tasks about the cathedral, such as cleaning, keeping the clock and acting as sexton. One was paid as 'assistant organist', which it is tempting to suppose was a grandiose term for pumping the bellows. Another was paid for cleaning the Chapter House and lighting a fire there when the Chapter met. Each year in accordance with the Statutes, the pensioners were provided with expensive coats, complete with fancy buttons and each decorated with a 'Rose', which was an elaborately-embroidered device made of silk, possibly depicting a Tudor rose, which would have been appropriate for an institution founded by Henry VIII. Each 'Rose' cost between 3s 0d and 5s 0d, and must have been intricate and time-consuming to make. New ones were purchased each year. In 1720 they were described as 'four Badges'.*

As was shown earlier, both the minor canons and the singing-men had other positions and served in other Bristol churches. The minor canons also had an additional source of income from conducting weddings in the cathedral. The cathedral Register of baptisms, marriages and burials begins in 1670, and between 1670 and 1700 there were 60 marriages conducted, mostly of persons who had no connection with the cathedral. During the same period there were only 4 baptisms and 8 burials [B.R.O. DC/A/10/1].

Payments were made for additional sermons, decorating the cathedral for Christmas and Easter and for annual commemorations such as the Gun Powder Plot on 5 November, the Execution of Charles I on 30 January and the Restoration of the Monarchy (Oak-Apple Day) on 29 May each year. The marble floor of the cathedral was regularly cleaned, and the eagle lectern, candlesticks and 'branches' or chandeliers were 'scoured' to remove the wax. Large numbers of tallow candles were purchased each year, and higher-quality wax candles were brought from London and were remarkably costly. Men were paid to carry the cathedral weapons at musters of the city-trained bands and to provide an escort for visiting royalty. Gifts were made to the poor of various parishes where the cathedral possessed estates or patronage; generally two parishes were chosen in turn each year. Regular fees and a salary were paid to Renatus Harris for work on the organ. Each year £1 1s 0d was paid to 'Mr Morgans keeper', but no explanation of this has been found; by the 1740s the same sum was paid to 'Lady Rachel Morgans keeper'. An entry in 1717 records the expenditure of £4 5s 0d on 'Lettice Wyer [Lattice Wire] for the painted window in the South Isle of the Colledge', showing that then, as now, wire guards were required to protect the windows.

An occasional heavy expense was the cost involved in visits by members of the Chapter to the widely-scattered cathedral properties. For example, in 1716 £13 17s 9d was paid 'for visiting the severall Estates belonging to the Dean and Chapter of Bristoll in the counties of Devon and Somerset by Dr Harcourt, sub-dean, and Mr Waterman, treasurer'. A similar visit to properties in Gloucestershire, Buckinghamshire and Wiltshire in 1719 cost £16 3s 11d.

The Particulars *show that the interior walls of the cathedral, together with the cloisters and Chapter House, were plastered and whitewashed. This must have given the cathedral a totally different appearance and atmosphere than that provided by the modern undecorated stonework. All the surfaces, including the roof, appear to have been whitewashed or 'white-limb'd', and entries show considerable expense in purchasing sailcloth to cover the organ and lay on the floors while the whitewash was applied.*

B.R.O., DC/A/9/2/1   **Book of Particulars 1699–1700**

Residencies from November 1699 to November 1700

		£	s	d
January	To Mr Cary	1	0	0
Aprill	To Mr Linesay	1	0	0
May	To the Deane	2	0	0
June	To Doctor Lye	1	0	0
July	To Mr Crespion	1	0	0
August	To Mr Crespion	1	0	0
September	To Mr Smyth	1	0	0
October	To Mr Towgood	1	0	0
		9	**0**	**0**

To Several Sums of mony laid out in repairacions & other expenses ordinary & exteraordinary from November 1699 to 30 November 1700

paid for a Rent role		5	0
paid Goody Whiting & Goody Whitfeild at Xmasse		10	0
paid Roger Adams Christmasse for Salry	1	10	0
paid John Holcomb Xmasse Salry	3	0	0
paid for a letter from Newport boat	–	–	1
paid Mr Edwards in part of his bill	18	0	0
paid Thomas Reynolds, mason as per bill		3	9
paid Hugh Jones, Tyler as per bill		1	6
paid Paul Powell for plucking Ivie from the church		1	6
paid John Holcomb Lady day Salry 1700	3	0	0
paid Roger Adams Lady day Salry 1700	1	10	0
paid John Goodred for bell ropes		12	6
paid Mr Edwards in part for Law	16	10	0
paid Richard Perryman for washing the communion linen		2	6
paid him for cleaning the leads and gutters		2	6
paid David Edwards for a watering pott		2	6
paid Graftons wife for a coat	1	0	0
paid for cloth for 3 coats more	2	12	6
	49	**4**	**4**

paid for a letter from Mr Edwards			3
paid for trimming the pentioners coats		7	8
paid Abraham Wood for 2 dozen Buttons		8	0
paid Hanah Daniell for 3 roses		9	0
paid for a bonefire 29 May 1700		7	0

	£	s	d
paid Callow for makeing 3 coats		10	6
paid Peter Wilkins in full of his Bill		15	0
paid Robert Hore, mason his Bill	1	10	0
paid Robert Naylor, joyner his Bill	1	4	0
paid John Avery, plumber in full of his bill	12	0	0
paid Richard Perryman his bill		13	9
paid the Choyer[choir] by your order	2	0	0
paid Paul Powell his bill for trees etc.	3	9	0
paid cleaning the ruble from the church		1	6
paid for a letter from Mr Edwards			3
paid Thomas Maddox for pitching before the church	1	2	6
paid Dr Lyes years rent for his garden Mich. 99	1	0	0
paid for Serving a Warrant against Nickolls		3	0
paid Mr Romsey a Fee	1	1	6
paid John Holcomb Midsomer Salry 1700	2	10	0
	29	**12**	**11**
paid Mr Richard Pennyman his bill 1s 2d,paid Robert Adams Midsomer Sal. £1 10s 0d	1	11	2
paid Capt. Devonshire to the Breife	5	0	0
paid Mr Morgans Keeper a Fee	1	0	0
paid Thomas Rennolds, mason his Bill	1	17	6
paid Mr French his Bill for nailes etc.		10	0
paid John Bramble for keeping the clock 2 years		10	0
paid Christopher Knight in full of arrears	6	0	0
paid Paul Powell & John Wyndy for carrying armes		7	6
paid Hugh Jones for White limbing the church	2	0	0
paid Mr Smyth & Mr Horns Executors	20	0	0
paid Robert Adams & John Holcomb Michaelmas Salry 1700	4	0	0
paid Richard Perryman for Whisks etc.		7	3
paid a Capuchien per Mr Towgood & Mr Carys order		10	0
paid and allowed Abingtons taxes to Lady day 1700	1	11	6½
paid Mr Edwards in part of his bill	18	0	0
paid for 2 post letters			5
	63	**5**	**4½**
paid William Jones, Glasier per the Deans order	1	1	0
allowed North & Head taxes for Michaelmas	3	5	3
paid Gardner for wax candles	6	1	0
paid for a letter from Gardner			3
paid and allowed Col. Wyndham			
for taxes Michaelmas	3	16	0
for collecting city rents 3		0	0
for collecting cuntry rents	3	6	8
usual allowance for entertaining Tenants		10	0
For 2 quire of paper		1	4

	£	s	d
paid Mr Grey for acquittances on payment of pencions		1	4
allowed Trevillian taxes for Ladyday 1700		4	6
allowed my Lord Poulett taxes Mich.	3	6	0
allowed Trevillian taxes Mich.	3	0	
	24	**16**	**4**

21 June 1701

This booke of particulars conteyning 5 pages
amounting to £175 18s 11½d was examined & allowed

by us	George Royse Deane
	Nathaniel Lye Subdean
	Stephen Crespion

1700–1701

A Transcript of the Booke of Particulars Residences from November 1700 to November 1701

		£	s	d
January	To Mr Cary	1	0	0
Aprill	To Mr Livesay	1	0	0
May	To Mr Deane	2	0	0
June	To Mr Sub Deane	1	0	0
July	To Mr Crespion	1	0	0
August	To the same	1	0	0
September	To Mr Smith	1	0	0
October	To Mr Towgood	1	0	0
		9	**0**	**0**

Severall Sums of mony laid out in repairacions
and other expenses ordinary and exterordinary
from November the 30 1700 to November 30 1701

	£	s	d
For a Rent role		5	0
an Auditt dinner to the Choyer	2	0	0
For Clock lines			6
For 10 yards of cloth for pentioners coates	3	10	0
For a letter from my Lord Pouletts Bayly		5	
paid Richard Perrymans bill		12	6
paid John Holcombe Xmasse Salry	2	10	0
paid Mrs Daniell for makeing 4 roses		12	0
paid Roger Adams Xmasse Salry	1	10	0
paid for a letter from Mr Drewe			3
paid for cleansing the branch and scocketts		2	6
paid for a letter from the Deane			5
paid for a letter from Gardner		3	
paid Abraham Wood for 12 dozen of Buttons		12	0
	11	**15**	**10**

paid Paul Powell for thorning & Staking trees		8	3
paid 2 Messengers goieing to Mr Towgood		10	0
paid Mr Phippin for triming 2 the pentioners coats		11	9
paid Mr Kellow for makeing the pentioners coates		14	0
paid Goody Perryman for washing the communion linen		2	6
paid for a letter from the Deane			5
paid Michael Symons cost on the [?] suit	11	10	0
paid for parchment for a proxy for the Convocation		2	0
paid for cleaning the leads to our Lady day		2	6
paid Richard Perryman for whiskes		1	3
paid Roger Adams Lady day Salry	1	10	0
paid John Holcombe the same	2	10	0
paid for a letter from Knight		3	
paid for a letter from the Deane		3	
paid Mr Taylor for a Sermon on the fast day 4 Aprill 1701	1	0	0
for goeing to Serve Nickolls with an order and expenses		10	0
Allowed Mr North taxes to Lady day 1701	1	7	6
	21	**0**	**6**
Allowed Mr Head the same		5	2
paid for a quire of guilt paper		1	6
paid Thomas Roath [?] for Iron worke		4	9
paid for fast bookes 4th Aprill		12	0
paid Dr Lye rent for part of garden Michaelmas 1700	1	0	0
paid William Coles by your order	2	3	0
Allowed Trevillian taxes to Lady day 1701		3	0
paid for a booke to enter alienations		4	0
paid for a booke to enter the booke of particulars		6	0
paid for a cash booke		4	0
paid for a booke to enter receipts in		3	3
paid Mr Berkins for tallow candles 1699 & 1700	1	5	6
paid Richard Langstone his bill		2	6
paid Roger Adams Midsomer Salry	1	10	0
paid John Holcombe Midsomer Salry	2	10	0
paid Mr Edwards by Sir Richard Reynalls rent	16	10	0
paid Peter Wilkins his bill		12	0
	27	**16**	**8**

paid Peter Wilkins for worke in the Cloysters		15	0
paid for a letter from Sutton Bonnington			6
paid for a piece of tape to tye up counterparts			9
paid for a letter from Mr Deane about Sutton Bonnington			5
paid Roger Adams Mich. Salry	1	10	0
paid Mr Edwards in part	18	0	8
paid Mr Abbotts for damage on his Tyle		2	0
paid Joseph Pope his bill		1	6
paid Mr North a years taxes Mich. at 3s per li 1701	4	2	5
allowed Mr Mead the same		15	0
paid for a letter from Mr North			6
paid for a letter from Mr Gardner			3
paid for a letter from Mr Crey			3
paid for a letter from Tredeger	1		
paid for collecting City Rents 1701	3	0	0
for collecting Country Rents 1701	3	6	5
paid Mr Edwards in full	1	8	0
	33	**4**	**7**

The usual allowance for entertaining Tenants		10	0
For 2 quire of paper		1	4
For 2 Stickes of wax		1	0
paid Mr Gardner for wax candles 1701	5	19	6
paid Mr Edwards by receipts		2	8
paid John Goodred for ropes as per bill	1	11	6
paid George Skuse as per bill for Smith's worke		5	0
paid William Jones, glasier his bill		16	0
paid for carryage of the wax candles 1700 & 1701		8	10
paid John Chesheir, glasier his bill		10	11
	10	**6**	**9**

22 June 1702
Then this booke of particulars of 6 pages
amounting to £113 4s 5d was examined and
allowed by us.

George Royse
Nathaniel Lye
Richard Towgood
Thomas Cary

paid for a letter from Mr Gardner			3
Allowed my Lord Pouletts years taxes Mich. 1701	9	18	0
Allowed Trevillian halfe a years taxes Mich. 1701		4	6
paid Hugh Jones, Tyler, for worke on the Sealing house		8	0
paid Goodred for a bell rope 10lb.		5	0
paid for 12 prayer bookes the fast day 19 Dec. 1701		12	0
paid Roger Adams Lady day Salry 1702	1	10	0

paid John Holcomb the same	2	10	0
paid for a letter from Mr North			3
paid for a letter from Mr Pratt			1
paid for a letter from Mr Abington			2
Allowed Col. Wyndham a yeares taxes Lady day 1702	3	16	0
paid by order of the Deane and Chapter to the School-boyes	1	0	0
paid for a letter from Mr Codrington			2
paid Mr Morgans keeper	1	0	0
paid for a letter from Mr Whatly			2
paid Mr Taylor for a Sermon 10 June	1	1	6
	22	**6**	**1**

paid 2 men to carry the Church Armes		6	6
paid Roger Adams Midsomer Salry 1702	1	10	0
paid Hugh Jones for mops,beisoms, brushes & whisks		4	0
paid for a quire of paper at the Auditt		0	8
paid Hugh Jones's bill		11	0
paid Joseph Popes bill		6	0
paid for a new belt etc.		6	6
paid for a Sheriffes Warrant against Nicholas		3	0
paid by order of the Deane and Chapter to Mr Massey	10	0	0
paid John Holcomb Midsomer Salry 1702	2	10	0
paid Mr Thorne for altering of the Dean & Chapters and Minor Cannons Stall	4	12	0
gave the workmen to drink	1	0	
paid for a letter from the Deane			5
paid Mr Berkins for candles		13	6
paid Mr Callow for makeing of coats		14	0
paid Geo. Skuses bill		8	6
paid for a letter from Wear			2
	22	**7**	**3**

paid for parchment and Stamp for a proxy for the Convocacon [Convocation] man		2	0
paid Joyce Ashby for clensing the Marble		2	6
Allowed Mr Abington taxes Lady day 1701	1	1	0
Allowed Trevillian taxes 1 yeare Mich. 1702		10	6
paid for Tylers worke on the Schoole		11	0
Allowed my Lord Poulett 1 yeares taxes Mich. 1702	13	4	0
Allowed Mr North 1 yeares taxes Mich. 1702	10	19	8
Allowed Mr Head the same	2	0	0
paid John Holcomb Mich. Salry 1702	2	10	0
paid Hugh Jones oyle & Soap to clean the marble			8
paid for a letter from Gardner			3

paid for carriage of the wax candles	3	10	
paid the porter			6
paid for wax candles	5	19	6
paid Peter Wilkins bill	1	3	0
paid for a letter from Mr Holford			5
	39	**18**	**10**

paid for a letter from Gardner			3
paid Mr Taylor for a Sermon 3 December 1702	1	1	6
paid Mr Cooke for painting the desks in the Choyer		5	0
for paper and sealing wax		2	6
Allowed Col. Wyndham a yeares taxes Mich. 1702	3	16	0
Allowed Mr Abington 1 yeares taxes Lady day 1702	1	1	1
for Collecting City Rents	3	0	0
for Collecting Country Rents	3	6	5
usual allowance for entertaining Tenants		10	0
paid the plumbers bill	22	5	0
paid the sextons bill		7	0
	35	**15**	**9**

27 June 1703

This Booke of particulars conteyning 6 pages amounting to £146 7s 11d was examined by us.

         Nathaniel Lye Subdeane
         Stephen Crespion
         Thomas Cary

The Booke of Particulars 1702–3

Residences from November 1702 to November 1703

January	To Mr Cary	1	0	0
Aprill	To Mr Livesay	1	0	0
May	To Ditto for the Deane	1	0	0
June	To Dr Lye Sub Deane	1	0	0
July	To Mr Crespion	1	0	0
September	To Mr Smith	1	0	0
October	To Mr Towgood	1	0	0
		7	**0**	**0**

Severall Sumes of money laid out in Repairacons
and other expenses ordinary and extraordinary
from 30 November 1702 to the 30 November 1703

For a Rent Role		5	0
For an auditt dinner for the Choyer	2	0	0
For cloth for the Pentioners coats	3	7	6
For trimming for them		9	0
Paid for a Letter from Mrs Holford			5
Paid for a Letter from Mr Day		0	2
Paid for four Roses		12	0
Paid for John Holcomb Mich. Sallry 1701	2	10	0
Paid Abraham Wood for buttons for the Pentioners		12	0
Paid for 2 Setts of prayerbooks for the last fast and Thanksgiveing	1	4	0
Paid for four Brushes for the Church		4	0
	11	**4**	**1**
Paid Mr Crey for 3 certifucates [?]		1	0
Paid Mr Avery in part of his Bill	10	0	0
Paid Dr Lye 1 year's Rent Michas. 1701	1	0	0
Paid Dr Lye another year's Rent Michas. 1702	1	0	0
Paid for a Letter from Mr Butterfeild			3
Paid for mending the Wheel of the Clock		1	0
Paid for a Letter to Mr Speeke		2	
Allowed for Mr North for Taxes Lady day 1703	5	9	10
Allowed Mr Head Ditto	1	0	9
Paid for Washing the Communion linen at Easter		1	0
Allowed Mr Abington 1 years Taxes Lady day 1703	1	8	6
Paid the School boys att the Gramer School	1	0	0
Paid for Wine there		6	0
Paid for Fast books 26 May 1703		12	0
Paid H. Jones for worke att the Gramer School	2	0	0
Paid for a Letter from Mr Day of Wells			2
Allowed Col. Wyndham taxes Lady Day 1703	3	16	0
	27	**16**	**8**
Paid Callow for makeing Pentioners coats		14	0
Paid for a Letter from Mr Day			2
Paid for a letter from Mr Evans			2
Paid for a quire of paper and a Stick of Wax		1	4
Paid 2 men for carrying Armes when the Queen came to Bristoll		4	0
Paid for cleansing the Armes and powder		2	0
Paid Goodred for Bell Ropes		13	0
Paid for a Letter to Dr Lye			2
Paid Mr Birkins for Candles		11	8
Paid Mr Pain for a Sermon 26 May 1703	1	0	0

Paid William Jones, glacier, for worke att the school		14	4
Paid him for worke att the Colledge	2	1	8
Paid Mr Avery in part of his Bill	15	0	0
Paid Mr Humbleston, Tyler, his Bill	7	10	0
Paid William Davis, Smyth, his Bill		11	6
Paid for mending the Lock of the Organ Loft			6
	29	**4**	**6**

Paid Mr Gravett for prayer books	4	12	0
Paid the Widow Gandys Bill		2	4
Paid Thomas Raynolds his bill	1	2	6
Paid for a Letter from Mr North			3
Paid for carrying away the rubble that lay against the Chapter house in Mr Towgoods garden		14	8
Allowed Mr Edwards for Taxes 1703		2	0
Paid Edward Jones for Whisks for the Organ loft			4½
Paid Alderman Swymmer for the highways	5	0	0
Paid for Two Letters from Mr Gardner			6
Paid for Carriage of the Wax Candles		4	0
Paid for porteridge			6
Paid for a Letter from the Deane			5
Gave the Workmen to drink		1	0
Paid Peter Wilkins in part	10	0	0
Paid for a key for the Choyer dore			6
Allowed my Lord Poulett 1 year's tax Mich. 1703	13	4	0
	35	**5**	**½**

Allowed Col. Wyndham taxes Mich. 1703	3	16	0
Paid for a Letter from Mr North			3
Paid Hugh Jones for dressing the Church twice with green		5	0
Paid for a Letter from Dr Lye			2
Paid Joseph Pope for Four Formes	1	6	0
Paid for a Letter from Dr Lye			2
Paid for a Letter to the Deane			2
Paid for a Letter from Gardner			3
Paid for a Letter from the Deane			2
Paid for a Letter with Deares Lease			6
Paid Roger Adams 1 year's sallary Mich. 1703	6	0	0
Allowed Mr North Taxes Mich. 1703	3	3	6
Allowed Mr Head Ditto		12	0
Allowed Trevillian 1 year's Taxes Mich. 1703		12	0
Allowance for entertainment of Tenants		10	0
	16	**6**	**2**

For Collecting City Rents	3	0	0
For Collecting Country Rents	3	6	8
For a Quire of paper			10
Paid for Wax Candles	6	2	0
Paid Mr Morgans keeper	1	0	0
Paid Peter Wilkins in part for Boards	12	0	0
Paid Goodredd for Bell ropes	1	0	0
Paid for a Letter from the Deane			5
Paid for a Letter from Mr Harly [?]			2
Paid for a Letter from Mr Pratt			2
Paid for a Letter from Mr Drewe			5
Paid Peter Wilkins for Works att the Schoole	1	13	0
	28	**1**	**8**

17th June 1704

The Booke of Particulars conteyning 7 pages
amounting to the Sume of £155 1s 3½d was
examined and allowed by us:　　　　　　155　　1　　1½

> George Royse, Dean
> Nathaniel Lye, Sub Deane
> Thomas Cary, Prebendary

The Booke of Particulars 1703–4

Residences from November 1703 to November 1704

January	To Mr Cary	1	0	0
Aprill	To Mr Livesay	1	0	0
May	To the Deane	2	0	0
June	To Dr Lye Sub Dean	1	0	0
July	To Mr Crespion	1	0	0
September	To Mr Smith	1	0	0
October	To Mr Towgood	1	0	0
		8	**0**	**0**

Severall Sumes of money laid out in Repairacons
and other expenses ordinary and extraordinary
from 30 November 1703 to 30 November 1704

For a Rent Role		5	0
For an Auditt dinner for the Choyer	2	0	0
For Cloath for 3 Pentioners Coats	2	10	0
For trimming for them		9	6
For 3 Roses		9	0
For 9 Dozen of Buttons		8	0
Paid Mr Callow for makeing		10	0
Paid for dressing the Church with Greens		5	0

	£	s	d
Paid Roger Adams 1 year's Salary Michas. 1704	6	0	0
Paid the Carpenters man for Christmasse Box		1	0
For 4 Hair Brushes		4	8
Paid Mr Taylor for a Sermon 19th Jan. Fast Day	1	0	0
Paid for Prayer Books		12	0
	14	**14**	**2**
Paid a Man 3 dayes setting up trees in the greene		4	0
Paid a Messinger to Winterbourn		1	6
Paid John Goodred for Ropes for the Organ	1	5	0
Paid Mr Taylor for a Sermon the 8th March 1703 Thanksgiving day	1	0	0
Paid for Prayer Books		12	0
Paid Edward Jones for mending the Lock of the Organ loft			6
Allowed my Lord Poulett taxes for Lady day 1704	6	12	0
Allowed Mr North the Same	3	3	6
Allowed Mr Head Ditto		12	0
Paid for a halfe hower Glasse			7
Paid for Washing the Communion Linnen att Easter 1704		1	0
Allowed Col. Windham taxes Lady day 1704	3	16	0
Paid the Scoole Boyes by order of the Deane & Chapter	1	0	0
Paid for a Letter from Mr Codrington			2
Paid Mr Morgans keeper's Fee	1	0	0
	19	**18**	**3**
Paid Vincent Lashley by your order		5	0
Paid Thomas Reynolds Mason in part and for limb	5	0	0
Paid George Townesend Free Mason in part	40	0	0
Paid Mr Birkins for Tallow Candles 1703	10	0	0
Paid for Canvass to naile about the Organ when the Church was White limb'd		8	0
Paid Hugh Jones for Scouring the Eagle and Branch		2	6
Paid Joyce Ashby for Scouring the Marble		4	6
Paid for a muskett		13	0
Paid for cleaning the Common shore under the House of Ease		10	0
Paid for a Post Letter from the Deane			5
Paid for a Letter from Dr Lye			2
Paid Mr Smith for a Thanksgiving Sermon in September 1704	1	0	0
Paid for Bookes		12	0
	49	**5**	**7**

Paid Peter Wilkins in full of his former Bill	4	10	0
Paid Head for mending the Lock and Barr of the Gate		5	0
Allowed Mr Edwards Taxes for his Quitt Rent 1704		2	0
Allowed my Lord Poulett half year's Taxes Michas 1704	6	12	0
Paid Thomas Reynolds more in part	8	0	0
Paid William Humblestone, Tyler, in part	5	0	0
Paid John Goodred for more Ropes	1	5	0
Paid Robert Sidwell, a smith, his Bill	1	13	0
Paid for a Letter to the Deane			2
Paid for a Letter from the Deane			5
Allowed Col. Windham Taxes Michas. 1704	3	16	0
Paid for a Letter from the Deane			5
Paid for a Letter from Mr Gardner			3
Paid Mr Gardner for Wax candkes	6	3	0
Paid for a Letter from Mr Gardner			3
Paid for a Letter from Mr Day of Wells			2
Paid Dr Lye a year's Rent for his Garden Mich. 1703	1	0	0
	38	**7**	**8**
Allowed Mr North half year's Tax Michas. 1704	3	3	6
Allowed Mr Head the Same		12	0
Allowed Trevillian 1 year's taxes Michas. 1704		12	0
For Collecting City Rents	3	0	0
For Collecting Cuntry Rents	3	6	8
For 2 quire of paper		1	8
For 2 Sticks of Wax		1	0
Usuall allowance for entertaining of Tenants		10	0
For a Letter for the Deane per post		5	
Paid William Jones, Glasier, in part	5	0	0
	16	**7**	**3**

23 June

Then this Booke of Particulars conteyning 6 pages amounting to £146 2s 11d was examined and allowed by us

	146	2	11

George Royse, Dean
Nathaniel Lye, Sub dean
Thomas Cary

Booke of Particulars 1704–5

Residences from November 1704 to November 1705

		£	s	d
January	To Mr Cary	1	0	0
May	To the Deane	2	0	0
June	To Dr Lye Sub Deane	1	0	0
July	To Mr Crespion	1	0	0
August	To Mr Livesay	1	0	0
September	To Mr Smith	1	0	0
October	To Mr Towgood	1	0	0
		8	**0**	**0**

Severall Sumes of money laid our in repairacons and
other expenses ordinary and extraordinary from
30 November 1704 to 30 November 1705

	£	s	d
For a Rent Role		5	0
For an Auditt Dinner for the Choyer	2	0	0
Paid for Cloath for 4 Pentioners Coates	3	10	0
Paid Mr William Swymmer for the High wayes	5	0	0
Paid for Trimming for the Pentioners Coates		11	10
Paid for a Letter from Mrs Holford			5
Paid for a Letter from Dr Lye			2
Paid for a Letter from Mr Livesay			6
Paid for a quire of Paper			10
Paid the Carpenters to their Xmasse box			6
Paid the Tylers men the Same			6
Paid for a Letter from Sir Thomas Bridges			3
	11	**10**	**0**

	£	s	d
Paid for a Letter from Mrs Holford			3
Paid for a Letter from Wells			2
Paid Abraham Woods for Buttons for the Pentioners		9	0
Paid for a Letter from the Deane			5
Paid for a Letter from Dr Lye			2
Paid for one to Dr Lye			2
Paid Thomas Callow for makeing Pentioners Coats		14	0
Paid for Letters from Mr Crespion & Mr Head			6
Paid for 4 Roses for the Pentioners Coats		12	0
Paid for a Quire of Paper			10
Paid for a Letter from Mr Crespion			3
Paid for another from him			3
Paid for a Letter from Mr North			3
Paid for a Letter from Mr Drew			2
Paid Hugh Jones for Greens & Scouring the Eagle		7	6
Paid for a Letter from Halberton			2

Paid for Levelling the Cloysters & Carring the Col [college] Armes	2	5	10
	4	**11**	**11**

Paid for a Letter from Mr Speeke			2
Paid for a Letter to Mr Speke			2
Paid for a Letter to Sumpsion, Freemason			2
Paid Esq. Morgans keeper his Fee	1	0	0
Paid for a Letter from Esq. Speke			2
Paid for a Letter from Wells			2
Paid for a Letter from Halberton			2
Paid for Carrying away the Rubble in the Cloysters		1	6
Paid for a Letter from Wells			2
Paid for a Letter from Banwell			2
Paid Dr Lye 2 years Rent for his Garden 1704 & 1705	2	0	0
Allowed Col. Wyndham half years taxes Lady day 1705	3	16	0
Paid for Brushes for the Church		4	8
Paid for Tallow Candles		11	0
Paid the Gramer Schoole boys	1	0	0
Paid the Deanes Expenses to Sir Thomas Bridges		8	0
Paid for parchment & Stamp for a Proxy for Convocation		2	6
	9	**5**	**0**

Paid for a Letter from Mr Blake			2
Paid Richard Townsend in full	7	3	6
Paid Mr Cary his Expenses	blank		
Paid Mr Payne for a Sermon fast day 4 April 1705	1	0	0
Paid for Prayer Bookes		12	0
Paid for a Letter from Mr Crespion			3
Paid for a letter from Mr Livesay			6
Paid William Jones, Glasier, in full of his Bill	6	9	0
Paid Thomas Sumpsion, Freemason, in part	40	0	0
Allowed Trevillian half year's Taxes Lady Day 1705		6	0
Paid Mr Baskervill by the Dean & Chapters orders	1	1	6
Paid for a Letter from the Deane			5
Paid for a Letter from Mr Head			3
Allowed Avington 2 year's taxes Lady Day 1705	2	16	0
Paid Thomas Sumpsion in full	20	0	0
Paid Thomas Reynolds, Rough mason in part	6	0	0
Paid Mr Livesay for a Sermon Thanksgiving day 23 August 1705	1	0	0
Paid for Prayer Bookes		12	0
	87	**1**	**7**

	£	s	d
Allowed my Lord Poulett half year's Taxes Lady Day 1705	6	12	0
Paid for Washing the Communion Linnen att Easter		1	0
Paid for a Letter from Mr North			3
Paid for a Letter from Mr Harrison			3
Paid for a Letter from Mr North			3
Allowed Mr North a year's Taxes Michas. 1705	6	7	0
Allowed Mr Head the Same	1	4	0
Allowed Col. Wyndham half year's Taxes Mich. 1705	3	16	0
Allowed my Lord Poulett half year's Taxes Mich. 1705	6	12	0
Allowed Trevillian taxes half yeare Mich. 1705		6	0
Paid Thomas Reynolds, Rough mason, in full	5	2	0

Book of Particulars 1705–6

	£	s	d
Paid William Humblestone, Tyler, in part	2	0	0
Paid for a Letter from Wells			2
Paid for a Letter from North			3
Paid for a Letter from Wells			3
Paid for a Letter from Gardner			3
Usuall Allowance entertaining Tenants		10	0
	32	**11**	**8**
For gathering the Cuntry Rents	3	6	8
For gathering the City Rents	3	0	0
For a Quire of Paper			10
Paid William Humbelstone, Tyler, in full of his Bill	1	4	0
For 2 Sticks of Wax		1	0
Allowed Mr Crey for 3 Receipts att Sarum for 1704 & 1705		2	0
Paid Gardner for Wax Candles	6	2	6
Paid for carriage & Porteridge of them		4	10
	14	**1**	**10**

16 June 1707
This Booke of particulers, conteyning 7 pages and amounting to £172-6s-4d was examined and allowed by us   172   6   4

> George Royse, Deane
> Nathaniel Lye, Sub Dean
> Thomas Cary, Prebendary

Booke of Particulers 1711–12

	£	s	d
Elizabeth Eynes	1	0	0
Jane Shore	1	0	0
Elizabeth Andrews	1	0	0
Deborah Deffield	1	0	0
Sarah Cary	1	0	0
Widow Gettoes	1	0	0
Mrs Godding	1	0	0
Mrs Lake	1	0	0
Elizabeth Clarke	1	0	0
Mrs Prigg	1	0	0
Widow Davis	1	0	0
Mrs Chamberlain	1	0	0
T. Williams	1	0	0
Mary Whitfeild	1	0	0
Widow Grafton	1	0	0
Widow Goodyard	1	0	0
Widow Watkins	1	0	0
Elianor Tuckey	1	0	0
Widow Prigg	1	0	0
Margaret Jones	1	0	0
	20	**0**	**0**

Disbursements of Residences 1711–12

July August & September	To the Deane	4	0	0
October & halfe November	To Mr Towgood	2	0	0
Aprill & halfe May	To Dr Lye	2	0	0
Half May & all June	To Mr Harcourt	2	0	0
January & halfe February	To Mr Waterman	2	0	0
October & halfe November	To Mr Towgood	2	0	0
		14	**0**	**0**

Severall Sumes of Money laid out in repairacons and other expenses ordinary and extraordinary from 30th November 1711 to 30th November 1712

Given to the Choir by order of the Deane and Chapter	2	0	0
For a City Rent Role		5	0
Paid Humphry Corsley for Cloath for the Pentioners Coats	4	2	6
Paid Mr Nicholas Hickes for triming for Pentioners Coats		10	6
Paid Abraham Wood for Buttons and Twist for the Pentioners Coats		11	8
Paid Humphry Cox for making the 4 Pentioners Coats		14	0
	8	**3**	**8**

	£	s	d
Paid for Four Roses for the Pentioners Coats		16	0
Paid Lynford the Pitcher on the College Greene	12	0	0
Paid Paul Powell for works done in the churchyard	6	0	0
Paid Mr Gardner for Wax Candles	9	12	2
Paid for Carridge and Porteridge of the same ?			8
Paid the Carpenters and Tylers men for their Christmas Box		1	0
For 2 Quire of Paper		2	0
For a Pint of Ink & a Stick of Wax		1	2
Paid Arthur Redwood for dressing the Church twice with Greenes		5	0
Paid Mrs Daniell for four Roses		16	0
	30	**1**	**4**

	£	s	d
Paid Arthur Redwood for Scouring the Eagle and Candlesticks etc.		2	0
Paid Mrs Jones for 8 lbs of Wax Candles att 2s 8d per lb	1	1	0
Paid Mr Arthurs for 6 lbs of Wax Candles att 2s 8d per lb		16	0
Paid Mr Coopy for a Sermon preach'd 8th of March the Queens Inauguration	1	0	0
Allow'd Mr Abbington half year's Taxes Lady Day 1712	6	12	0
Allow'd Col. Wyndham half year's Taxes Lady Day 1712	3	16	0
Paid for a Sermon the 5th November 1711	1	0	0
	15	**1**	**0**

	£	s	d
Paid the Deane for 3 Sermons (viz.) Easter and Whitsunday 1711 & 1712 3		0	0
Allow'd Esq. Trevillian halfe a year's Taxes Lady Day 1712		6	0
Paid Mr Hippsley for prayer Bookes 5 severall tymes	1	10	0
Paid Jones the Glasier his Noat		6	10
Paid Benjamin Long for new hanging the Great Bell etc.	3	3	0
Paid Thomas Reynolds, Mason, his Noate for Masons Works in and about the Church	1	13	0
	9	**18**	**10**

	£	s	d
Allow'd Esq. Trevillian halfe yeares Taxes Michas. 1712		6	0
Allow'd Col. Wyndham halfe yeares Taxes Michas. 1712	6	12	0
Allow'd my Lord Poulett halfe yeares Taxes Michas. 1712	6	12	0
Paid for Beasoms		1	0
Paid Dr Lye 1 year's Rent of his Garden	1	0	0
Paid Mr Matthew Pomfry for Tallow Candles	1	2	10
Paid Mr Harcourt for 6 Prayer Bookes for the Prebendarys	3	3	0
Paid Jones the Glasier in full	9	10	0
Allow'd by Chapter to the Servants 5s and for Fire etc. the Last Auditt 5s		10	0
	26	**0**	**10**

Transcript of Entries in the Book of Particulars for 1724, 1735 and 1742

Book of Particulars 1724

The particular account of the money given Ordinarily to the Poor

		£	s	d
Jane Hopkins		1	0	0
Widow Berryman		1	0	0
John Buckeridge		1	0	0
Mary Stibbe		1	0	0
Widow Lloyd		1	0	0
Betty Howell		1	0	0
Widow Tuckey		1	0	0
Widow Godier		1	0	0
Widow Edwards		1	0	0
Widow Lutton		1	0	0
		10	**0**	**0**

	£	s	d
Given to the Poor at Bathampton and Ford	2	2	0
Given to the Poor at Bradford	3	3	0
Given to a Poor Clergyman	4	15	0
	20	0	0
To the Repaire of the Highwayes etc.	20	0	0
	40	**0**	**0**

Disbursements for Residences for the year 1724

October & ½ November	Mr Waterman	2	0	0
½ November & December	Mr Dean	2	0	0
January & ½ February	Mr Livesay	0	0	0
½ February & March	Mr Head	2	0	0
April & ½ May	Dr Harcourt	2	0	0
½ May & June	Mr Sutton	2	0	0
July & ½ August 28, 2006	Mr Dean	2	0	0
½ August & September Mr Casberd		2	0	0
		14	**0**	**0**

Disbursements for Sermons on Publick dayes 1724

December 25th	Dr Harcourt	1	0	0
January 30th	Mr Waterman	1	0	0
Easter day	Mr Rogers	1	0	0
May 29th	Mr Sutton	1	0	0
November 5th	Mr Dean	1	0	0
		5	**0**	**0**
	Total of this page	**19**	**0**	**0**

Severall Disbursements in Ordinary
Reparations etc from November 30 1723 to November 30 1724

Date	Description	£	s	d
Dec 8	Paid to the Choir by order of the Dean & Chapter	2	0	0
	For two Roses		10	0
	A Quire of Paper, Ink etc.		2	6
	For a Rent Roll		5	0
Jan 16	George the Taylors Note	1	14	6
24	Coreys Note for looking after the Chapter house etc.		12	6
28	Audit Dinner	5	7	6
Feb 12	Paid to the Churchwardens of All Saints an Arrear for a Gout [drain]	1	0	0
Mar 7	To Mr Edward Boothe for transcribing the Charter, the Statutes of this Cathedrall on Vellum	10	10	0
28	Mr Harris Organ builders Salary to Lady Day	3	0	0
Apr 2	Coreys Second Note		12	1
	A Quire of Paper etc.		2	6
	For money advanced for the Prompt Payment of the Choir	10	0	0
May 15	Expenses in Visiting Bathampton, Ford & Bradford	4	12	0
	Paid to Mr Bayly	1	1	0
Aug 15	For Wax Candles	10	7	10
	For Carriage of them from London and Porterage		6	6
	Given to Mr Morgans Servant	1	1	0
Sep 19	Paid to John Cole, Tyler, for plaistering & washing the Sealing Roome and Cloysters	8	12	0
	Given to his men at severall times		5	0
21	To Mr Serjeant Eyre his Fee as Standing Counsell for the Dean & Chapter	1	5	0
	For his Opinion on Mr Shottleworths & other Leases	1	1	0
Sep 30	Mr Harris Organ builders Salary to Michas	3	0	0
Oct 1	Coreys 3rd Note	1	2	0
15	For Coal		16	3
Nov 3	To Michael Sidnet [?] Freestone Masons Note for repairing the Cloysters	2	7	0
17	To Mr Priest for the Advancement of his Salary	6	0	0
Dec 2	To Cossley for Prayer Bookes at the Communion Table etc.	7	13	0
19	To Mr Carter for the Advancement of his Salary	18	10	0
21	Thomas Maddocks Carpenter Note	1	10	0
27	To Gibbs for Pensioners Cloath	4	10	0
	Taxes allowed to Col. Wyndham for 1 year to Midsomer	3	16	0
	Earle Poulett for 1 year to Michaelmas	6	12	0
	Mr Trevillian for the same time		6	0
	Sir William Compton for the same time		14	0
	Mr Buckler for the same time	1	0	0
	Mr Hill for the same		18	0

Allowed to Mrs Crew for two Acquittances	1	0	
For Letters sent and receaved	1	0	0
Entertainment of Tennants	1	0	0
Collecting the City Rents	3	6	8
Collecting the Country Rents	3	6	8
Paid to Matthew Mattocks, Chorister	4	0	0
By an Arrear of One Quarter of Sir Thomas Reynells			
Rent upon altering the time of Payment	8	5	0
Given to the Revd Mr Hart by order of the Chapter	5	5	0
For two Almanacks		1	0
For looking after the Green & for Trees	2	8	6
To England the Pitcher	1	1	6
To the Pensioners for Washing & Cleansing the			
Sealing house		2	0
	88	**11**	**7**

Fears Rent not paid for the halfe year ending			
att Michaelmas		10	0
Expenses in placeing out Anne Badman, a poor Child			
from Churchill	6	8	0
Jones the Glaziers Note	5	12	6
Watkins for Tallow and Candles	1	19	0
To Mr Oldfeild his Bill of Charges in Severall Law Suites			
and other Affaires	36	0	0
	50	**9**	**6**

Payments made by the Treasurer as by the Precedent			
Pages it Appeares	19	0	0
	64	7	11
	88	11	7
	50	9	6
In all	**222**	**9**	**0**

Received by the Treasurer for the use of the			
Deane & Chapter			
By the Overplus of Banwell	20	0	0
From the Parish of Churchill towards placeing out			
Anne Badman	2	0	0
By a Vacancy in a Singing Mans Place	4	0	0
By Taxes deducted out of the Pension paid to Sir Thomas			
Bridges Executors	8	10	0
Received from the Revd Mr Waterman on Dr Lyes			
Account towards Law Charges	4	10	0
	39	**0**	**0**

22 February 1724

Then this Book of Particulars consisting of Seven Pages, the 2nd 3rd 4th & 5th whereof amount unto the Sume of Two hundred and twenty two pounds and Nine Shillings (Out of which the above Sume of Nine and thirty pounds being deducted there remains the Sume of One hundred Eighty three pounds & Nine Shillings) was examined and allowed by us

Robert Boothe, Dean
Hugh Waterman
Henry Head
John Sutton

Book of Particulars 1735

John Sutton, Treasurer

To the Poor

Widow Berriman	1	0	0
Widow Edwards	1	0	0
Widow Nurse	1	0	0
Widow Barton	1	0	0
Widow Howell	1	0	0
Widow Rowley	1	0	0
Widow Hicks	1	0	0
Mrs Grosean	1	0	0
Mrs Rogerson	1	0	0
Mrs Thresher	1	0	0
To the Poor of Peterston	5	0	0
To the Poor of Kingston	5	0	0
	20	**0**	**0**
To the Highways etc.	20	0	0
	40	**0**	**0**

To Residences for the year 1735

Half November & December	Mr Dean	2	0	0
January & February	Dr Harcourt	2	0	0
Half February & March	Mr Sutton	2	0	0
April & half May	Mr Dean	2	0	0
Half & June	Dr King	0	0	0
July & half August	Mr Casberd	2	0	0
Half August & September	Mr Livesay	0	0	0
October & November	Mr Waterman	2	0	0
		12	**0**	**0**

To Sermons upon Publick Days for the year 1735

December 25th	Dr Harcourt	1	0	0
January 30th	Dr Harcourt	1	0	0
Upon Ashwednesday	Mr Sutton	1	0	0
Easter Day	Dr Harcourt	1	0	0
May 29th	Mr Sutton	1	0	0
Good Friday	Mr Waterman	1	0	0
November 5th	Mr Dean	1	0	0
		7	**0**	**0**

Ordinary Disbursements for Reparations and other Expenses from November 30th 1734 to November 30th 1735

To the Choir upon St Andrew	2	0	0
Paid the Sexton per Note	1	16	5
To Col. Morgan's Keeper	1	1	0
For Haling wood		4	0
For a Bell Rope as per note		6	6
Paid Mr Osborn's Note		5	0
The Sexton's Note		4	6
The Glaziers note	1	9	11
Oil for the Lamp as per Note		12	0
Col. Morgans Keeper	1	1	0
Paid Mr Palmer as per Note	1	13	0
Cole the Tilers Note	3	10	11
Paid Mr Nash for the Pensioners Cloath as per note	4	4	0
	20	**15**	**3**

Paid Mr Sutton his Allowance for Prompt payment	10	0	0
For collecting the City & Country Rents	6	13	4
For Entertaining Tenants	1	0	0
For letters sent and received	1	0	0
For his Way to the Palace	1	0	0
For his Stable	1	6	8
For paper, pens & wax etc.		5	0
For a Rent Roll		10	0
For a Rope for the Clock		4	9
The Sexton's Note	1	5	0
Mr Carter for Pricking Anthems	1	10	8
To make up his Allowance		2	0
The Carpenter's note	3	1	0
For a wire Lattice for the painted Window as per note	6	16	0
Paid the plummer as per Note	3	19	0
Cole's note for the school	1	15	0
Paid Cole a second note		10	0
Paid Mr Mugleworth per note for Cushions	23	3	0
	64	**1**	**5**

Disbursements continued

Paid Brooks for Collecting City Rents	2	0	0
Paid his note		5	6
The Curate of Broadwoodwigger	10	0	0
Mr Cossley for Books for the Choir as per note	9	11	0
Mr Smith for Cleaning the Clock	2	0	0
Robine the Gardiner for looking after the Green	3	0	0
Mr Adams Note for Candles	10	14	0
Dr Harcourt for the Revnd Mr Hart at Xmas 1734	5	5	0
To Pembruge by Order of the Dean and Chapter	3	0	0
To the Organist to make up his salary £40	4	5	0
To Capt. Wheeler's Account	6	12	7½
To four Roses		10	0
To Capt. Wheeler gone	100	0	0
To Bearpacker	4	0	0
	161	**3**	**1½**

Taxes Allowed for the Year at two Shillings in the Pound

To the Earle Poulett	6	12	0
To John Trevilian Esqr.		6	0
To Sir William Compton		14	0
The Revnd Mr Hill		18	0
The Revnd Mr Smith	1	0	0
	9	**10**	**0**

Taxes Received by John Sutton, Treasurer

Taxes Deducted out of the Pension paid Sir Thomas Bridges Executors	8	11	0
Received of Mrs Crey for Taxes Allow'd by the Bishop, Dean and		6	0
Chapter of Sarum	**8**	**17**	**0**

[Total Expenditure	**274**	**9**	**9½]**

To be Deducted

Taxes	8	17	0
Roads	20	0	0
Carter	2	6	0
Mary Port		5	0
	31	**8**	**0**

16th Aprill 1736

Then this Book of Particulars amounting to the Sum of
£274 9s 9½ d out of which the Sum of £31 8s 0d being
Deducted there remains the Sum of £243 1s 9½d was
Examined and Allowed by us

> Samuel Creswicke, Dean
> Hugh Waterman
> James Harcourt, Treasurer

Book of Particulars Anno Domini 1742

Henry Waterland, Treasurer

To ten Poor Widows	10	0	0
To the Poor in Olveston	5	0	0
To the Poor in Ilminster	5	0	0
To the Repairs of High Ways	20	0	0
	40	**0**	**0**
John Albin's Bill January 23rd	3	10	0
Philip Tyler's December 19th		17	0
Philip Tyler's June 24th		6	0
John Cole's Bill September 12th	1	4	0
William Bradford September 29th	5	9	0
Philip Tyler December 21st	2	0	0
Mr John Smith January 3rd	3	1	0
Mr Lewis August 27th	2	9	0
Part of Samuel Gilberts	1	4	0
	20	**0**	**0**

Residences in the Year

October & half November	Mr Waterman	2	0	0
Half November & December	The Dean	2	0	0
January & half February	The Dean	2	0	0
Half February & March	Mr Casberd	2	0	0
April & half May	Mr Sutton	2	0	0
Half May & June	Mr Billingsly	2	0	0
July & half August	Mr Castleman	2	0	0
Half August & September	Mr Waterland	2	0	0
		16	**0**	**0**

Sermons on Publick Days

December 25th	Mr Tucker	1	0	0
January 30th	Mr Waterman	1	0	0
Good Fryday	Mr Waterman	1	0	0
Easter Day	Mr Castelman	1	0	0
May 29th	Mr Pritchard	1	0	0
June 11th	The Dean	1	0	0
November 5th	The Dean	1	0	0
November 10th	Mr Waterman	1	0	0
		24	**0**	**0**

Ordinary Disbursements for Repairations etc. from November 30th 1741 to November 1742

To the Choir on St Andrews Day	2	0	0
For four Roses		10	0
An Almanack			6
Ballance of last Year's Account	14	12	7
Interest thereof		14	0
Rent Roll, Paper, Ink etc.		15	0
Mr Sutton for the Way to the Palace	1	0	0
For his Stable	2	13	4
To the Curate of Broadwoodwigger	10	0	0
Mr Nash for the Pensioner's Cloth	4	4	0
Mr George Making the Coats	1	10	6
Mr Cray for Acquittances		1	0
Carter for writing Anthems		8	8
Augmentation of Minor Cannon's Salary	16	0	0
To make Mr Morley's Salary £40	3	13	4
Augmentation of Gantony's Salary	1	0	0
Prompt Payment of the Choir	10	0	0
Letters	1	0	0
Entertainment of Tenants	1	0	0
Collecting Country and City Rents	6	13	4
John Ganthony's Salary	3	0	0
	80	**16**	**3**

Deducted for Mr Suttons Way to the Pallace & £1 6s 8d wrong Charged	**82**	**6**	**8**
	78	**9**	**7**

Taxes allowed at 4s per pound:

To Lord Poulet	13	4	0
To the Revd Mr Smith	2	0	0
To the Revd Mr Harris	1	16	0
Half Taxes allowed to Hurditch	8	13	6
To the Curates of Churchill & Puxton	32	0	0
To Elizabeth Clements of Order of Chapter	32	17	9
Interest allowed by the Chapter	1	10	0
Paid Mrs Jones for Candles	10	16	0
4 Acquittances to Bishop & Arch Deacon of Landaff		1	4
Lady Rachel Morgan's Keeper	2	2	0
Part of the Money paid to S. Gilbert	3	0	0
To Williams the Glazier	1	11	6
Mr Swarbock 2 Years Salary due Xmas 1742	12	0	0
To the Revd Mr Evans	2	0	0
The Dean's Bill for Bradford	4	1	8
Mr Cobb's Bill		8	4
Salary as Auditor	6	13	4
As Chapter Clerk	4	0	0
Allowed Mr Castelman Hurditch's Tax	4	13	6
For Mr Sutton's Stable	2	13	4
	146	**2**	**3**

Arrears for the Year 1742

The Revd Mr Philips 3years	3	4	0
Loyd's Executors Tenement in Week		12	0
The Chamber of Bath		5	0
Mr Elly, rectory of St Catherine's	3	16	0
Marlow Rents	[blank]		
Ralph Gunnell & Charles Truss		4	0
Lord Lymington		1	0

Arrears of City Rents

Hugh Grove		8	0
Charles Vann		5	0
Thomas Maddox	1	13	4
William Lowden	1	10	0
James Saunders	4	7	0
William Swymmer & Elizabeth Ewen overcharged in the Computum		3	6
	14	**8**	**10**

Wee do allow that fourteen Pounds Eight Shillings & ten Pence being Arrears for the year 1742 as in Page 5 be added to the Ballance of £188 10s 11d

	14	8s	10d
	202 19s	**9d**	

Taxes received by Henry Waterland, Treasurer

From the Pension paid the Executors of Sir Thomas Bridges	17	0	0
From the Payments to the Bishop and Dean & Chapter of Sarum	12	0	
From Banwell above the Rent reserved in the Computum	34	0	0
Received of Widow Brooks for 1 Years Rent of Cantocks Closes due Michaelmas 1740	4	7	0
Received of Mr Castelman 1 Years Rent from Sir William Compton	6	1	5
Aaron Rance ½ Year			6
	60	**0**	**11**

Page 2	£24 0s 0d				
Page 3	£78 9s 7d	248	11	10
Page 4	£146 2s 3d				

Taxes etc. to be deducted as by Page 6	60	0	11
	188	**10**	**11**

13 March 1743

Then this Book of Particulars consisting of six Pages whereof Page2, 3, & 4 amounting to the Sume of £248 11s 10d out of which the Sume of £60 0s 11d being deducted, there remains the Sume of £188 10s 11d, was examined and allowed by us

> Thomas Chamberlayne, Dean
> Hugh Waterman Prebend
> Joseph Casberd, Prebend

EIGHTEENTH-CENTURY DESCRIPTIONS OF THE CATHEDRAL AND BISHOP'S PALACE

The Cathedral in 1727

Bristol was one of the cathedrals visited and described by the assiduous antiquary, Browne Willis, during the early 18th century. The results of his research were published under the title A Survey of the Cathedrals of York, Durham, Carlisle, Chester, Manchester, Lichfield, Hereford, Worcester, Gloucester and Bristol, *2 vols., (1727). He listed the clergy and offices of the cathedral as prescribed in the original deed of foundation, and then proceeded to a description, starting with the cathedral precinct.*

Has a Dean, Six Prebendaries or Major-Canons, six Minor Canons, six Lay-Clerks or Singing-Men; one Master of the Choristers; one Subdeacon, six Choristers; two Masters of the Grammar School; four Almsmen; one Subsacrist or Sexton; one Porter who shall be Verger; one Butler, two Cooks; in all 39. by Hen. VIII's Foundation , which bears Date as abovemention'd, and is referred to in *Rymer*; tho' the Places of the inferior Members being but small, they are seldom kept entirely filled, as provided for in the Statutes, which are *mutatis mutandis*, the same with those of *Gloucester* already mentioned, and others of the new Foundation, which may be all judg'd by those of *Rochester*, printed in an *Octavo* Account of that Church, *An.*1717. But I will for the better Information of the Curious, insert the Statute Words at length, forasmuch as they expressly describe the limited Members of the Church......

The Bishop has a large, tho' no very convenient House, here appropriated to him, adjoining to the Cathedral, being what was heretofore the Abbacy; it opens into the East Cloister, and consists of several Rooms, divers of which were well repaired and fitted up by the last Bishop Dr *Smallridge*: The Chapel is very small, being only 15 Foot long, and 11 broad; and notwithstanding there is in the Windows a good deal of painted Glass, as there is likewise in other Parts of the House; yet there being to be seen the Names and Arms of two or three of the last Abbots, and first Bishop, it plainly shews the Building is of no antient Date.

The Deanary which stands at the West End of the Church, appears to be a better House than the Episcopal Palace, and the present yearly Value of it is esteemed as good as the reserved Rents of the Bishoprick. The six Prebendaries have all Houses within the Cathedral Limits; tho' the Minor Canons and Singing-Men are now destitute of Habitations within the Church Precincts, if they ever had any.

The West and South Sides of the Cloisters are pulled down, the Scite and Extent of them are yet visible. The East and North Cloisters would probably have been likewise demolish'd, but that the first serves for to carry you into the Chapter-House and Bishop's Palace: 'tis but mean, and is covered at the Top with a sloped Roof like a Shed, which perhaps was not the original Roofing, but put up for Conveniency: In the Middle of it, leading out of the Church, is an opening into the Chapter-House: This is an elegant Building, and has a very handsome Stone Roof of two Arches, and is in Length, 46 Foot, the Floor was lately raised four Foot, by the laying of a Deal or Timber Floor above the Pavement, to obviate any Objections of the Members to the Damp of the Stones, and make it more commodious for their meeting and dispatching the Church Business, which they now transact altogether here, and have fitted up a Press for their Register Books, and in Place of the old Circular Window, have put in four large Sash Ones; and set up over the Door, this Inscription:

> *Capitularis haec domus reparata & ornata fuit, A.D. 1713,*
> *Honorabili & Reverendo* Roberto Bothe, *S.T.P. Decano,*
> Jacobo Harcourt, *S.T.P. Vicedecano,* Hugone Waterman,
> *A.M. Thesaurario.*

....

As to a Description of the Fabrick, the best Idea of it will be form'd from the Draughts here annex'd: It is truly no elegant Structure, being reputed one of the meanest Cathedrals in the Kingdom; However, by the Generosity and Zeal of the present set of Members, it is so well adorn'd, that it wants for no Cost or Art to render it beautiful, and is daily improving, and may be said to be kept in as good Repair as any Church whatsoever.

The Organ is large and good, the Choir Stalls very regular, the Altar which is ascended to by black and white Marble Steps, and laid with Pavement of the same, is embellish'd with costly Painting and Gilding; and the East Window being large, and glaz'd with painted Glass, looks very magnificent: and indeed, the whole Structure is kept so decent, that the example of this Chapter, is worthy to be recommended to the Imitation of our richest and most antient Cathedrals.

The Bishop's Palace

By the 18th century the bishop's mansion, adjoining the cathedral, which had been the lodging of the Augustinian abbots, had become dilapidated and was in great need of refurbishment. Most bishops stayed at Bristol only three or four years before securing a more lucrative bishopric, and they had little incentive to spend money on the repair and maintenance of the bishop's palace. Not all were neglectful of their diocese. One particularly energetic bishop was Thomas Secker (bishop of Bristol 1735–7). Although he only stayed for two years before becoming bishop of Oxford and later archbishop of Canterbury, Secker was remarkably active in the diocese. Within a year of his consecration he carried out a careful visitation of the whole diocese, recording the results, including information on the population of each parish, the condition of the church building, the frequency of services and the number of dissenters in a notebook. His notebook also contains his uninhibited opinions of the clergy and of parochial conditions [Elizabeth Ralph & Joseph Bettey, 'Bishop Secker's Diocese Book', <u>Bristol Record Society</u>, XXXVII, 1985, 21–78].

Like many of his predecessors, however, Secker did little to improve the condition of the bishop's palace. It was finally restored at great expense by one of the most distinguished of the bishops of Bristol. This was Secker's former school-friend, Joseph Butler, who was bishop from 1738 to 1750, an unusually long time for an 18th century bishop, most of whom stayed at Bristol for only three or four years before securing a more lucrative bishopric. When he arrived in Bristol Joseph Butler had

Fig. 7 The Memorial to Bishop Joseph Butler, who died in 1752 and was buried in the cathedral. The heraldry shows the arms of the bishop impaled with those of Bristol where he was bishop from 1738 to 1750, and of Durham where he was bishop from 1750 to 1752. The inscription was written by the Bristol poet, Robert Southey, and refers to Butler's theological work and to his influential book <u>The Analogy</u>.
(Photograph by Philippa Johnson).

already published his book, The Analogy of Religion, Natural and Revealed, to the Condition and Course of Nature, *which became the leading Anglican theological work of the 18ᵗʰ century. He combined the bishopric of Bristol with the much better paid position of Dean of St Paul's cathedral, and as a bachelor had no pressing need for a larger house in Bristol. Nonetheless, he devoted a great deal of money and effort into virtually rebuilding the bishop's palace together with its chapel, at a cost of some £5000. His work included the creation of the garden. He exchanged the land known as the Bishop's Orchard, east of the palace and cathedral with the Dean and Chapter in return for land on Canons' Marsh, so that his garden, which he laid out with secluded walks and arbours, stretched down to the river Avon, 'south to the common Shore'. Evidence for his work on the house is contained in the preamble to the Deed of Exchange drawn up in 1743. This includes the following:*

B.R.O. EP/E/2/1

Whereas the said Reverend Father [Bishop Butler] hath lately made and almost compleatly finished large Improvements and alterations in the Mansion House and Garden of the said Reverend Father, situate and being in the City of Bristol aforesaid and known by the name of the Bishop's Palace, by taking down great part of the said House which was very ruinous and out of Repair and rebuilding the same at his own Expense and Charge.....'.

The Bishop's work on his private chapel included covering the walls with a wainscot of cedar wood, although he faced criticism in Bristol for placing a cross on the altar, at a time when anything more than two candles, generally unlit, was regarded as dangerously popish. Sadly, Bishop Butler's work was totally destroyed when the palace was wrecked and burnt by rioters in 1831. Further details about the improvements made by Bishop Butler are contained in The History and Antiquities of Bristol *which was published in 1789 by William Barrett.*

William Barrett (1727–1789) was a surgeon who spent his whole career in Bristol. He became greatly interested in the history of Bristol, and since no general history of the city existed, Barrett resolved to remedy this defect. As a well respected surgeon, Barrett gained access to the houses of many of the local gentry and merchants, and had many opportunities to collect historic records which might other wise have perished. Barrett's work was spoilt by his acceptance of the mass of totally spurious 'evidence' concerning numerous aspects of medieval Bristol foisted upon him by the young solicitor's clerk and poet, Thomas Chatterton. Chatterton claimed to have discovered a wealth of medieval material among the records at St Mary Redcliffe. Barrett was so pleased to have so much hitherto unknown documentary evidence that he failed to demand to see the originals or to notice the inconsistencies, mock medieval spelling and invented names. When Barrett's book, his life's work, finally appeared in 1789, a reviewer in The Gentleman's Magazine *mercilessly attacked the inaccuracies and obvious fabrications which Chatterton had cynically persuaded Barrett to include in the book. Barrett was so devastated by the ruthless criticism of the work to which he had devoted so much effort over so many years that within a few weeks he sickened and died on 13 October 1789.*

Notwithstanding the serious shortcomings of Barrett's book, it does contain valuable material, especially on the topography, markets, docks, churches and secular buildings of Bristol during his lifetime. His plans and descriptions of the churches, including the cathedral, show the interiors, furnishings, positions of monuments and layouts before all the changes caused by later restorations. His work provided the inspiration and formed the basis of the authoritative publications of his younger friend, Samuel Seyer.

Like many other 18th authors, Barrett maintained a darkly romantic and sinister view of the medieval church and especially of the monastic institutions. This explains why he included in his book the story of a supposed scandalous discovery made while the bishop's palace was being renovated. This is included in the extract which follows. The so-called 'dungeon' which Barrett describes was no doubt part of the elaborate and well-built system of water-courses and drainage channels which are commonly found in monastic institutions, being so constructed that they provided easy access to the drains or water supplies [Joseph Bettey, The First Historians of Bristol: William Barrett & Samuel Seyer, Bristol Historical Association, 2003].

William Barrett's Description of the Bishop's Palace, Deanery, Cloisters and Chapter House 1789

In the endowment of this church the bishop had a large though not very convenient house appropriated to him, adjoining to the cathedral, which was formerly the abbacy or abbot's lodgings: it opens into the east cloister and consists of several spacious apartments, many of which were well repaired and neatly fitted by Bishop Smalridge, since his time it was suffered to go to decay, but a late worthy and generous Bishop, Dr Butler, in 1744, had great part of it taken down and rebuilt, at the expence of near £5,000.

Many of the apartments are large and ornamented in a grand manner, and the whole house is now exceedingly convenient, by means of the prebendaries receiving certain lands of his lordship, which lay behind the south side of Trinity-Street for their's, which lay contiguous to his palace: this enabled him to add to the palace a handsome garden and walks. The chapel which is in the house is also very neatly repaired, and wainscoted with cedar: it is very small, being only fifteen feet long and eleven broad; in the windows is a great quantity of painted glass, which was lately repaired, and there is more in other parts of the house yet to be seen, with the names and arms of two or three of the last abbots and the first bishop. The whole fabric is a handsome and commodious dwelling, which his lordship and the succeeding bishops have made their place of residence for about five months in the year, during which time once a week they keep an open table for all the clergy and gentry: and Bishop Butler, in expending so large a sum upon the fabric of the palace then going to decay, which he knew himself should not long enjoy, shewed his most noble and generous spirit and proved him worthy of his high office.

In 1744, whilst the palace was rebuilding a parcel of plate fell through the floor in one of the rooms, which by this accident was found to be decayed, and occasioned the floor's being taken up, when to the surprize of the workmen a room appeared underneath, in which were found a great many human bones, and instruments of iron, it was supposed to punish the refractory and criminals. At the same time was discovered a private passage to this dungeon, originally constructed with the edifice, being an arched way just large enough for one person to pass in at a time made in the thickness of the wall, one end terminated in the dungeon, and the other in an apartment of the house, which by all appearances had been used as a court; but both entrances of this mural passage were walled up and so concealed that no one could suspect it to be any other than one solid thick wall.

The deanery which stands at the west end of the church appears to be a good house; it was repaired in the time of Dean Creswick, and almost entirely rebuilt by Dean Warburton. The present yearly value of the deanery is estimated to be as good as the reserved rents of the bishopric. The six prebendaries have all houses within the cathedral limits, but not residing, they let them out at good rents. The minor canons and singing men are now destitute of habitations within the church precincts, though the chapter-books for1529, folio 33, mention the petty canons' chambers in the inner green near the dean's garden.

The west and south sides of the cloisters are pulled down, the site and extent of them are still to be seen. The east and north cloister would probably have been likewise demolished, but that the first leads into the chapter-house and bishop's palace. What remains of the cloister is covered with a sloped roof of stone like a shed, which was not the original roofing, that being formerly of lead. The whole formed an handsome and elegant square, but makes now a very mean appearance; for in the year 1655, Walter Deyos being mayor of Bristol, the lead was taken off from the cloisters as well as from the cathedral, and deposited in the chamberlain's hands; but a stop being put to any farther spoil, an order was made the 8th of January 1655, that the lead removed from the cathedral and cloisters adjoining should be sold, and laid out in the necessary repairs of the said cathedral. [Tolzey Book, p. 99]. This was the second pillage this cathedral has suffered since the general sack in Henry 8th's reign. In the middle of the cloisters leading out of the church is an entrance into the chapter-house, which is a very elegant curious building, and has a very handsome stone roof of two arches, the pillars being adorned with curious twisted carved work in the Saxon stile of architecture, and it is in length 46 feet and in breadth 26 in the inside, and was as much in height till the floor was lately raised four feet by laying a deal floor above the pavement, to render it less damp and make it more convenient for the chapter's meeting upon business, which they now transact altogether here; and they have fitted up a press for their books and registers, and in place of the fine old circular window have put in four large modern sashes. ....

The square of the cloisters was 103 feet every way, there is a door yet leading out of the west part of the church. Adjoining to the deanery is a noble gate-house, remarkable for its well-turned arch and curious workmanship. ....

BISHOP THOMAS NEWTON (1704–1782),
BISHOP OF BRISTOL 1761–1782

In contrast to most 18th century bishops of Bristol, Thomas Newton remained for more than 20 years. Like many other bishops, he had risen in the Church through his diligence in ingratiating himself with influential patrons, and had become a canon both of Westminster Abbey and York Minster, had been appointed to several wealthy livings, and eventually achieved the rich prize of the Deanery of St Paul's which he kept when he was appointed Bishop of Bristol in 1761. The Bristol chronicler, John Latimer, wrote of him 'he possessed all the arts by which the adroit

clergymen attained worldly distinction' [John Latimer, <u>Annals of Bristol in the 18th</u>
<u>Century</u>, 1893, 345–6]. *Bishops were appointed by the government of the time with
as much concern for their support in the House of Lords as for any suitability they
might have for high ecclesiastical office. competition for bishoprics was fierce and
they were only to be obtained by constant reminders to patrons. Thomas Newton's
method can be seen in the following extract from one of a succession of letters he
wrote to the Duke of Newcastle, who was at the hub of contemporary political
patronage. The bishopric of Bristol was already vacant, and clearly Newton also
cherished a hope of the archbishopric of York.*

> 7 August 1761
> I think it my duty to acquaint your Grace that the archbishop of York lies
> a-dying, and as all here think cannot possibly live beyond tomorrow
> morning, if so long; upon this occasion of two vacancies, I beg, I hope,
> I trust your Grace's kindness and goodness will be shown to one who has
> long solicited your favour.

*Newton's persistence was finally rewarded when on 8 December 1761 he was named
as bishop of Bristol* [Mary Bateson, 'Clerical Preferment under the Duke of
Newcastle', <u>English Historical Review</u>, VII, 1892, 694. *For an account of Thomas
Newton's life see* <u>Oxford D.N.B.</u>].

　　*As is clear from the extract which follows, he was constantly preoccupied by
concern for his health, and seems to have regarded himself as an invalid during a
long period at the end of his life. He was, nonetheless, a prolific author, producing
an edition of Milton's works which was for long regarded as the most authoritative,
and writing a large number of theological tracts. One of these was entitled*
<u>Dissertations on the Prophecies which have been fulfilled and at this time are</u>
<u>fulfilling in the World</u>. *In spite of its title, this became a popular work since it
appealed to contemporary patriotism by extolling the position of the Church of
England and containing a strong denunciation of Catholicism. It ran to several
editions and was his best-known work.*

　　*Thomas Newton devoted the last years of his life to arranging all his publications
and these were published in three large volumes shortly before his death. This
collection of his* <u>Works</u> *was preceded by a lengthy account of his life which reads
rather oddly since it is written in the third person. It does however contain an
interesting section on his time in Bristol, with scathing criticism of the cathedral
clergy, their pluralism, non-residence and general neglect of their duties. The
bishop's strictures should be viewed against the prevailing ethos of the
contemporary Church, and also against the fact that he was himself a pluralist and
used his alleged ill-health as an excuse to be absent from St Paul's for long periods.
Since when in Bristol during the summer months he resided in the bishop's palace
adjacent to the cathedral, it is significant that he says that he attended Sunday
services only when his health and the weather permitted. He also seems much more
concerned about the effect that the absence of senior clergy from the cathedral
would have on gentry visiting the Hotwells Spa than any consequence it might have
for regular worshippers at the cathedral or on the religious life in Bristol. The
Bishop evidently had a very poor opinion of the Dean, Cutts Barton. He served as
Dean from 1763 until his death in 1781, and is remembered as the Dean who*

presented the High Cross which had stood on College Green to Henry Hoare of Stourhead. The High Cross had been removed from the ancient centre of Bristol to College Green in 1733, and was demolished again in the 1760s.

Thomas Newton <u>Works</u> 1782 pp94–7

From the time that he was first made Bishop, he constantly went to Bristol every summer, and usually stayed there the three months intervening between his last residence at St Paul's and the next following; and when he was no longer able to go to St Paul's, he continued at Bristol four or five months, and went to church as often as his health and the weather would permit. In the summer of 1766 the Duke of York lodging at Clifton did him the honour of dining with him, and besides Lady Charlotte Edwin to accompany Mrs Newton, there dined at the same time the Mayor and Sir Abraham Elton, and some principal merchants and other persons. ...

After dinner the Duke and Lady Charlotte Edwin and the Bishop being retired into a bow-window in the drawing room, the Duke among other things asked the Bishop what might be the yearly value of his bishopric, and the Bishop answered that the fines were very uncertain, sometimes more, sometimes less, and sometimes none at all; the certain clear income was £300 a year, and a little more. How then, said he, can you afford to give me so good a dinner? ...

The Bishop never failed going to Bristol every summer till the year 1776, when contrary to the advice of many friends he went upon his fifth visitation into Dorsetshire, and visited and confirmed at Blandford, and at Dorchester, and at Bridport; and by these exertions, it is supposed, he burst a vessel, and had a profuse spitting of blood, which lasted a week, and much alarmed his wife and all his friends. In this distress however it was some comfort, that he was at the house of his good old friend and Archdeacon, Mr Walker of Spetisbury, where he had good help from Dr Pulteney of Blandford, and was almost as well accommodated as he could have been at home but he was not able to proceed any further in his visitation; the Archdeacon visited for him at Shaftesbury; and the visitation at Bristol he was forced to send and put off, and to order his servants who were there with his baggage to return to London, as he himself did by easy stages, as soon as he was in a condition to be moved. This was his first failure of going to Bristol; and by living and residing there so much, he was in hopes that his example would have induced the other members of the church to perform also their part, and to discharge at least their statutable duties. The deanery is worth at least £500 a year, and each prebend is worth about half that sum, and their estates are capable of good improvement: and for these preferments the residence usually required is three months for the Dean, and half that time for each Prebendary. But alas! never was church more shamefully neglected. The Bishop has several times been there for months together, without seeing the face of Dean, or Prebendary, or any thing better than a Minor Canon. The care and management of the church were left to Mr Camplin, Precentor or Senior Minor Canon, and to the Sexton. His example having no kind of effect, he remonstrated several times, that their preferments deserved a little better attendance, as they would well bear the expence of it; their neglect was the more conspicuous and culpable, being in the second city in the Kingdom; and that their want of residence was the general complaint not only of the city, but likewise of all the country; that great numbers resorted every year to the Wells [i.e. Hotwells], and generally came, at least on a Sunday, to see the cathedral; that they were astonished at finding only one Minor Canon both to read and to preach, and perhaps administer the sacrament; that this was not a time for such relaxation and neglect of all order and discipline; that the Church had too many enemies, and Deans and Chapters in particular; that they furnished their adversaries with the strongest arguments against themselves; that there were those who contended for the worthlessness and uselessness of Deans and Chapters, and they could not point out a more flagrant instance of good pay received and little duty done than the church of Bristol. ....

But the Bishop of Bristol's remonstrations had no better effect than his example, and [to] do more than to say what was right and practise it himself was not in his power. The power of Bishops is thought to be something, and it is really nothing. The Bishop is their visitor, vocatus sive non vocatus, but he can only admonish and reprove, he has not the power of inflicting any penalty in case of failure.

While the Deans of Gloucester, Norwich and Peterborough, to their honor, were improving and adorning and beautifying their churches, poor Bristol lay utterly neglected, like a disconsolate widow, saying My lovers and my friends have forsaken me. Upon the Dean's death the Bishop forbore adding what he might have added with truth and justice; for it was contrary to his nature and temper to say severe things of any man: but yet he was of opinion, that something ought to remain as his Protestation against such men and such measures. It is to be hoped that a better race is springing up, and that the new Dean, Dr Hallam, who bears an excellent character, will rectify all these irregularities, and restore the good old order and discipline of the Church.

CHAPTER BUSINESS 1751–1801

The only surviving Book of Particulars ends in 1745, and no other similarly detailed accounts exist. The Chapter Minutes and the Computa *or account books continue throughout the 18th and 19th centuries, but the entries are mostly brief and formal and without the interesting details contained in the Particulars, although the Minutes and Accounts after 1745 include references to Books of Particulars which no longer exist. Most of the entries in the volume of Chapter Minutes 1751–1801 are concerned with noting the periods of residence assigned to each canon, granting or renewing leases on cathedral properties, and the appointment of minor canons, the organist, schoolmaster, singing men and other members of the cathedral staff. Only occasionally do matters of more general interest appear in the Minutes. One such occasion occurred during the years 1749–52. This was in consequence of a profound disagreement between the Dean, Thomas Chamberlayne, and the other members of the Cathedral Chapter. The Dean claimed that the right to appoint minor canons and other members of the cathedral staff rested solely in him. The prebendaries assembled in the Chapter House objected strongly to the Dean's claim, and it was because of this dispute that extracts from the Chapter Minutes relating to such appointments during the years 1542 to 1751 were inserted in the volume of minutes covering the years 1663–1751. The dispute continued unresolved for many months, and the delay in settling it contributed even more to the anger and irritation on both sides. Meanwhile the Dean continued to appoint minor canons and incumbents to cathedral benefices himself, without any reference to the Chapter. Not until 1752 was it agreed by all parties to submit the matter to the arbitration of the bishops of London, St David's and St Asaph. The result appears in the Chapter Minutes on 31 March 1752.*

B.R.O. DC/A/8/2

    The Act of the Chapter before the Revd Mr Chapman
    Sub-Dean, the Revd Doctor Waterland, Treasurer &
    Receiver, and the Revd Mr Castelman, Prebendary and
    Proctor for the Revd Mr Aylmer, Prebendary

On which Day was produced to the Chapter an Arbitration under the Hands & Seals of the Lords Bishops of London, St Davids and St Asaph, Dated the 23 Instant in relation to the Differences and Disputes between the Revd Doctor Chamberlayne, Dean of this Cathedral Church and the Chapter of the same, which Arbitration is ordered to be Copyed in the Minute Book and is as follows:

Whereas Differences & Disputes had arisen between the Reverend Dr Chamberlayne, Dean of the Cathedral Church of Bristol, and the Chapter of the said Church touching the right of Naming the Precentor, Minor Canons, Grammar Schoolmaster, Lay Clarks or Singingmen, Choristers, Subsacrist or Sexton of the said Church, they the said Dean and Chapter did by an Act of Chapter dated the 19th of August 1751 Submit the said dispute to the Arbitration and Determination of the Lords, Bishops of London, St Davids & Norwich in Case he should be able to attend, if not the Lord Bishop of St Asaph.

And Whereas the Lord Bishop of Norwich has 'by reason of his Constant Attendance upon the Prince of Wales & Prince Edward' declined the said Arbitration. We the said Bishops of London, St Davids & St Asaph have accepted and do hereby accept of the said Reference & Arbitration in virtue of the aforesaid Act of Chapter and also of two Subsequent Acts of Chapter bearing date 30 November 1751 and the 2nd March 1752 and the said Acts of relation being thereunto had, may more fully appear.

And we the said Arbitrators having Considered the Case laid before us by the Dean of Bristol on the one part and the Prebendaries on the other, and also the Papers and Documents delivered on each side in support of their respective Claims, particularly and especially the Charter of Foundation of Henry the 8th bearing date the 4th of June in the 34th year of his Reign, and also the Body of the Statues given by commissioners to the said Dean and Chapter bearing date the 5th July in the 36th year of his Reign, and we are of opinion and do determine that the right of naming the Precentor, Minor Canons, Grammar Schoolmaster, Lay Clerks or Singingmen, Choristers and Subsacrist or Sexton of the Cathedral Church of Bristol is in the Dean and Chapter, and the Dean being absent in the Vice Dean & Chapter of the said Church. In Witness whereof we have hereunto set our hands & seals this twenty third day of March in the Year of our Lord one thousand seven hundred and fifty two.

                Tho. London
                Richd. St David's
                R. Asaph

Postscript

And to prevent any future Dispute in relation to the Choice of other officers and Ministers of this Church not mentioned in the before-going Arbitration, it is ordered and Agreed that the Dean's Declaration under his hand dated March 6th 1752 be likewise Copied in this Minute Book which is as follows:

March 6 1752

These are to assure my Brethren the Prebendaries of Bristol, that as I never have insisted so I never will insist on the Sole Nomination of the following Officers in the said Church, Namely the Sub Dean, the Treasurer, the Receiver, the Auditor, the Chapter Clerk, and the Organist.

Thomas Chamberlayne

This arbitration was accepted by both sides, but it may be significant that Dean Chamberlayne did not attend any more Chapter meetings for more than a year, and in his place the Sub-Dean, John Castleman (or Castelman) presided.

Following the arbitration and its acceptance by the Dean, some of the minor canons and officials appointed without reference to the Chapter were suspended.

31 March 1752

It is ordered and agreed That the Dean's sole nomination of Thomas Bolt as Subsacrist or Sexton of this Cathedral Church on 11 April 1749, of the Reverend John Davie as Minor Canon of the said Church, on 29 June 1749 of the Revd John Camplin and Isaiah Jones as Minor Canons on 27 January 1749 and of the Revd Benjamin Hancock as a Minor Canon on 12 June 1750 is Unstatutable and Invalid.

At the Chapter meeting 15 April 1752, however, the Chapter relented and agreed to accept the validity of the various appointments.

The Cathedral Library

Another matter of more than routine business which was recorded in the Chapter Minutes for 24 June 1755 was the decision to establish a library in the cathedral. It seems odd that a library did not already exist, but no reference is made to any books. The entry in the Minute Book is as follows:

The Revd Doctor Hamond having proposed to establish a Library in the Chapter house for the benefit of the Residing Prebends and Canons and at the same time having paid for that purpose Ten Guineas in Lieu of a Treat [?] usually given by a Prebendary on his Admission, the Dean and Chapter desired Doctor Hamond to lay out the said Ten Guineas in such Books as he shall think proper

At a Chapter meeting on 27 August 1760 it was noted that the library had been

'......brought to some perfection, and a number of Books accordingly placed in the Chapter House, and such a Library is likely to meet with a great increase. It is necessary that a Librarian should be named to regulate and take care of the books placed in the said Library and compleat a catalogue of the books in the said Library.

The Rev John Camplin, precentor, was appointed as librarian, with an honorarium of 40s a year. The library was housed in the Chapter house, where bookcases or 'presses' were installed for its reception.

The order made by the Chapter in 1760 was as follows:

That Presses for Books be continued at the Expence of the Chapter at the East End of the Chapter house uniformly with the present Shelves and made by William Hopkins, Carpenter, who was employed in making the present Presses.

Sadly, most of the books, together with many of the cathedral manuscripts, were destroyed or lost during the 1831 Riots.

Dr Josiah Tucker (1713–99)

One prebendary who achieved a national reputation as an economist and political theorist was Josiah Tucker. He became curate of St Stephen's church in Bristol in 1737, rector of All Saints' 1739, and vicar of St Stephen's in 1750. In 1738 he was made private chaplain to Bishop Butler, and through the Bishop's influence obtained a minor canonry at Bristol cathedral in 1742. He was an important and original writer on economic matters, including taxation, foreign trade and colonial policy, arguing that it was in Bristol's long-term economic interest to give independence to the American colonies. His reputation and political influence secured him a prebend at Bristol in 1756, and in 1758 he was created Dean of Gloucester, combining this with his position as vicar of St Stephen's [Oxford D.N.B.].

Miscellaneous Chapter Business

Another quarrel between Dean Chamberlayne and the members of the Chapter occurred in 1757 when consideration was given to the best way of wiping out a debt of £250 which had built up in the accounts. The prebendaries proposed that the next substantial fine to be received for the renewal of a lease should be used to extinguish the debt, rather than being shared out among the members of Chapter as had been the long-established custom. The Dean, however, objected strongly and the Minutes record that he stated '...it would take him a long time to consider the proposal, namely, till next winter'. At the Chapter meeting in September 1757 the Dean finally agreed with the proposal, but by then he was already extremely ill, and died a few days later.

Entries in the Chapter Minutes for 8 November 1759 and 11 September 1761 give
some indication of problems at the cathedral, although they also indicate that the
Chapter continued to be concerned with the care and maintenance of the building.

8 November 1759

On which day it was ordered that Mr James Boult, Sacrist of this Church, shall
forbid any person to hang Cloaths in the Churchyard of this Cathedrall Church or to
Enter into the same for any other private purpose without apprising the Sacrist
thereof and obtaining Leave for such purpose. And it was also ordered that the
Churchyard shall be kept shut up next to Trinity Street and that the Hole made in the
Churchyard wall by or by the order of Mr James Foord be Stop'd up and that the said
Mr Boult shall employ a Mason to do it.

11 September 1761

Whereas It has been represented to the Dean & Chapter by the Minor Canons of the
Church That their Attendance at 7 o'clock Prayers during the Winter Season is very
dangerous and detrimental to their Health, and that the Congregation they are to read
to at that Time, consists of very few persons. The Dean & Chapter have therefore
thought it proper to dispense with that part of the Minor Canons Duty, and to excuse
their reading the Early Prayers from the first day of November to the last day of
March, provided that they attend diligently at Early Prayers for the other part of the
year.

Whereas Complaint has been made to the Dean & Chapter That Numbers of loose
and disorderly people meet together in the Church Cloisters as soon as it is dark, to
the great Scandal and Annoyance to the Neighbourhood. It is therefore ordered that
the Revd Doctor Waterland and Mr Aylmer or one of them may rectify that
Grievance by causing the Gates to be nightly shut up or otherwise as they or either
of them shall think fit.

The Dean & Chapter having thought it proper and necessary to clean and beautify
the Cathedral Church by white washing and painting and by mending and repairing
the windows, the Expense of which amount to the Sum of £100 14s 11d as appears
by the Bills & Receipts viz[t] :

	£	s	d
Joseph Thomas, Tyler & Plaisterer	68	12	10
Benjamin King, Glazier	25	7	6
William Hopkins, Carpenter	4	0	4
John Jones, Smith	2	3	9
Thomas Bolt, Sexton		10	6
	100	**14**	**11**

Which sum is not to be added as an Onus on the <u>Computum</u>, already too much
loaded, but to be taken out of the Fine to be paid by William Morgan Esq[r] to be

delivered into the hands of Mr Tyndall [Chapter Clerk] who is desired to discharge the aforesaid Bills and to deliver them with their Receipts to the Chapter.

William Morgan leased the manor and rectory of Peterstone (Mon) and the fine amounted to £342 10s 0d.

In 1762 the Dean and Chapter considered the matter of burials within the cathedral. The number of 18th century memorial slabs which remain on the floor of the cathedral is a reminder of how popular such burials were among those who could afford the fee charged. The memorials show that, as well as Bristolians, many of those buried beneath the floor had come to Bristol in an unsuccessful attempt to restore their health by taking the waters at Hotwells. A remarkable number came from the West Indies.

Archaeological work during repairs to the floors has revealed large numbers of graves, many of them in quite shallow excavations. Up to 1762 the fee for such burials had been £10 for the choir, and £5 for the nave or cloisters. In 1762 these fees were reduced to £5 for the choir, £3 for the nave and £2 for the cloisters. In 1776 the fees were restored to £10, and in 1802 they were increased to £15.

31 May 1774

Abraham Hooper, one of the Singingmen, having Several Times been admonished for Neglect of Duty without Effect, the Dean and Chapter order that on the next Complaint made against him, the said Abraham Hooper to be turned out immediately from being any longer a Singingman of this Church.

26 June 1775

On which day the Subdean & Chapter admonished the Singingmen of this Church in General for Neglect of Duty and laid a Mulct or Punishment of 6d for every time they absent from the Divine Service of this Church and orders that on the next complaint made against any or either of them they or he will be immediately turn'd out from being any longer a Singingman of this Church.

24 July 1780

Whereas frequent complaints have been made against the Choristers for Misbehaviour during the time of Divine Service, Order'd by the Subdean That a Book be provided entitled <u>Merricks Translation of the Psalms</u> to be kept in the Vestry, and that every Chorister so offending shall be by the Senior Minor Canon present (if no Prebendary be present) be confined in the Vestry from the time of Morning Prayers till the Evening Prayers of the same day. And that he have a portion of one of the said Psalms given him to be learn'd by Heart, not less than Twenty Lines nor more than Thirty at any one time, at the Discretion of the Person so confining him. And that if he shall neglect or refuse to learn the same during his first Confinement, that his Confinement shall be repeated in the same manner Day after Day between the times of Morning and Evening Prayer till he can repeat his Task perfectly. Order'd also that if any Chorister so Confined shall wilfully Spoil or deface the Book provided for this purpose, the Chapter Clerk shall provide another Book of the same kind and pay for it out of the Sallary of the Chorister so offending.

7 December 1789

Ordered that as Abraham Hooper, one of the Singingmen of this Cathedral, did not attend the service of the Choir this day, nor has attended it for the last two years and upwards, there will be imposed on him a Mulct of a Portion of his Salary from Michaelmas last proportionate to the times of his non-attendance, to continue in the same proportion, till his regular attendance and behaviour shall recommend him to the approbation of the Chapter.

Notwithstanding the entirely formal nature of most of the entries in both the Chapter Minutes and the <u>Computa</u> *during the later 18th century, and the repeated reminders that the conduct of services, residence of clergy and diligence of lay-clerks fell far below the accepted standards of later periods, occasional references, such as those quoted above, show that the cathedral continued to be well maintained. Tradesmen such as masons, carpenters, plumbers and glaziers were regularly employed and much care was taken over the maintenance of College Green and the Lower Green, including regular tree-planting and the spreading of gravel on the paths. In June 1771 William Symons, one of the cathedral almsmen, was appointed to be 'Conservator of the Colledge Green and to impound any Cattle straying therein'. In 1774 the Chapter Minutes show that it was agreed to pay James Morss £5 per annum 'from This time for his Trouble in looking after the Workmen of this Church'. In 1791 a major problem became apparent in the condition of the tower, which for the previous three centuries had been deprived of the support on its western side which had been provided by the medieval nave. The Dean and Chapter ordered a survey to be conducted by Henry Emlyn of Windsor, and on 9 April 1791 agreed that:*

> The Defects affecting the Stability of the Fabric of the Church be repaired in the Manner prescribed in the Survey of Mr Emlyn of Windsor delivered to the Chapter, and that the Deputy Treasurer do remit to the said Mr Emlyn the sum of £10 for his trouble in making such Survey.

Henry Emlyn's Particular of Necessary Repairs to the various parts of the College Church at Bristol 7 April 1791

Tower
The upper Story on each side in many parts are defective and spread out (though it may stand some years longer). I think it necessary to tie them in with a frame of timber with proper Iron bands and Bolts and make good the several defects in the stone piers and arches to prevent rain from getting in.
A Calculation of the Expence for a frame of Timber for Securing and Tying in the Tower at the College and making good the Joists and Plate at the end of the Isle behind the Dial, agreeable to Instructions received:

Carpenters' Work may cost near about	£130–0–0
Masons' Work	£ 60–0–0
Smiths' Work	£ 90–0–0

This work together with various minor repairs to the chance, and north side of the cathedral was carried out according to Emlyn's recommendations.

Apart from the two Greens, much of the area surrounding the cathedral was gradually covered with houses during the 18th century. The land to the east, between the cathedral and the church of St Augustine the Less, which had been known as the 'Masonrie', was transformed by the building of Trinity Street during the 1750s. In 1753 the wealthy merchant and banker, Thomas Tyndall, was granted a lease of the cathedral's land on St Michael's Hill, known as Cantocks Closes. There he began to lay out an extensive park around the elegant mansion which he had built on the site of the Royal Fort. In 1770 an Act of Parliament was obtained enabling the bishop to lease for building purposes the land to the west between the cathedral and Brandon Hill. This was soon divided into building plots and covered in tenements, including the buildings along College Street.

A Scheme to increase the Income of the Cathedral

A proposal for major development of the cathedral land on the slopes of St Michael's Hill was agreed by the Dean and Chapter in 1791–2. If the proposed scheme had succeeded it would have secured the financial future of the cathedral, and provided a regular major source of income. Unfortunately, the plan failed because of the outbreak European war and a total collapse of financial confidence. During the 1780s Bristol had experienced a period of building mania, as rising population and commercial prosperity fuelled an ever-increasing demand for houses. There were major building projects in Clifton, and many houses were begun around Berkeley Square and along Park Street, Park Row, Great George Street and Charlotte Street. In 1791 the Dean and Chapter attempted to benefit from this situation, and to secure the financial future of the cathedral by a major housing development on 24 acres of their land on St Michael's Hill, known as Cantock's Closes. They petitioned Parliament for an Act enabling them to grant a thousand-year lease of the land and to proceed with an imaginative scheme. This was to lay out a whole new suburb consisting of:

.......a Crescent Square, Circus, several Streets and other buildings upon a Regular Plan ...the same would form a regular and grand Plan of Building which would very much improve the said City and the said lands of the Dean and Chapter. (BRO DC/E/40/48/2)

This plan had been drawn up by a consortium consisting of Thomas Griffith Vaughan, merchant and banker, John Weeks, vintner, and James Weekes, gentleman, and the whole concept was to be designed by James Wyatt, the leading and most fashionable architect of the time. If these ambitions had been realised they

*would have rivalled similar schemes which had been developed in Bath. They would
also have brought a greatly increased income to the Dean and Chapter, since they
were to receive one-third of all the income from the properties. The buildings would
have created an imposing landmark on the hillside overlooking Bristol.*

A proposal for this purpose was prepared for presentation to Parliament in 1792.

B.R.O. DC/E/40/48/2 [32 Geo III 1792]

An Act for Enabling the Dean and Chapter of the Cathedral Church of the Holy and
Undivided Trinity of Bristol, to grant a Lease of Part of the Lands of the said Dean
and Chapter, in the Parish of Saint Michael the Archangel, in the City of Bristol for
the Purpose of Building thereon. ......

(*The lands are*) very conveniently situated for Building Houses upon for the use of
the Inhabitants of the said City, and if they were to be laid out together the same
would form a regular and grand Plan of Building which would be an Ornament and
very much improve the said City, and the said Lands of the said Dean and Chapter
would be thereby made to produce to them and their successors a very large Increase
of Rent to the amount of several hundred Pounds per annum, and which could not
be effected in any other manner.

*Unfortunately for the Dean and Chapter, these proposals could not have come at a
worse time. The outbreak of war with France in 1793 led to a rapid recession in
trade and an evaporation of financial confidence. The result was that the property
boom collapsed. Numerous builders and developers, including Thomas Griffith
Vaughan, became bankrupt and for the next few years many parts of Bristol and
Clifton presented the melancholy spectacle of half-finished houses. As late as 1807
a visitor commented that the scene resembled the desolation 'occasioned by a siege,
or the ravages of a plague'* [James Malcolm, 'First Impressions 1807, quoted by W.
Ison, The Georgian Buildings of Bristol, 1952, 27–8].

Competition for Seats in the Cathedral

*The consequence of the cramped and inconvenient accommodation for the
congregation provided by the cathedral is illustrated by the following two items
relating to seats for the Bishop's household and for the wives of Minor Canons.
Pews in the cathedral were kept locked and were only available to those who
appropriately rewarded the sexton or verger; all others sat on forms or benches.
Moreover, the whole congregation had to move out of the chancel and into the
transepts to hear the sermons. At a Chapter meeting on 31 May 1774 the following
agreement was made:*

B.R.O. DC/A/8/2

The Dean and Chapter caused the following order in Compliment to his Lordship the
Bishop of this Diocese. Vizt. The right to the little pew immediately under the

Bishop's Throne in the Quire having been lately called in Question, It is hereby recognized and declared that the Bishop has a just right and Title to the same pew and that not only this pew and the new pew erected by him in the Quire, but also the other pews which have constantly been appropriated to him in Body of the Church, do properly belong to the Bishop for the Sole Separate Use of him and his Family during the residence of his Lordship.

In 1800 the Chapter received a petition from the Minor Canons asking for reserved seats to be allocated for their wives in the same way that seats were set aside for the wives and families of the prebendaries. The petition again shows the crowded conditions in the cathedral, the inconvenience of having to move for sermons, and the reluctance of the canons' wives to mix with the crowd of common worshippers who evidently assembled for the services.

BRO DC/A/13/4

21 June 1800

The Minor Canons on behalf of their wives, take the liberty of laying before the Revd the Dean and Chapter –
    That their Wives have no certain Sitting in the Body of the Cathedral. That either during the Communion Service they must (contrary to Piety and Decency) go out of the Quire into the Body of the Church to secure a Seat. Or if they postpone leaving the Quire till after the Nicene Creed is ended they run the hazard of having no Seat or at least are obliged to stand a considerable time among the People before they are admitted into one.
    They pray therefore that One of the short Pews under that which the Prebendaries and Minor Canons sit in during the Sermon may be allowed them. Each of these Pews will contain four Persons and not more. The Pew which opens to the North Aisle is that which they wish to be appropriated to their sole use. By each having a Key (the expense of which with permission they will defray themselves) they may from the North Aisle very conveniently let themselves in without walking through the crown or waiting till the Sexton comes. And though that Seat will contain four Persons and all the Minor Canons may not have Wives, it will nevertheless afford those who do attend the advantage of taking a part of their family if the Seat be not filled. The Seat being solely appropriated to their Use they will have it in their power mutually to accommodate each other in that respect.

Chapter Dinners

According to the Cathedral Statutes a meeting of the Chapter should have been held every three weeks, but by the late 18th century such frequent assemblies had long since been abandoned. Because so many members of the Chapter held other appointments, often at considerable distance from Bristol, Chapter meetings were irregular, often at intervals of two or even three months. Not all members attended every meeting, but appointed other canons to act as their proxies. Two General Chapters were held each year, one in June and the other in November. These were meetings at which all really important business was discussed, the accounts were audited, and surplus funds allocated to cathedral maintenance, charity, any exceptional expenses, and the residue shared as a dividend to the members of the Chapter. These General Chapters often lasted for more than one day, and at the conclusion of each day's business, it was the practice for members to have dinner together at one of the local inns. The receipts for some of these dinners survive, and the following are examples from the late 18th century.

B.R.O. DC/A/9/6/6

White Lyon 24 & 25 June 1776

		£	s	d
24 June	Bread etc.		1	0
	Wine		10	0
	Chicken Pye		7	6
	Beef Steaks		1	6
	Beans & Bacon		2	0
	Pease etc.		2	0
	Lobster		2	0
	Cucumber		4	
	Cheese, Butter, Pye		1	6
	Beer, Porter & Cyder		2	6
	Coffees		3	0
	Suppers		4	0
	Fruit, Cream, Sugar		3	0
25 June	Bread		1	0
	Wine		7	0
	Three Chicken Boyld		6	0
	Bacon, Collyflowers etc.		2	6
	Legg Mutton		5	6
	Pease, Butter etc.		1	6
	Chiny [?shin beef]Pye		2	6
	Cheese & Butter		8	
	Beer etc.		3	0
	Fruit, Cream & Sugars		3	0
	Coffees		3	0
	Suppers		7	0
		4	13	8
	Servants		6	0
		4	**19**	**8**

White Lyon 15 July 1778

		£	s	d
	Bread		6	
	Wine		12	6
	Turbott, Whiteing, Lobster & Shrimp Sauce	1	1	0
	Couple ducks & dressing		5	0
	Pease, Butter		2	0
	Cheese, Butter			4
	Beer & Porter		2	2
	Fruit, Sugar		2	0
		2	5	6
	Servants		**4**	**0**
		2	**9**	**6**

White Lyon 23 June 1779

		£	s	d
23 June	Bread & Cheese		1	4
	Wine		10	0
	Fish Sauce		6	0
	Couple Chickens Boiled		4	6
	Ducks Rosted		5	6
	Pease & Bacon		2	6
	Rasberry & Currant Pye		3	0
	Calleflower & Butter		1	0
	Porter & Beer etc.		2	8
	Paper			2
	Tea & Coffee		4	2
	Suppers		2	6
	Porter & Wine		3	6
	Wine for Clerks		2	6
24 June	Bread & Cheese			10
	Wine		7	6
	Neck Mutton Rosted		3	6
	Cupple Chickens		4	6
	Beans & Bacon		1	6
	2 Cucumbers, Oil etc.			9
	Beer & Porter		1	6
	5 Coffees		3	9
	Suppers		3	0
	Negus		1	6
	Porter, Ale etc.		1	4
	Paper			2
		3	**19**	**2**

25 June				
	Bread & Cheese			6
	1 pair Soles Dressed			
	& Sauce		3	0
	Beef Steaks		1	6
	Beer & Porter			10
	Wine		5	0
	Strawberry, Cream etc.		2	0
	5 Teas & Coffee		3	9
	3 Suppers		3	0
	Porter etc.			10
	Wine		2	6
		5	2	1
	Waiters		7	6
		6	**6**	**4**

26 June				
	Bread & Cheese		6	
	Wine		3	9
	Fowl Boyld & Mushrooms		3	0
	Beef Stakes		1	6
	Beer & Porter		1	0
	Strawberry & Cream		2	0
	Suppers		1	0
	Porter & Beer		1	0
	Punch		3	0
		5	18	10
	Waiters		7	6
		6	**6**	**4**

Bush Tavern 3 July 1792

	Dinners	3	0	0
	Beer & Porter		3	6
	Cyder		4	6
	Port		12	6
	Madeira		13	6
	Punch		5	0
	Tea & Coffee		5	0
		5	4	0
	Waiters		5	0
		5	**9**	**0**

London Inn 28 Nov. 1799

	Fish & Dressing		3	0
	Fowls & Dressing		6	0
	Bacon		1	0
	Steaks		4	6
	Butter & Sauces		2	0
	Pastry		2	6
	Bread & Cheese etc.		1	6
	Port		7	0
	Sherry		4	6
	Beer		1	0
	Biscuits		6	
	Tea & Coffee		4	0
29 Nov.	Fish & Dressing		4	0
	Soup		2	6
	Turkey & Dressing		7	6
	Pastry		2	6
	Butter & Sauces		2	0
	Garden Stuff		1	0
	Port		7	0
	Sherry		4	6
	Beer		1	0
	Tea & Coffee		4	0
	Waiters		3	0
		3	18	0

London Inn 24 June 1800

Dinners for 12 @ 5/- each	3	0	0
Port	1	10	0
Sherry		9	0
Beer & Cider		8	0
Fruit & Biscuits		7	0
Tea & Coffee		12	6
Servants		3	6
	6	10	0
Dinners	1	2	6
Port		11	3
Sherry		4	6
Beer		2	0
Fruit & Biscuits		4	0
Tea & Coffee		6	3
	2	10	6
Waiters		7	6
	9	8	0

London Inn 28 Nov. 1801

28 Nov.				
	Bread & Cheese		3	0
	2 Fowls & Dressing & Oyster Sauce		7	0
	Beef Stakes		6	6
	Apple Pie		4	0
	Jelley		1	6
	Vegetables, Pickles & Butter		2	6
	Beer & Porter		3	0
	Port		15	0
	Sherry		4	6
	Fruit		3	6
	Servant		2	0
	Teas		6	3
		2	18	9

1 Dec.				
	Dinners	1	0	0
	Beer & Porter		2	0
	Sherry		4	6
	Port		11	3
	Fruit		3	6
	Coffee		5	0
	Porter for Calling Coach			6
	Waiters		5	0
		5	**10**	**6**

NOTES ON THE HISTORY OF THE CATHEDRAL
BY DR HENRY BEEKE (1751–1837),
DEAN OF BRISTOL 1813–1837

Henry Beeke was a distinguished scholar and writer on economic affairs, taxation and finance. He was born in 1751 at Kingsteignton, Devon, where his father, Christopher Beeke, was the vicar. After education at Oxford, he became a Fellow of Oriel College in 1775 and was Regius Professor of Modern History at Oxford between 1801 and 1813. He also progressed through the Church, becoming vicar of St Mary the Virgin, Oxford (1762), rector of Ufton Norcot, Berkshire (1789), Dean of Bristol (1813) and vicar of Weare, Somerset (1819). He was a man of profound learning and wide interests. A contemporary described his popularity in Bristol and wrote of him:

> Small in stature, the little dean, as he was called, was a paragon of information. Omniscience was his forte without being his foible. There was no sort of knowledge with which he was not said to be familiar. The commanding officer of a cavalry regiment in Bristol found him as well

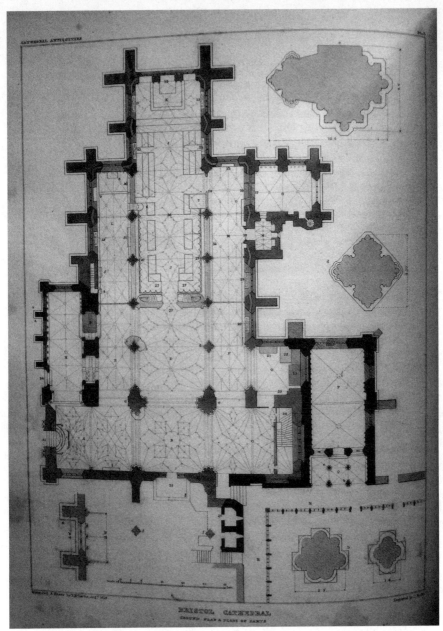

Fig. 8　Plan of the Cathedral in 1830 from John Britton's <u>History & Antiquities of Bristol Cathedral</u>. This shows the remarkably small space within the cathedral, further constricted by the central pulpitum, and by the numerous monuments whose position is marked on the plan. The main entrance was through a door in the north transept; the Elder Lady chapel was virtually unused, and the Berkeley Chapel was made into a vestry.
(Photograph by Philippa Johnson).

versed in farriery as did his friend Mr Vansittart when Chancellor of the Exchequer, as a consultee in matters of finance.

[Lord Teignmouth's Reminiscences, II, 266, quoted in Nicholas & Taylor, II, 82]

His reputation as an economist was acquired through the publication in 1779 of his book Observations on the Produce of the Income Tax, and on its Proportion to the Whole Income of Great Britain. *This was written during the fierce public debate on William Pitt's introduction of a tax on incomes above £50 in 1799 to help pay for the war against France. Throughout his life Beeke continued to correspond with politicians and other influential persons on economic matters, and in his Oxford lectures during the early 19th century he may well have been the first person to deal with the subject of political economy at the University. He died at Torquay on 9 March 1837.*

During his long time as Dean of Bristol, Henry Beeke took a great interest in the history of the Augustine abbey, the cathedral and in the estates which formed the endowment of both institutions. He made copious notes on the records which, until the destruction and dispersal which they suffered during the Riots of 1831, were kept in the Chapter House. Among his notes are detailed comments on the dimensions of the abbey church and buildings as measured by William Worcestre in 1480, and about the houses built on the site of the nave during the late 16th century. He also studied the documents relating to churches where the cathedral possessed the patronage, and to various estates, and he made detailed notes on Somerton, Merriott and Bathampton. He was particularly interested in the original foundation of the cathedral, in the Statutes, the methods of appointing minor canons and other members of the cathedral community, and in the ways in which the practices had departed from the original intentions of Henry VIII in 1542.

The following extracts and notes made by Dean Henry Beeke are based on the work of Dr William Hill, who was a prebend of Bristol 1607–21. His survey of the earliest arrangements for the cathedral made in 1609 has not survived, so Dean Beeke's notes are particularly valuable. A survey of the cathedral estate at Olveston made by Dr William Hill in 1610 does survive [BRO DC/E/21/1].

B.R.O. DC/A/7/9/1

From Dr Hill's Notes on the Cathedral Establishment in 1542

	£	s	d
Dean			
William Snowe	100	0	0
6 Prendaryes			
John Goughe	20	0	0
Roger Edgworth	20	0	0
Henry Morgan	20	0	0
Roger Hewes	20	0	0
Richard Browne	20	0	0
George Dogeon	20	0	0

6 Petticanons

Sir Thomas Allen with 40s to him assigned for exercising of the Sextons office	12	0	0
Sir John Browne to have	10	0	0
Sir William Penne	10	0	0
Sir John White	10	0	0
Sir John Dyer	10	0	0
Sir William Bowden	10	0	0

The Gospeller & Epistoler Clark

Sir John Somer, Gospeller	6	13	4
Sir Richard Bowyer, Epistoler	6	13	4

Six Singing Men to have

John Moore	6	13	4
Thomas Sexton	6	13	4
Nicholas Crepulgate	6	13	4
John Morgan	6	13	4
John Badle	6	13	4
John Archard	6	13	4

The Master of the Choristers

Thomas Sennes	10	0	0

Six Choristers

John Tison	3	6	8
Raph Snowe	3	6	8
James Bonifant	3	6	8
Thomas Estcourt	3	6	8
William Hungerford	3	6	8
Edward Lilling	3	6	8

The Schoolmaster & Usher of the Grammar School

William Eden, Schoolmaster	8	6	8
Richard Lee, Usher	6	8	4

Four poor men decayed in the Kings Wars or in his Guards Service

Richard Cooke	6	8	4
John Puther	6	8	4
John Philips	6	8	4
Adam Williams	6	8	4

The Alms yearly

Item to be distributed in Alms yearly	20	0	0

For makeing & mending the highe Ways

Item for making of high Ways	20	0	0

	£	s	d
The Reparations there			
Item the reparations there yearly	53	6	8
The Steward of the Lands			
William Button to have yearly	6	8	4
The Auditor there			
Griffin Tindall there to have	10	0	0
The Porter there			
John Collins the Porter to have for his Wages & Diet	6	8	4
The Butler there			
Robert Bremer for his Wages & Diet	6	0	0
To Cookes to have for their Wages & Diet			
William Unt, cheife Cooke to have	6	0	0
David ap Watkin, under Cooke to have	3	6	8
The Cator there			
Thomas [blank] for his Wages & Diet	6	0	0
Extraordinary Charges			
Item for extraordinary Charges	20	0	0
Sum of all the charges aforesaid over & besides the			
Bishops Portion	570	0	0
Whereto is to be added to bear the Tenths	57	0	0
The first Fruites	28	10	0
And so to beare all charges & to pay tenths & first			
fruits it may please the Kings Majestye to indow the			
Church with	655	10	0
Item, the Bishops Portion before not charged			
with £33 6s 8d to him allowed for the tenths	366	13	4
	1022	**3**	**4**

Marginal Note
The Rents & Receipts being £679 3d 11d take away
the yearly Allocations   £655 10s 0d there remaineth
but   £23 13s 11d for Suites in
Law and many other extraordinary Charges

Observations – H[enry] B[eeke]

There is somewhere an inaccuracy in the Statement which gives as the sum total £570 whereas the particulars only amount to £569 13s 4d. I suppose that the former sum was considered as a sufficiently near approximation to the latter.

I have not discovered the time when the Dean & Chapter ceased to appoint the two reading Clerks.

The Master of the Choristers undoubtedly was also the Organist when an Organ was erected, but when that was done I cannot find.

Considering their statutable services the Pensions of the four poor men were large.

It has long been the practice to divide the £20 for Alms in three parts giving £10 annually to poor Widows & £5 each to be distributed in two of the Parishes where we have Estates or Advowsons, not exactly in rotation, but having regard to two circumstances – the times of Renewals & the Population.

The point most worthy of observation is that in this original arrangement about a twelfth part of the whole regular annual income was allocated for Repairs. The value of Money had already begun to diminish when the Cathedral was founded, but not so as to have any great effect on prospective calculations. If when Renewals were afterwards made the annual rents had been increased in proportion to change of the value of money, instead of increasing the Fines, the annual Income by regular Rents would now have been very much greater & in Justice the Allocations should have been regulated accordingly. In that case a sum corresponding with £53 6s 8d heretofore would have been an ample Fund for all Repairs.

It appears to me to have been in contemplation that this sum should properly have been separated & any unemployed surplus should have remained in hand, so that the greater expense of one year might be defrayed by the part of former savings. I know not when this was first omitted, but it was in my opinion a very mischievous departure from the original intention.

Christopher Pacey, Treasurer, Extraordinary Charges 1581 to 1582 that is during one year from Michaelmas to Michaelmas

	£	s	d
Paid to Mr Reads man for bringing a Doe to the Dean & Chapter		4	0
To Mr Hawles servant for bringing a Box			6
For two double Draughtes of wood to make a fyre upon her Majesties day		6	0
For bread for the ryngers		2	4
For a kynderkyn of beer for them		2	0
For a rounde of befe & a rounde of pork for their supper upon Thursday night & for dressing the same		2	4
For a cheese for their dinner and supper upon Fryday			10
For milke & wheat and butter for them			11
For parsenepes for them			4
For salt fyshe		10	
For their Rynging		4	0
For bread distributed to the poore		6	8
Given to Richard Rice by the agreement of the Dean and Chapter for goyng divers tymes in the house busynes		5	0
Given to Anthony Pryn by the sayde[?] consent for charges layed out by him in his jorney in providing some meter [?] choristers for our Choir		5	0

Given at Christmas for the Dean and Chapter to the maiors [mayor's] & Sherefes [sheriff's] servantes and to the waytes [carol-singers]		10	0
Paid to a messenger 5th of February for carrying a letter to the Archdeacon of Dorset about the house busynes		2	6
Paid the 22nd of Marche to a messenger sent to Mr Sands with a letter touching the Advocation of Somerton		2	4
Given by Mr Deanes consent 6th of April to a minister which laboured to have a petty canons place in our church		3	4
Given the 12th Aprill by Mr Deanes consent to the Tawlest man of our souldyours then newly come from Ireland		2	0
Paid 25th of Aprill to Gilbert Roberts and Whitfeld for their horses & their own charges in ryding to Wells to serve Mr Sands and John Smythe with proces touching excheker matters		blank	
Paid to Mr Carye for money laid out by him for resting of Seamen		blank	
Given 5th of August by Mr Deanes consent to Stafford		blank	
Paid the 25th of August by Mr Deanes appointment to a Sent with letters to the Lord of Gloucester touchinge the libell [?]		2	6
Gave 5th of September by Mr Deanes appoyntment to a poore singinge man		2	0
Paid to Mr Greene by the agreement of the Deane and Chapter for charges layed out by him in dyvers tymes journeying to London about the house busynes as it now playnly appears by his bill of particulars	10	17	0
Paid 22nd of September for a pottle of Ipocres to present the Earle of Pembroke & xiid for whight wyne and sugar layed out by Nicholas Morgan upon my Lords gentlemen		4	0
Paid to Mr Deane for charges layed out by him in ryding up to London about the house busynes	5	12	6
Paid by the Dean and Chapters consent to Gylbert R. in consideration of his bearing the Rodde & keeping good order in the Church		6	0
Paid to Sadler for keepinge clean the Leades and gutters of our Church	1	0	0
Paid to Gualter Gleseon for parchment to engross the last years bookes of Accompt		4	0
Paid to Mr Sawle [?] and to myselfe £4 a piece granted to us heretofore in consideration of our charges by our continuall residence here	8	0	0
Paid to the plummer for his fee		10	0
Paid to Laidler for his paynes about the house busynes		6	8
Summa omnium extraordinari　　**xxxii-li-xs -id**			

Paid the weekly Almes to the poore after 10s the week which ryseth in the whole for the yeare	26 0	0
Paid to Mrs Harrys wydow	13	4
Given 16 of November by Mr Deanes consent to a poore craftsman [that] have fallen blynd	2	6

Computa before Sequestration in 1642

The earliest Computum that I have found was for the year ending at Mich. 1550. This with those for the following years are separate and on paper. Those from 1556 to 1582 remain very neatly transcribed on Vellum, excepting that 1560 and 1571 are missing. From 1583 to 1592 the original Computa remain written on paper. From 1594 to 1602 all are missing, excepting that for 1595. From 1603 to 1619 they are extant in two large quarto facicules written on Parchment as from 1556 to 1582. From 1620 they are for many years irregularly deficient; those for 1633 to 1641 and part of 1642 are in one volume but the last page of the latter is unfinished.

Nota: The Statutes were promulgated by royal authority in July 1544, wherefore the first statutably appointed Nov^r [?November] Chapter was probably in the latter part of that year & the computa for 1544, 5, 6,7, 8 & 9, six in number and rather important as respecting the early history of the Cathedral are missing.

Revenue after the Restoration

1660:   The Restoration was on the 29th of May, at which time only two remained of the Dean & Prebendaries of Bristol, namely Weeks and Williamson, the former received the Income of his Prebend till his death, but does not appear to have been present at any Chapter; the latter survived many years, & appears to have had considerable influence with his Bretheren.

The Computum for this year 1660 is described in its Title Page as 'a Festo D Johannis Baptistae ultimum praterrito & in redditu Seremissimi Domini nostri Caroli secundi Magnae Britannae Franciae & Hiberniae Regis auspicissismi huiusque nostri hemispharae solis splendidissimi, qui Regnis lisce et Ecclesiis pene expirantibus per eius adventum, & divina faventi benignitate, novam lucum vitamque prebuit, ad Fcstum Michaelis huius Anni 1660'.

As the Capitular Body had not been re-constituted till after Midsummer & was not immediately assembled & in Possession a small Receipt only could be expected for these few Months; and only a small part of the Computum for 1661 & no part for 1662 was ever transcribed into the Book, but a blank Space was left for them. It appears from the Chapter Minutes that there was a very slow progress in auditing the Accounts of these two years & I have not yet found the rough Copy of them, if indeed it be still extant.

		£	s	d
1660	Receipts	171	10	10½
	Disbursements	122	10	10
	Surplus	49	0	0½
1663	Receipts	1043	7	6½
	Disbursements	1029	8	0
	Surplus	19	19	6½
1664	Receipts	1136	4	9
	Disbursements	1118	8	5
	Surplus	17	16	4
1665	Receipts	934	16	3½
	Disbursements	898	7	3½
	Surplus	36	9	0
1666	Receipts	910	16	8½
	Disbursements	902	9	5
	Surplus	7	7	3½
1667	Receipts	874	1	8
	Disbursements	850	15	0
	Surplus	23	6	8

I have no doubt that the reasons why the Accounts for the years 1661 & 1662 were so slowly audited – not till late in the Spring of 1663 – were the irregularity and slowness of the Receipts from the Tenants reluctantly submitting to pay Rent for Estates which for some years they had held as if the sole Proprietors. This seems to have been the case of Doves the Lord Farmer of the rectorial manor of Tisbury. The Cathedral also, after fifteen years of Abuse & Neglect must have wanted many & expensive Repairs, and the slow Progress in them & in auditing the Charges for them might be another reason for the Delay.

I conjecture that the Receipts of the two subsequent years 1663 & 1664 exceeded an Average in consequence of the preceding deficiency, & that the three subsequent years 1665, 1666 & 1667 of which the average was a Receipt of £906, & a Disbursement of £884 — a Surplus £22, give very nearly the actual, average state of both if the Accounts had included a longer Period.

But this was exclusive of the contingent & regularly periodical Fines of which the respective Account seems to have been always apportioned and received or receivable at the time of sealing the leases. The transaction of fixing the sum to be paid was not till many years after inserted in the Capitular Minutes, nor can any thing respecting them be now discovered. Only the subsequent Practice leaves no doubt that in conformity with the Statute which gives two shares of the Dividend of the Surplus remaining at the Audit to the Dean & one to each prebendary, they were divided into eight shares when the number was full untill by a voluntary Arrangement it was agreed that one ninth of them should be added to the annual Receipts, which were then unequal to the annual Disbursements, so that during many Years the annual Accounts carried over from Audit to Audit a large Debt to the Chapter Clerk as Deputy Treasurer.

More recently by Sale of Lands etc. to redeem their Land Tax & by a systematic though slow and reversionary increase of the reserved Rents, having added both to the annual Income, brought to Account at the Audit, the Receipt has been & will be still more materially increased, & it is by this only that we have been able to increase the stipends of the Organist, the Schoolmaster, the Minor Canons etc. etc..

Dean Henry Beeke's Notes Concerning the Houses built on the Site of the former Nave

Respecting the Houses and Ground on the West of the present Cathedral Church

The work of rebuilding the Church of the Monastery of Saint Augustine which began at the eastern part in the reign of Edward the second, had slowly extended westwards so that the present Tower was not built till the reign of Henry the sixth. When this was building great part if not the whole of the west end of the antient Church must have become useless, for the Buttresses are so constructed as to extend into it and include the Arches or parts of them which were intended as the commencement of the new Church on that site.

We may therefore be nearly certain that a more rapid Decay must have followed after the Disuse of this Building, and not many years were necessary to its Fall & Destruction. This had been so complete that all but a small part of it had become neglected till it was inclosed by a new Wall on the two open sides not long before the year 1583. In that year a lease was granted by the Dean & Chapter to Nicholas Hill thus describing the Premises:

> 'All that little Messuage with the Appurtenances with a Cellar or Vaute under the same, together with the Chambers and Buildings thereof situate & being in the said city of Bristol at the west end of the said Cathedral Church & adjoining to the same. And also all that their Garden or Ground adjoining to the said Messuage, newly inclosed with a new Wall which Garden or Ground containeth in length from the Wall of the said Cathedral Church unto the Wall at West end near unto the now dwelling House of Christopher Pacie, Clerk, one of the Canons of the said Church 118 feet or thereabout, & in breadth from the Cloister Wall of the said Church unto the said new Wall 90 feet or thereabout, which said Messuage was in the occupation of William Blomer & the said Garden or Ground lately was in the occupation of the said Christopher Pacie, Clerk and are now in the occupation of the said N. Hill. The lease is for a term of 40 years, the annual reserved rent 26s 8d. The lessee covenants within four years

ensuing to edify & build one convenient dwelling House in & upon the same ground or part thereof at his or their proper cost and charges. Subsequent leases on surrender of those preceding were granted:

To Israel Gleson, the Chapter Clerk, -three years after in	1586
Again to the same Israel Gleson	1600
And again in	1613
To George Gough in	1622
To [blank]	1641
To William Haynes	1660
To Richard Northen with licence to build a House	
50 foot long	1664
To the same Richard Northen	1668
To Susannah Northen	1693'

This latter lease however was not granted without serious objections & after considerable delay. The impropriety of leasing for houses or any secular uses a part of the site of the antient Church seems not to have been so seriously thought of as to have caused any Capitular Minute on the subject till the year 1688 when the Dean (Dr Levett) the Revd John Chetwynd, Richard Towgood & John Rainsthorp made the following Order:

'Whereas there is one or more Houses of Office upon or against the Wall of the West end of the Church belonging to the Tenements now in the possession of Mrs Northen or her Assigns, which do greatly annoy the Church and very much endanger the Foundation of the Tower & west part of the Church – ordered that the Chapter Clerk forthwith give notice to Mrs Northens Tenants or Servants now being on the Premises that they take care to remove the same annoyance by our Lady Day next or otherwise to be proceeded against according to Law, and that Mr Thomas Oldfield be employed as an Attorney therein.

Chapter 20 June 1690. Ordered that the Window in Northens House near the Door going into the Cloisters be forthwith stopped up by Renalls the Mason.

Chapter June 23rd 1690. Ordered that the Lease of Northens Houses be no more renewed, but suffered to expire for there being built on the west part of the Cathedral are very inconvenient and do greatly annoy the Church.

Chapter 29 December 1690. Ordered that the Virger in the name of the Dean and Chapter do forbid Northens Tenants throwing Dust etc. into the Cloister Yard which is a great Nuisance.

Chapter 9th July 1692. Present the Dean, Horne, Towgood, Chetwynd. Mrs Northen desired to renew the Lease of the Houses on or near the West End of the Cathedral Church.

The said Dean & Chapter did agree to abide by their former Resolution.'.

In the Interval before the next Capitular Resolution on this subject, Dr Royse had become Dean, vice Levett, & Livesay & Cary Prebendaries, vice Chetwynd & Rainsthorp.

Chapter 14 March 1693. Present the Dean, Horne, Towgood & Livesay & Lye. Mrs Northen did agree with the Dean & Chapter to renew her Lease dated 4th June 1668 of several Tenements near the west end of the Cathedral Church for the Fine of £120. N.B. Against this Bargain Mr Towgood & Mr Livesay did deliver in Chapter a Protest & their reasons against sealing Mrs Northens Lease of her Houses in writing which Mr Towgood read, & they desired it to be entered in the Chapter Book. The Dean (Royse), the Subdean (Horne), Dr Lye & Mr Cary voted against it. Eodem Die: Mrs Northens lease was sealed & the Fine paid.

Chapter 4 August 1712. Mr Pomphrey desiring a Lease to be renewed of some Houses standing upon the West End of the Cathedral Church which Lease was some years since denied to be renewed a Protest being formerly made and read to the Chapter by Mr Richard Towgood and Mr Charles Livesay, Prebendaries, against the renewing of it, which Protest was this day again read and repeated. It is now agreed by the Dean and Chapter that the said Protest shall be registered in their Chapter Book, and they do again for the same several reasons refuse to renew the said Lease intending likewise to crave the Opinion & Determination of the Lord Bishop of Bristol in his visitation or otherwise.

The Protest is this

We, Richard Towgood & Charles Livesay, Prebendaries of the Cathedral Church of Bristol, do hereby enter our dissent from this Contract or Bargain, not out of any obstinate & perverse opinion of our own but remaining unsatisfied:

In conscience because one part of the Houses now contracted for is built upon Consecrated Ground & that which either has been or was designed to be part of the very body of the Church, which is visible by some Pillars & antient Monuments thereof now standing therein. And some part of the same has been & is at this time enjoyed to the most sordid Uses, such as Houses of Office & the like, besides some Chimnies built up against the Walls of the Church which do not only annoy but impair and endanger the Fabrick, all which we think to be a very great Desecration of the place, & several Chapter Acts have been made against renewing the Lease for these and many other reasons of the same nature.

We are not satisfied that this Lease can be valid in Law for by the Statutes Deans & Chapters are limited to make Grants 'de Dimissis & Dimissilibus' so that though a Lease has been obtained thereof, yet if it be not demiseable in its nature, such a Lease will be void in itself & we cannot imagine that the scite of the Church (of which the ground on which these Houses now stand is a part) is in its nature demiseable by the Ecclesiastical (which in these cases will be consulted) or municipal Law, & the latter has sufficiently declared its sense in this matter when by a particular Statute Fairs are prohibited to be kept in Cemetaries, even in a Churchyard. And if this Bargain should proceed we take leave to declare that we will not apply our shares or proportions to our private use, but do intend they shall remain in the hands of the Chapter Clerk until we shall be advised to dispose thereof to some such uses as may atone for any guilt which may fall on us in this matter though not consenting to it.

And we do further declare that our dissent is purely for the reasons above mentioned, & we shall be glad at any time or in any manner to contribute our proportions to recompense the present Tenant for the Term she has on the said

Houses & the Damage she may sustain for not renewing this Lease, to the end that the said place may be restored to its primitive religious use & design, so that if any pious person should be disposed to complete the Fabrick of the Church thereupon, the Ground may without any pretence of right be ready for such a structure.

Nine years after the entry of this Protest and the Capitular Resolution connected with it, a considerable change having taken place in the Dean & Chapter during the interval.

> Chapter 18 November 1721. The Dean & Chapter did seal Matthew Pomphreys Lease, his Fine having been first paid, which Lease has in it several special
> Covenants and Agreements.
> After this four Renewals have been successively made
>
> | | |
> |---|---|
> | To Sarah Pomphrey | 3rd August 1708 |
> | To George Pomphrey | 3rd August 1732 |
> | To Matthew Pomphrey | 30 November 1781 |
> | To Martha Pomphrey | 30 November 1793 |

In this last Lease the way into the Cloisters was especially excepted & has now been many years shut up. That part of the Premises which is near to it having become very notoriously a Receptacle for Prostitutes. To prevent this during the remainder of the Term, the Sub-Sacrist with the concurrence of the Dean etc., took an Under Lease of that part, & it was also I hope, finally decided never to grant another Renewal. The existing Lease will expire on the 30th of November 1835.

August the 3rd 1829   H. Beeke, Dean

CHAPTER MINUTES 1818–1831

B.R.O. DC/A/8/4

During Dr Beeke's period as Dean the Chapter Minutes are almost entirely concerned with the granting or renewal of leases and with other matters of estate management. There are few references to repairs or maintenance to the cathedral building, and no Computa *survive from these years. Charity continued to be given as usual, the canons kept their periods of residence and the services were duly performed by the minor canons and lay-clerks or singingmen. In 1818 an additional Sunday service was instituted when the Dean & Chapter agreed to sell part of their land at Addercliff in Bedminster for a new gaol to replace the notoriously hideous conditions in which prisoners were kept at Newgate. The site was sold for £1133 13s 0d, and the Chapter Minutes record that it was agreed to:*

> ....establish an afternoon sermon in the Cathedral Church on Sundays and to apply the interest from the said sum of £1133 13s 0d to pay the Minor Canons for preaching such afternoon sermons

It is clear from the Minutes for this period that the Dean & Chapter continued to have great trouble with the attendance and behaviour of the singingmen and almsmen. There are frequent references to irregular attendance by the singingmen and threats of reduction of stipend or dismissal. Much of the problem lay in the fact that several singingmen served in various Bristol parish churches as organists, choir-masters or clerks and found it difficult to adequately fulfil the demands of their dual offices. One solution was to allow those singingmen with additional positions to appoint deputies to perform their duties in the cathedral. An example of this is given in the Chapter Minutes of 23 June 1818 when it was:

Resolved that John Barrett, one of the Singingmen of this Church, having been appointed Clerk to the Parish Church of St Augustin, be permitted to provide a Deputy to attend in the Cathedral, such Deputy to be approved of by the Dean and Chapter.

The behaviour of the four almsmen also gave rise to frequent complaints and warnings. For example, another entry in the Chapter Minutes for 23 June 1818:

Resolved that an admonition be given by the Dean to William Gray, one of the almsmen of this Church, for Drunkenness and Striking the Sub-Sacrist in Church on 29 May last, and for other improper conduct.

Five years later, on 25 June 1823 the Chapter Minutes record a formal warning given to all the almsmen or pensioners.

Admonition to the Pensioners

B.R.O. DC/A/8/4

By the Statutes of the Cathedral given by its Founder King Henry the eighth, it is Ordered that there shall be four Poor Men appointed by him and his successors under his sign manual. Disabled Soldiers are to have a preference, and their Duty is thus described in the same Statute. Every day in the year unless prevented by sickness or unless they have from time to time leave of absence from the Dean or Vice Dean they are to be present at divine service and are to wait on and serve the Officiating Clergy, they are also to cleanse the cathedral from all dirt and are to assist the subsacrist in attending to the Lights and extinguishing them and in ringing the Bells to the utmost of their ability. Also they are to obey the Dean and Vice Dean in such things as belong to the decorum of the cathedral. If they are found neglient in these Duties the same Statute authorizes the Dean or in his absence the vice dean to punish them as they may think fit.

The same Statute goes on to direct that if any one of the Poor men now called Pensioners shall absent himself, and shall not reside either within the bounds of the Cathedral or at least very near to it, he shall lose his Stipend in proportion to his absence, but it allows that the Dean or in his absence the Vice Dean may for a cause approved of, give once in a year leave of absence for twenty days.

The same Statutes of the Cathedral allow to each of the four poor men a yearly Pension of Six Pounds three shillings and four pence and three yards of Cloth at three shillings and four Pence a yard to be made up at their own expence.

Fig. 9 (*above*) **& 10** (*opposite*)   Medieval Reredos to the Altar of St Maurice from Samuel
Seyer's <u>Memoirs Historical and Topographical of Bristol</u>, Vol. II, 1823. This reredos, which
is at the east end of the north choir aisle, was totally mutilated in 1821 to accommodate the
large Codrington monument of 1618, which had been removed from the chancel. The
window above the Codrington monument shown in Fig. 10 was erected by Dr Henry
Glemham (Dean 1660–1667). It depicts various biblical scenes including the Resurrection
and Ascension.
(Photographs by Philippa Johnson).

The yearly Pension and Cloth is the whole of the antient Payments to you; nor have you any legal Perquisites; and all else that you now receive from Fees in the Cathedral or by gift of the Dean and Chapter is not appointed in the Statutes and may at any time be altered or taken away at their discretion.

You hear by the Statute that all of you should attend divine service every day in the cathedral, and you have also been told what is your Duty there – I must now add that the subsacrist is by the Statutes and has always been invested with authority to order you what to do and you are bound to obey him in the things before mentioned.

If you have any cause to complain that he orders you to do what the Statutes have not appointed, you must speak to the Dean or Sub Dean or in their absence to the Prebendary in residence who will take care that you suffer no injustice.

And now it is my duty to admonish you Gray and you Ricketts that for a long time you have both and you Gray more especially have neglected your Duty, and nothing but compassion has prevented your expulsion- both of you have been most shamefully drunk in the Cathedral, the House of God, for whose presence you seem to have no regard, and I find also have often left the Cathedral during Divine service – even on Sundays. Such profane and scandalous behaviour deserves to be very severely punished, I now therefore assure? you [and for your own sakes I wish you to remember] that I have taken care to be well informed if ever this should again happen, and if it does, the keeper of any Publick House which you frequent will be in danger of losing his Licence and you will most certainly be expelled, for after this admonition the offence will be inexcusable.

THE RE-POSITIONING OF THE CODRINGTON MEMORIAL 1821

In an attempt to make more room in the cramped chancel of the cathedral it was decided in 1821 to move the elaborate monument of 1618 to Robert Codrington & his family which was fixed to the north wall. The monument commemorates Robert Codrington, gentleman, of Wapley, one of the Chapter properties, in south Gloucestershire who died in 1618, his wife Anne, and their 17 children. It includes two kneeling figures and two standing angels pulling back the curtains from a large semi-circular canopy, together with a long Latin inscription. Robert Codrington's father was vicar of Didmarton in south Gloucestershire, and one of the 17 children included on the monument, Christopher Codrington, established the sugar plantations in Barbados which were to make later generations of the family extremely wealthy [B.R.O. 17125/6]. Unfortunately, the monument was moved to the east end of the north aisle where the magnificent reredos of an altar had recently been discovered. This altar had been part of the furnishings of the abbey church, and had been dedicated to St Maurice in honour of Lord Maurice de Berkeley, one of the benefactors of the abbey. He had died in 1281 and was buried nearby. Also buried nearby was Lord Maurice Berkeley who died in 1368 of wounds received at the battle of Poitiers. The reredos had been covered by plaster, possibly during the period following the Reformation, since it no doubt originally contained statutes of saints. When the covering was removed this proved to be a superb piece of late medieval work with many of its original colours still intact. Latimer quotes an unnamed local newspaper report which described it as

'a very superb piece of workmanship, the gilding and colours of which were remarkably bright, and the fluted columns very perfect. There are niches on each side with small pedestals'.

[J. Latimer, Annals of Bristol in the 19th Century, 1887, 91]

With total disregard for this fine piece of medieval craftsmanship, much of the reredos was hacked away in order to accommodate the ornate Codrington monument. This destroyed an interesting and attractive survival from the

Augustinian abbey. Later four marble memorial tablets were placed around the Codrington monument. No reference to the re-positioning of this monument occurs in the Chapter Minutes.

THE BRISTOL RIOTS 1831

The ferocious riots in Bristol which lasted from Saturday 29 October to Monday 31 October 1831 caused immense damage in the city, including the sack and burning of the bishop's palace and the destruction of many of the archives and much of the library of the cathedral. The riots were caused by a combination of frustration over local economic recession, unemployment, food shortages and poverty, and were triggered by anger at the rejection by the House of Lords of a bill promoting reform of Parliament. That the bishop, Robert Gray, was an opponent of reform and that the votes of the bishops were widely believed to have ensured the bill's defeat, ensured that he would be an object of hatred by the rioters. On the Sunday morning the bishop had preached in the cathedral and then left the city. It was then left to William Jones, the bishop's butler, to attempt a defence of the palace when it was attacked by the rioters on Sunday evening, 30 October. In spite of his strenuous efforts, the rioters, numbering more than hundred, gained entry to the house and set about its destruction. They stole wine from the cellar, smashed furniture, porcelain and glass and set fire to beds and curtains so that the house was soon ablaze. The rioters were prevented from entering the cathedral by the courage and determination of the sub-sacrist, William Phillips, who managed to bar the door between the cloister and the south transept, where his brave action is commemorated by a wall plaque. This did not stop the rioters entering the Chapter House where the cathedral archives and library were kept. Many of the books and documents were thrown on to the fires in the bishop's palace, while others were carried away or cast into the harbour as part of an orgy of destruction which enveloped the whole central area of the city. The cathedral was saved, but the bishop's palace was left as a burnt-out shell, countless books and irreplaceable documents were lost or destroyed and the Chapter House and adjacent cloister were badly damaged. [G. Amey, <u>City under Fire: The Bristol Riots,</u> (1979) 67–9].

The Chapter Minutes 1831–41 [B.R.O. DC/A/8/5] *contain few references to the riots and the damage caused. On 30 November 1831 it was noted that the Chapter meeting was adjourned to the Dean's house.*

'by Reason the Chapter House being unfit to transact business in from the damage done to it during the late Riots on the 30th October last. .... The window in the small Muniment Room in the Chapter house and also the Presses [i.e. bookcases] be immediately repaired under the direction of the Dean as soon as conveniently may be under the like directions'.

Chapter meetings were resumed in the Chapter House from November 1833.

During the years 1832–6 a great deal of work was carried out on the Chapter House, cloisters, roof of the cathedral, and in demolishing the houses which stood

*on the site of the former nave. It is not possible to distinguish in the surviving
accounts payments which were made for work on specific parts of the building.
Moreover, not all the work done, for example, on the Chapter House, was
necessarily to repair the damage done by the rioters, since much work was done on
the floor, during which the Anglo-Saxon stone-carving depicting the 'Harrowing of
Hell' was discovered. A water-closet and drain was also installed. The following
entries from the accounts give some indication of the scale and expense of the work
carried out.*

B.R.O. DC/F/1/2

	£	s	d
1832 For repairs to the Chapter House	780	1	0

*[This was certified by the architect R.S. Pope, and paid by the sub-sacrist, William
Phillips, who had prevented the rioters entering the cathedral].*

	£	s	d
For pulling down old houses against the west wall of the south transept and tower, including painting, scaffolding, repairs to the roof of the cathedral and chapter house	110	9	9½,
Greenway & Taylor for work on the Chapter House, library and muniment room	329	3	4
Joseph Keyes, carpenter	147	17	2½

1835 Account from R.S. Pope, architect. 3 December 1835
For drawing specifications and superintending artificers
on the Chapter Room

	£	s	d
Mason – Godwin & Higgs	123	4	0
Carpenter – Marshall	91	16	0
Plasterer – Trickey	14	18	11
Gaslight – Breillat	7	17	3
Smith – Stevens	87	15	0
Glazier – Mitton	2	10	6
Smith – Poole	12	5	0
Picture Frame – Hatherley		10	0
	340	**16**	**8**
340–16– 8 @ 5% =	17	0	9
+ Specification for sale of old houses =	2	0	0
	19	**0**	**9**

IN MEMORY OF

WILLIAM PHILLIPS,

SUBSACHRIST OF THIS CATHEDRAL

45 YEARS:

OBT 2ND APRIL 1849. Æ. 79.

ON SUNDAY OCTOBER 30TH 1831. THIS CATHEDRAL WAS PRESERVED FROM DESTRUCTION DURING THE RIOTS, BY HIS UNFLINCHING COURAGE. LEST THIS BE FORGOTTEN, THESE WORDS WERE ADDED BY THE DEAN AND CHAPTER, JANUARY 1905.

Fig. 11 Memorial Plaque to William Phillips whose prompt action on the night of Sunday, 30 October 1831 in closing the door from the cloister, thus preventing the rioters from entering the cathedral, saved the building from suffering the same fate as the bishop's palace. The memorial is appropriately situated by the cloister door.
(Photograph by Philippa Johnson)

It had evidently been anticipated that the rioters might attack the cathedral. A hastily-scribbled and barely-legible account records that William Phillips the sub-sacrist, and several other men were paid £6 10s 6d for mounting guard in the cathedral during the period of the riots. Afterwards they were paid 'for assisting in collecting books and for cleaning churchyard and cloisters, and hauling loads of rubbish'. In addition William Phillips was paid 13s for providing beer and porter for the men while they kept watch in the cathedral. After the riot attempts were made by the Chapter to recover some of the books and records dispersed by the rioters. There is an account from the Bristol newspaper Felix Farley's Bristol Journal *for an advertisement inserted in December 1831 offering rewards for the return of books and records taken from the Chapter House. Some material was returned, and, for example, James Wood was paid £5 in June 1832 for 'saving deeds taken by the rioters' [B.R.O. DC/A/9/6/9].*

As late as 1869 Canon John Norris was able to purchase loose pages of a register of leases 1542–73 from Thomas Kerslake, a Bristol bookseller. He had them re-bound and noted inside the front cover 'I bought these loose and crumbling leaves of Kerslake bookseller in Park Street, February 1869'. [B.R.O. DC/E/1/16].

Sydney Smith's Description of his house in Lower College Green, and his Sermon on 5 November 1828

An indication of the accommodation provided by the prebendal houses in the cathedral precinct, as well as a brief description of some Chapter members, occurs in the correspondence of Sydney Smith, the celebrated wit and author, who was a canon of Bristol from 1828 to 1831. Sydney Smith was evidently pleased with the house which was provided for him in Lower College Green and described it in the following letter to Lady Holland:

N.C. Smith, Letters of Sydney Smith, 2 vols., 1953
Vol. 1, 478

Letter to Lady Holland

Bristol 17 February 1828

My dear Lady Holland

An extremely comfortable Prebendal house, seven-stall stable, room for four carriages, so that I can hold all your cortege when you come; looks to the south, and is perfectly snug and parsonic; masts of West-Indiamen seen from the windows. The collegues I have found here are a Mr Ridley, cousin to Sir Matthew; a very good-natured agreeable man, and the Duke of Bedford's Randolph, deaf, tottering, worldly-minded, vain as a lawyer, noisy and perfectly good-natured and obliging. The little Dean I have not seen Dr Beake, he is as small as the Bishop they say. It is supposed that one of these ecclesiastics elevated upon the shoulders of the other, would fall short of the summit of the Archbishop of Canterbury's wig. The Archbishop of York is forced to go down on his knees to converse with the Bishop of Bristol just as an elephant kneels to receive its rider.
....

Your sincere and affectionate friend,

Sydney Smith

As well as Dean Henry Beeke, the other colleagues mentioned are Henry Ridley (canon of Bristol 1816–32), and Francis Randolph, (canon of Bristol 1791–1831) who was a protégé of the Duke of Bedford. The Bishop of Bristol from 1827 till his death in 1834 was Robert Gray.

Sydney Smith was a passionate advocate of parliamentary reform and religious toleration, and caused great offence to the ultra-conservative members of Bristol Corporation by his sermon in the cathedral on 5 November 1828. They expected the usual denunciation of Popery, and instead were enraged to be treated to a sermon on Christian charity, advocating toleration for all religious opinions.

The circumstances, content and reception of his sermon were described by Sydney Smith in letters to Lord and Lady Holland.

N.C. Smith, Letters of Sydney Smith, 2 vols., 1953, vol I, 480–1

Letter to Henry Holland   Bristol, 28 August 1828

...You will be amused by hearing that I am to preach the 5th November sermon at Bristol, and to dine at the 5th November dinner with the Mayor and Corporation of Bristol. All sorts of bad theology are preached at the Cathedral on that day, and all sorts of bad toasts drunk at the Mansion House. I will do neither the one nor the other, nor bow the knee in the house of Rimmon.

Letter to Lady Holland   Lower College Green Bristol, 5th November 1828.

...Today I have preached an honest Sermon (5th November) before the Mayor and Corporation of Bristol, the most protestant Corporation in England. They stared with all their Eyes. I know your taste for Sermons is languid, but I must extract one passage for Lord Holland to show that I am still as honest a man as when he first thought me a proper object for his patronage.

> 'I hope in this condemnation of the Catholic religion in which I sincerely join their worst Enemies, I shall not be so far mistaken as to have it supposed that I would convey the slightest approbation of any Laws which disqualify and incapacitate any class of men for Civil offices on account of religious opinions. I consider all such Laws as fatal, and lamentable mistakes in Legislation. They are the mistakes of troubled times, and half barbarous ages..... I cannot discuss the uses and abuses of this day without touching upon the errors of the Catholic faith from which we have escaped; but I should be beyond measure concerned if a condemnation of Theological Errors were construed into an approbation of Laws so deeply marked by the Spirit of Intolerance......'.

The Catholic Emancipation Act, freeing Catholics from most of the civil restrictions which had for long been imposed upon them, was passed by Parliament in April 1829. Sydney Smith combined his canonry at Bristol, at first with the benefice of Halberton in Devon, and from 1829 with the vicarage of Combe Florey in Somerset. He came to Bristol only for his statutory periods of residence, and attended few meetings of the Chapter. In spite of his pleasure at his house in Bristol, he soon let it to a tenant and resided at Gloucester Place, Clifton, when he came to Bristol.

THE CHAPTER'S RESPONSE TO THE REQUEST FOR A LARGER ROOM FOR THE CONSISTORY COURT 1838

From the establishment of the cathedral in 1542 the sessions of the episcopal court for ecclesiastical causes were held in a small room to which access was gained by a flight of steep stone steps which had formerly been the night stairs of the Augustinian abbey. The stairway was reached through a narrow door in the south transept and was not easy to find since the same area was crowded with pews and a gallery. The court room itself measured only 11 feet by 30 feet and was barely adequate for the Chancellor who presided over the court, the various court officials who were known as proctors, and the numerous litigants and offenders who were summoned to appear. The court records which survive from 1545 show the wide range of ecclesiastical jurisdiction, covering many aspects of daily life, from marriage disputes and probate matters to heresy, immorality, slander and tithe disputes [B.R.O. EP/J/1/1–EP/J/1/45]. *It was the passage of the feet of the innumerable persons attending the court over the centuries that has caused the stairs to be so badly worn. In an attempt to improve the cramped conditions, the furniture and fittings of the court were renewed by the diocesan Registrar, Edward Pownall in 1667. As part of this refurbishment, the door of the court room, which dates from the 12th century and was part of the original furnishings of the Augustinian abbey, was altered by having oak panels fixed to its exterior side and the date 1667 marked by nails. Two centuries later, the date 1867 was also marked by nails on the face of the door* [Joseph Bettey & Hugh Harrison, 'A Twelfth-Century Door in Bristol Cathedral', B.G.A.S. Trans, 122, 2004, 169–71]. *On 10 April 1838 the Deputy Chancellor of the Court S.J. Milford, wrote to the Dean and Chapter with the not unreasonable request that in view of the cramped conditions and inconvenient situation of the Court, a larger room might be found for it. As the following letters show, his plea received a firm refusal from the Chapter.*

B.R.O. DC/A/6/11

22 Broad Street Bristol
April 10th 1838

Very Reverend Sir

As Deputy Chancellor of the Consistory court of the Bishop of Gloucester & Bristol I have been requested by the Deputy Registrar and Proctors of that Court to call your attention and that of the Chapter of the Cathedral Church to the very small and inconvenient room which is now allotted for holding its sittings and to the propriety of a larger and more convenient place being provided for that purpose.

At Present there are only seats sufficient for 5 proctors and these are almost always occupied. The number of proctors will probably ere long be encreased when there will not be seats enough for them and the space allotted to the public is so small that nothing can be taken from it for the accommodation of the proctors. The concealed situation of the court is another reason why it is desirable that it should be removed from its present scite as the public must have considerable difficulty in finding it when called there by business. If I might suggest a place which would be desirable for a new court and obviate the inconveniencies I have mentioned I should point out the Lady Chapel it is not used for any other purpose at present and when the Court is not sitting it might be closed as it now is.

The communication of this application to the Chapter will greatly oblige Very Reverend Sir

Your obedient Servant
S.J. Milford Deputy Chancellor
of the Episcopal Court of Bristol

To The Very Revd Dr Lamb D.D.
Dean of Bristol

At a Chapter meeting on 23 June 1838 the request was considered and the Chapter Clerk was directed to respond by a firm refusal, as shown by the following copy of his letter in the Chapter Minutes.

B.R.O. DC/A/8/5
Chapter Minutes 1831–41

25 June 1838

Sir

            I am desired by the Dean and Chapter to inform you that they have had your letter under consideration in which you request that a larger space may be allotted in the Cathedral than there is at present for the holding of the Episcopal Court.
            The Dean and Chapter direct me to state that upon all the information they have obtained they do not deem it advisable to make any alteration in the present Court; and that they would particularly object to the use of the Lady Chapel or any part in the Body of the Cathedral for the purpose proposed.

Following this refusal, the Court continued to meet in the inconvenient room with its difficult access until 1920 when it was moved to the new Diocesan Church House in Queen's Road, Clifton [Joseph Bettey & John Lyes, 'The Consistory Court of Bristol Diocese', B.G.A.S. Trans., 124, 2007].

CONDUCT OF SERVICES AND RELATIONS WITH BISHOPS

A curious dispute over the way in which prayers should be offered in the cathedral occupied much time during Chapter meetings in 1848–9. The incident illustrates the often difficult relationship between the Chapter and successive bishops of Gloucester and Bristol. It had for long been the practice that certain prayers, petitions and responses should be sung or chanted by the Precentor or one of the other Minor Canons, together with the choir. It appears that in 1848 the Revd Sir Charles Macgregor was appointed as a Minor Canon in spite of the fact that he was or claimed to be unable to chant or intone the appropriate parts of the service. Faced with this situation, the Chapter took a remarkable decision and at its meeting on 5 December 1848 'Ordered that the portion of the Service hitherto chaunted in the Cathedral by the Minister shall from and after the 8th Instant be read'. The sequel to this declaration is found in the volume of Chapter Minutes covering the years 1841–57 [B.R.O. DC/A/8/6] *and from John Latimer's* Annals of Bristol in the Nineteenth Century, *1887, 308–9. The Chapter decision appears to have been taken without any consultation with the Precentor, the Revd R.L. Caley, or any other of the Minor Canons. They objected to the order on the grounds that it would violate the oaths which they took on their appointment concerning the reverent and appropriate conduct of the worship within the cathedral. They were also concerned that the*

Statutes ordered services to be accompanied by music and the singing of psalms and hymns; and they argued that the Litany should be chanted in the time-honoured manner. One of the Minor Canons, the Revd. James Carter, therefore appealed to the Bishop of Gloucester and Bristol, Dr James Henry Monk (bishop 1837–56), since according to the Statutes *he was the visitor of the cathedral. In addition a memorial supporting the Revd Carter was sent to the bishop by the Mayor and Sheriff of Bristol and by members of the Cathedral congregation.*

The response of the Chapter to these protests was stubbornly to repeat their previous decision. On 13 February 1849 the following order was issued by the Dean, Dr John Lamb:

B.R.O. EP/V/6/1

I, John Lamb, Dean of the Cathedral Church of Bristol do hereby order that those parts of the Liturgy appointed by the Rubricks to be said or read by the Minister or Priest be read by him in the Cathedral Church without any intonations or adding any thing in the matter or form thereto. Also that the Litany appointed by the Rubrick to be read or sung be read by the Minister in the Cathedral Church.

Bishop James Henry Monk acted quickly to over-rule this decision of the Dean & Chapter. On 27 February 1849 he held a formal visitation of the cathedral in the Chapter House, summoning both the Minor Canons and the Dean and Canons to appear before him. Having heard the arguments on both sides, he ruled firmly in favour of the Minor Canons, adding to his judgment the exhortation to the Dean and Chapter to take more care before appointing Minor Canons in future, and to ensure that they could perform the duties required of them. The Chapter Minutes record the grudging acceptance of this episcopal judgment.

B.R.O. DC/A/8/6

'The Order of the Chapter of the 5th December last vizt. "that the portion of the Service hitherto chaunted in the Cathedral by the Minister shall from and after the 8th Instant be read" be now rescinded.

Ordered that notwithstanding any invalidity which may legally attach to the said order it was in strict accordance with the ordinances of the Church and well calculated to promote and maintain the devotion due to the service of Almighty God'.

This was signed by the Dean, Dr John Lamb. The fact that the Dean added the second paragraph is a measure of his reluctance to admit the Bishop's authority to order the services to be conducted according to ancient tradition. At the next meeting of the Chapter on 10 May 1849 the matter was again discussed and the Minutes contain a long account of the objections of the Chapter to the Bishop's interference in their affairs. The Chapter Clerk was ordered to send a Resolution to the Bishop suggesting that he had been badly advised and including the statement that:

'...the celebration of the choral services in the Cathedral Church be upheld and maintained according to the usages and practice of the said Cathedral Church by the Choristers, Men and Boys, under the direction of the Precentor, as prescribed by the Statutes. That with respect to the celebration of other parts of the Church service vizt. The Prayers and the Litany, the Minor Canons be enjoined to pay strict attention to the Rubrics of the Book of Common Prayer in compliance with the Act of Uniformity'.

The dispute was brought to an end by the fact that in November 1849 the Revd Sir Charles Macgregor resigned as a Minor Canon, and that in 1850 Dr John Lamb died and was replaced by the Revd Gilbert Elliot. Under Elliot, the conduct of Chapter meetings, the regular attendance of prebendaries (who were now known as canons) and their much more detailed involvement in the affairs of the cathedral, and a new regime of governance was introduced. The dispute with the Bishop during 1848–9 was in part due to the continuing pluralism and only occasional residence in Bristol of the Dean and Chapter. Dr Lamb, for example, was Master of Corpus Christi College, Cambridge and spent the greater part of each year there, while the other canons came to Bristol only for the period of residence each year and for the meetings of the Chapter. During his early years as Dean, Elliot was constantly resident in Bristol and the other canons lived nearby or came to Bristol frequently, as well as fulfilling their periods of residence and service in the cathedral.

REVIVAL, REFORM AND RESTORATION 1836–1877

In 1836 the reformed House of Commons took action to overcome some of the inequalities and abuses which had for so long affected the Church of England. For Bristol, as for other English cathedrals, this brought about a major re-organisation in its personnel and management. The unworkable arrangement whereby the county of Dorset was part of the diocese of Bristol, a situation which had survived since the creation of the diocese in 1542, was finally abandoned. Dorset once more became part of the diocese of Salisbury. The surviving part of the diocese of Bristol, consisting mainly of the parishes within the city and county of Bristol, was amalgamated with Gloucester, with one bishop, who was based in Gloucester. As a major trading city and port, with a rapidly rising population, Bristol was permitted to keep its own cathedral, but no longer had its own bishop. The number of canons was reduced from six to four, and the income thus saved was vested in the Ecclesiastical Commissioners who had been established in 1836 to administer and redistribute Church property. In 1837 James Henry Monk became the first bishop of the new joint see of Gloucester and Bristol. The surroundings of Bristol cathedral were also transformed. The bishop's house had been badly damaged by the rioters and was never rebuilt, and the houses with their associated gardens, privies and other outbuildings which had for long disfigured the site of the former nave were soon to be demolished. For the cathedral itself, however, significant change came only after the appointment of Gilbert Elliot as Dean in 1850, he was to remain as Dean until his death in 1891.

Gilbert Elliot (1800–91) came from a family of distinguished soldiers, administrators and diplomats. His father had been an ambassador in Germany and

Italy, and was later Governor of Madras. Elliot's family connections, particularly with the prominent Whig dynasty of the Russells, ensured his rapid rise in the Church. He was presented to a succession of wealthy benefices, eventually in 1846 becoming rector of Holy Trinity, Marylebone. An impressive figure and an effective preacher, Elliot was autocratic and austere, tending to inspire respect rather than affection among his colleagues. He was a low churchman, resolutely opposed to ritual, ornaments and to the Tractarian or Oxford movement within the Church. He refused to allow a cross or candles on altars and was vehemently opposed to anything that suggested catholic practice or influence within the Church. Evidence of Elliot's views can be seen in remarks he made to a meeting of Bristol clergy on 6 November 1850, soon after his arrival in Bristol. He vehemently attacked the Tractarians for doing the work of the Roman Catholic Church.

What hope have we to countervail this direct effort to lead to Rome if the Bishops will not interfere? Is it not high time that the Tractarian treason should no longer be permitted to train converts to Rome, that Tractarian presumption should no longer be permitted to ride roughshod over the really faithful and mourning servants of the Church?

[Bristol Mirror 9 November 1850, quoted by Peter Cobb, The Oxford Movement in Nineteenth-Century Bristol, Bristol Historical Association, 1988].

As Dean he soon became involved in numerous projects in Bristol, including the creation of new parishes to cater for the rapidly-growing population of the city, and in the encouragement of educational provision. Later he was to be enthusiastically involved in the campaign to establish a University in Bristol, and he became the first President of the University College in 1876.

Elliot's arrival, his high standards and his conscientious approach to his duties brought a new atmosphere to the Chapter and a new style of governance for the cathedral. During his early years as Dean Elliot was constantly resident in Bristol, and at the outset he refused to accept the offer to hold the benefice of Olveston in addition to the Deanery as his predecessor had done [B.R.O. DC/A/8/6. Chapter Minutes 27 June 1850].

The major deficiency of the cathedral of which Elliot became Dean in 1850 was the lack of space for congregations. Elliot was also concerned about the stability of the tower. As early as June 1850, only a few months after his appointment, he invited Isambard Kingdom Brunel, who was then involved in a multitude of engineering projects in Bristol including the railway, docks and shipbuilding, to survey and report on the tower of the cathedral. Brunel's hectic lifestyle and various business interests are evident in his reply to the Dean's request. Brunel wrote that he was able

'...to give a couple of hours for a cursory inspection to form some opinion of the subject. I can be at the Cathedral at 5 o'clock on Tuesday morning next, having to leave Bristol by train to Exeter at 7.50 a.m.
[R.A. Buchanan, 'Brunel in Bristol' in P. McGrath & J. Cannon, eds., Essays in Bristol and Gloucestershire History, 1976, 249–50]

The Chapter Minutes for the 28ᵗʰ June 1850 record that a report on the tower had been received from 'Mr Brunel, Civil Engineer' and that he had recommended a few repairs, but had concluded that no major work was required 'the next or following generation will probably be called upon for more extensive repairs and restoration'. Brunel's assessment was considerably over-optimistic, but it was accepted by the Chapter who asked him 'to cause the repairs he recommended to be carried out immediately' [B.R.O. DC/A/8/6].

Elliot next set about raising funds to pay for a re-organisation of the interior. In 1859 the Dean and Chapter applied to the well-known church architect, George Gilbert Scott for his advice on creating more space for congregations within the cathedral. Scott's report was as follows:

Report from George Gilbert Scott

British Library Add. MSS 31, 382

"To the Very Reverend the Dean, and the Reverend the Chapter of Bristol.

"Reverend Sirs, –

"I have, at your request, carefully considered the questions proposed to me in reference to the re-arranging of your cathedral, with a view to increased accommodation.

"The question as it applies to the majority of our cathedrals is one of considerable difficulty. These vast edifices are evidently far beyond the dimensions suited to a single congregation according to the services of the Church of England, which pre-suppose that every person attending them should be able distinctly to hear every part. They were designed for a different service, and were also, for the most part, intended especially for the uses of a great Clerical Body sufficient to occupy a very large choir, and who screened themselves round to such an extent as to be invisible from the nave.

"At the Reformation, when the Clerical Staff was usually reduced and the services rendered more congregational, the choir became the place for both clergy and congregation, – the remainder of the church remaining wholly unused, and thus involving the inconsistency of having vast temples capable of containing immense multitudes, but only a minute portion of which, about as large, perhaps, as a college chapel, made any use of, and the remainder treated as a mere ambulatory, or place to receive monuments.

"Let us for a moment consider what a cathedral suited to the uses of the Church of England ought to be.

"Being the great central and typical church both of the diocese and the city, it should, in the first place, I think, be marked by the following characteristics:- it should in the first place, be emphatically the *Diocesan Church*, -that at which the clergy of the diocese are from time to time called together to meet their Bishop, and in which the people of the diocese may assemble in almost unlimited numbers, to join in these especially solemn and diocesan services. It should be the church in which any other especial services of a diocesan character would most naturally and most conveniently be held, and, consequently, that which would contain the greatest congregation. In the same way of the city itself, - it is its great central church, distinct from its many parochial churches, in not being intended for a fixed congregation, but being equally open to all the inhabitants. It is the church at which the services are celebrated in their highest form, and should, therefore, have arrangements suited to this peculiarity, not only for the smaller requirements of every day, but for the more extended wants of special occasions. Again, as especially the Church of the People, its arrangements for congregational uses, and particularly for preaching, should be on the most ample and extended scale, – in short, it should be fitted to contain the greatest possible and the most promiscuous congregations, spreading over a surface the very greatest which the human voice can possibly fill.

"Now, in your church, all this may be provided for in a considerable degree, without being perplexed with that excess of space beyond what it is possible to use, which is involved in the opening out of our larger cathedrals. From the fact of the non-completion of the nave, the dimensions of the church are moderate; while the fact of its being only one half of an entire cathedral removes that architectural necessity for a screen of a very marked character, which exists in more perfect cathedrals; indeed the building will be better without any very pronounced division of choir and nave. On the other hand, the fact of the cathedral being placed amidst so vast a population, demands even more than usual consideration of its congregational requirements; in short, its primary demand is for a *nave* of the greatest possible capacity, - a wide area, in which a great assembly may both attend the church services and be addressed from the pulpit.

"To effect these great objects, the arrangement which naturally suggests itself is a limited choir at the eastern end, quite unobstructed towards the nave, being parted from it only by a low metal rail or screen, and the whole of the remainder of the church left open to the congregation, who may be provided for partly by light benches, and partly by chairs....

*   *   *   *   *   *   *   *   *   *   *   *

"I may mention, though it is a secondary matter, that the design of the interior of the cathedral is one which ill bears any marked division, and needs good scope to see it to advantage; but that with this, its effect will be both beautiful and unique.

"I have the honour to be,
"Reverend Gentlemen,
"Your very faithful servant,
"GEORGE GILBERT SCOTT

"*London, June 28th, 1859*

The work on the cathedral was carried out under the supervision of a local architect, T.S. Pope, at a cost of more than £15,000. It was certainly successful in creating additional space, and the available accommodation was increased from about 300 to 1,000. The work involved the destruction of the Tudor screen or pulpitum, which had been given to the cathedral in 1542, and the removal of the fine Renatus Harris organ of 1682 which had stood on top of the screen. The organ was re-erected in the north aisle. In place of the massive stone pulpitum a light screen was erected further to the west, freeing all the area east of the transepts for congregation and choir.

Chairs replaced the previous large pews, thus providing even more space. The large monument to Lady Joan Young and her two husbands, which occupied a great deal of space in the south-east corner of the choir, was dismembered and removed, later to be rebuilt on a smaller scale in the north-west corner of the new nave. Its removal made it possible to reconstruct the medieval sedilia which had been cut back to make room for the monument in 1603. New floors were laid, involving the destruction or removal of most of the medieval encaustic tiles, many of them decorated with the arms of the Berkeleys and other benefactors of the Augustinian abbey.

Finally, Dean Elliot took the opportunity to remove some of the medieval misericords or lively carvings from beneath the seats in the choir stalls. These he regarded as indecent or improper, although from surviving illustrations they do not seem to have been particularly objectionable or obscene.

The results of this work provoked a great deal of criticism, and Scott himself was at pains to declare that it did not accord with his intentions. The influential journal The Ecclesiologist, *while acknowledging the difficulties involved in providing more accommodation, declared that it 'has not met with unqualified success'. It condemned the way in which the scheme had been carried out, and suggested that it would have been far better for the Dean and Chapter to raise funds to rebuild the nave. Even more critical was the writer of a letter published in* The Ecclesiologist *in 1861. Calling himself 'P.Q.' he ignored the fact that the great Tudor screen had been demolished, but found little to admire in any other aspects of the work.*

The Ecclesiologist, 22, 1861

To the Editor

SIR, – It may be worth while, though it will afford you no pleasure, to give you some idea of the alterations that have taken place (under the name of "restoration") at Bristol Cathedral.

The plan of the building is doubtless familiar to you, and the old arrangement of seats, organ-screen, and sanctuary. The altar was formerly considerably raised above the nave: it is now lowered to one step only. This alteration was effected, it is said, to bring the base of one of the monuments on the north side into view: but it appears to me that this base has had to be increased, *in consequence*, by the introduction of a new chamfer: at all events, it has been extended more than was necessary or correct: and the bases of the three arches along the lower part of the east wall, (of late post-reformation date, which have been retained, and are, to say the truth, more satisfactory than the present new work) have been elongated too in the most awkward manner. The sedilia have been restored. The sanctuary alone has been repaved: the pattern and materials are such as would disgrace a railway-station, or the show-room of a cheap lath and plaster warehouse: there is no footpace, but the whole space from the *one* step which goes across the entrance to the sanctuary, is laid with plain white, yellow, brown, and blue or green tiles, in mere draughtboard arrangement, and without any pattern tiles.

By the way, some eight or nine months ago, while the work was going on, I recollect seeing two or three heaps of old encaustic tiles, lying in the choir; may I ask what has become of these? Why have they not been re-used, or preserved for sacred purposes?

The choir monuments have been scraped completely, with the usual results. The modern renovator appears to have been unable to comprehend the foot of one of the angels holding up the mitred head of an abbot or bishop, and has taken away the instep and produced a sort of fringe for the toes. There was a great talk about the Dean's intention to have one of these monuments coloured up again "at his own expense entirely" after its scraping. This was done, (though I have good authority for saying not without questions being asked as to the names of "what the abbot had on", and a display of utter ignorance of common ecclesiology), but the figure came out far richer and gaudier than the Dean had ever contemplated: so the paint was ordered to be removed, and thus the sculpture has had a second dose of the tool. The stalls have been retained with the addition of a row of new desks supposed to tally with the old, but the springings of the tracery placed at different levels. The choir it appears are to be placed at the extreme west end of the stalls. The organ is in the north side under the arches into side chapels: the old Jacobean work being in the main preserved – a luxury when compared with the new choir organ.

Two bays of the choir westward of stalls are unaccounted for: but at the west end (one bay from the present west wall) is a new stone screen with marble shafts; there are no screens at the sides, nor could I make out definitely whether such things were contemplated, so the appearance of the choir reminds one of a gate to a field, with the hedges taken away.

While in the building I was struck with some immense blocks of stone about 2 ft 7 in. square, of hideous and ridiculous design; these are for gas standards. The colouring of the vaulting is tame, and the stringcourse round the sanctuary miserable.

It appears to me that the sole object of the new western screen is to keep the *people in*, to mark no distinction between priests and people. As it is, it is a most absurd and unnecessary waste of money, and without the side screens of no use whatever. A better arrangement, it strikes me, would have been to erect a temporary roodscreen at the west end of the stalls (in case of a future rebuilding of the nave) and thus prevented the indiscriminate boxing up of clergy, choir and congregation on *one level*. Such an arrangement would have spared the expense of side screens, and the elaborate one at the west end, increased the accommodation, and allowed a little money towards fitting up the splendid north First-Pointed chapel, now in such a disgraceful condition. (This might well have served for a wayfarer's chapel.) I have no doubt that Mr Scott though his name has been freely mentioned, is not responsible for these things.

Yours, &c.,
P. Q.

The cathedral was re-opened with a civic service attended by the Mayor and Corporation on 27 June 1861. The bishop of Gloucester and Bristol, Charles Thomas Baring, might have been expected to preach on this occasion, but refused to do so. His relationship with Dean Elliot was already strained, and he was opposed to the idea of creating more space in the cathedral on curious grounds. According to The Ecclesiologist *of 1859 writing before the project had been carried out:*

'The Bishop has, with singular ill grace, fulminated against the whole scheme, as a vain attempt to recommend an unprofitable cathedral service

Fig. 12   An example of the painted plasterwork saved from part of the Old Deanery
before its demolition in 1901. All the paintings illustrate scenes from the Old and
New Testaments. This one shows the Raising of Jairus's Daughter, with the text in Latin
'She is not dead, but sleepeth' and King Saul casting his javelin at David with the text
'The Lord preserved David'.
(Photograph by Philippa Johnson).

in preference to unadorned parochial worship. Against this extraordinary
opposition our warmest sympathies are with the Dean and Chapter; and
we can only regret that the plan which their architect has advised them to
adopt is not one which we can unreservedly support'.

For future generations, the destruction of the medieval screen which, as explained
earlier in this volume, had come originally from the church of the Carmelite friars
in Bristol, is an unmitigated tragedy. Only a few fragments of the screen now survive
in the cathedral to attest to its quality. For Dean Elliot, however, the stream of
criticism which greeted his praiseworthy endeavour to increase the accommodation
within his cathedral, no doubt deterred him from any further projects of that sort,
and may well explain his totally negative response to the proposals to rebuild the
nave.

During the period 1847–53 Elliot suffered a succession of personal tragedies. In
1825 he had married Williamina, the daughter of Patrick Brydone F.R.S.. The
marriage produced one son and three daughters. Sadly, his eldest daughter, Mary
Elizabeth, died in 1847 at the age of 13, and in 1851 his son, Gilbert, who was a
lieutenant in the Royal Navy, was drowned at sea off the west coast of Africa, aged

22. *Two years later, in 1853, his wife died and was buried in the cathedral. Elliot continued to live in the fine deanery house west of the cathedral and facing on to College Green. In 1860, however, he decided to leave the ancient house, alleging that it was unhealthy and unsuitable, moving instead to Clifton, first to Royal York Crescent and later to the Mall. For a time the deanery was used as by the Y.M.C.A., but in 1865 it was demolished to make way for a new road built by the Corporation, providing a new route from the city centre to Hotwells. Part of the deanery survived, but this was demolished in 1901 to make way for the new City Library. It was from this part of the deanery that 13 large plaster panels with elaborate decoration and Latin texts were saved. Dating from the late 16ᵗʰ century, they illustrate various Biblical and allegorical stories, and are now preserved in the cathedral, leaving doubts as to what other treasures existed in the deanery and were destroyed with it.*

Meanwhile in 1863 Elliot had re-married. His bride was Frances Dickinson, a member of a wealthy west-country family, who in 1838 while still a minor had inherited the manor of Queen Charlton, near Bristol, and several other properties. She had previously been married to a Scottish landowner, John Geils of Geilston on the Clyde, by whom she had four daughters. This marriage had ended in divorce in 1848. She was a lively, active woman, the friend of Charles Dickens, and had acted with him in a play which he had written with Wilkie Collins in 1857. This rich vivacious divorcée seems an unlikely choice of partner for the staid, low-church Dean, who was more than 20 years older than his new wife. It is hardly surprising that the marriage was not a success, and that it brought great unhappiness to both partners. A series of increasingly bitter disputes with his wife inevitably occupied much of Elliot's attention. Moreover his wife was an inveterate traveller. One of her daughters was married to a Spanish Marquis, another to an Italian aristocrat, and she frequently visited them, accompanied by the Dean. As a result of her travels she produced two books, The Idle Woman in Spain, *and* The Idle Woman in Italy. *All this meant that after his marriage the Dean spent long periods away from Bristol, and took little part in the momentous decisions which were to lead to the triumphant rebuilding of the nave of the cathedral [For further details of Elliot's career see* Joseph Bettey, 'Constrasting Clerics in Nineteenth-Century Bristol', in Joseph Bettey, ed., Historic Churches and Church Life in Bristol, *2001, 196–201].*

The Demolition of the Medieval Water Conduit in the Cloister 1853

From its foundation in 1140 the Augustinian abbey was supplied with plentiful, good-quality water from a spring on Brandon Hill which was piped to a conduit or fountain in the centre of the cloisters, and was from there distributed throughout the monastic buildings. After the dissolution in 1539 this conduit continued to supply the cathedral, the bishop's palace and the houses which were built on the site of the former nave and around the Lower Green. A description of the cathedral written in 1634 which was quoted earlier in this volume describes 'In the Cloystare is a fayre Conduit of Freestone, and leads with many Spouts, which continually runs, and waters all the Colledge with that sweet Rockwater'. A decision taken by the Chapter in 1853 led to the demolition of what must have been an attractive feature of the cathedral precinct. This was a lease of the source of the water at Jacobs Wells to Richard Abbot for 21 years. In return Richard Abbot undertook to carry out the work specified in his letter dated 24 December 1853 which was copied into the Chapter Minute Book. The plan referred to in his letter is not included in the Minute Book.

B.R.O. DC/A/8/6

Waterworks at Jacobs Wells

A Lease to Richard Abbot of the Springs of Water at Jacobs Wells for 21 years from the 21st Instant (the former Lease of 21 December 1832 granted to George Rogers having expired) at a Rent of 25/- and upon the terms and conditions contained in his letter to the Chapter Clerk copied at the foot of these proceedings. ....

Sir

Bristol 24th December 1853

Waterworks at Jacobs Wells

    Being desirous of obtaining a Lease of these Works from the Dean and Chapter of Bristol I am willing to undertake and execute under the conditions hereinafter mentioned the following work.

    To take down and remove the present Reservoir and the Water House in the Cloisters and to level and Gravel the site thereof.

    To erect and completely finish a new Reservoir (capable of containing two Tons of Water) with all proper Buildings, Works and conveniences connected therewith upon the site of the Room used for the cathedral Library.

    To lay down new Iron pipes of two Inch bore in the direction shown on the Plan hereto annexed from the Spring head to the new Reservoir so to be erected as aforesaid and reinstate and connect the service pipes to the Cathedral, Deanery and Canonical Houses and Stables and to find and provide all labor and material and execute all the work free of charge.

    The works to be completed and finished within 6 Months from the date hereof.

    To provide and keep constantly laid on to the Cathedral, Deanery, Canonical Houses and Stables a supply of pure and wholesome Water at all hours and during all repairs necessary to be done to the Works, at the yearly payment by the Dean and Chapter of £20 and in default of such constant supply Lease to be forfeited.

    The Lease to be held by the Dean and Chapter until the whole of the Work is completed to the satisfaction of their Surveyor.

    To keep Pipes, Reservoir and Works in substantial repair during the whole term and to deliver same at the expiration of the term in good order and condition.

    All which I undertake to do upon condition of my being allowed to take to the whole of the old Pipes, Reservoir and the old material forming the before mentioned Water House, and upon condition also that the Dean and Chapter will grant me a Lease of the Works for a term of 21 years without payment of

Fines from the 21st day of Dec. instant on the terms and conditions above mentioned at a Rent of £1. 5. 0 per Annum and containing all usual & proper Covenants & Agreements.

The Costs of Lease and Counterpart Plans etc. to be borne by me.

(signed)   Richard Abbot

Robert Osborne Esqr
Chapter Clerk

Restoration Work on the Cathedral Tower

In spite of the assurances which Isambard Kingdom Brunel had given following his rapid survey in 1850, by 1860 the condition of the late-medieval tower began to give serious concern to the Chapter. The demolition of the cathedral nave during the Reformation period had left the western side of the tower inadequately buttressed, and urgent work was required to prevent its collapse. To its credit, the Dean and Chapter undertook this task energetically. The Chapter Minutes for 1862 record that £6,000 was set aside for the project; work was immediately commenced and lasted for the next few years. The Chapter was able to afford this sum because £8,500 had been received for the sale of the land on St Michael's Hill known as Cantocks Closes and Jockins Closes to Mr Thomas Tyndall. Dean Elliot later reported that £6315 had been expended to save the tower [B.R.O. DC/A/8/7 Chapter Minutes 1858–79, entries for 1862; DC/F/1/4]. The task of making the tower stable was much more difficult than had been thought. Work on it continued for many years, and it was still giving cause for concern when the rebuilding of the nave was started in 1868.

The Rebuilding of the Nave

The creation of a new road across College Green and close to the north side of the cathedral during the 1860s which had involved the demolition of most of the deanery, had the effect of revealing the former north porch and part of the foundations of the wall of the medieval nave of the Augustinian abbey. The discovery had a profound effect upon a recently-appointed canon of the cathedral, John Pilkington Norris who became the leading figure in the campaign to once again create a nave for the cathedral, and he was to be the most enthusiastic and successful fund-raiser for the project. John Norris (1823–91) was an accomplished classical scholar and prolific author. Much of his early career had been devoted to the promotion of education in Church schools. He was appointed as a canon at Bristol in 1865, where he remained for the rest of his life. In 1877 he also became vicar of St Mary Redcliffe, and in 1881was appointed Archdeacon of Bristol [Oxford D.N.B.]. As soon as the medieval foundations of the nave were uncovered, Norris sought an interview with the Mayor and councillors of Bristol and persuaded them to move the route of the new road slightly to the north so that a new nave and north porch could be built on the old foundations. Having secured their agreement, Norris then inserted the following notice in all the Bristol newspapers.

BRISTOL TIMES AND MIRROR, JULY 21, 1866

NOTICES

RESTORATION OF THE NAVE OF
BRISTOL CATHEDRAL

Chapter House, Bristol, July 1866

At the last meeting of the Chapter, a Resolution was unanimously passed that the restoration of the Nave of the Cathedral should be commenced, and I was authorised to take measure during my residence for making this generally known.

It is judged advisable, for two reasons, that the restoration of the Nave should proceed along with the restoration of the Tower.

1. – It will be the best and, indeed, the only way of buttressing the Tower, which, ever since the demolition of the old Nave (300 years ago), has been more or less unsafe.
2. – By carrying on the two works together a considerable saving of expense will be effected.

For the restoration of the Tower no appeal to the public is made: the Dean and Chapter set apart £6,000 for the purpose four years ago.

As this involves the members of the Chapter in a considerable sacrifice of income for some years, an appeal is now made to the public *for the restoration of the Nave.*

The expense (including Western Towers) is estimated at £30,000.

Two offers of £1,000 have been made on condition that eight others be forthcoming.

That all will be interested in it need not be doubted. We shall be planting Christ's Gospel conspicuously, as it ought to be planted, in the heart of this great city, and testifying at the same time to our faith in the permanence of His Church on earth.

Our Chancel, the most spacious in England (not excepting even Canterbury), is admirably adapted for choral worship, but is painfully ill-suited for the sermon. In a nave of five bays double the number of people might hear the preacher without difficulty.

It is proposed to proceed with the building as the money comes in. Some may prefer to pay their subscriptions by instalments.

Subscriptions or promises of subscriptions will be received by the Canon in residence, the Chapter Clerk (Chapter–office, 10, College green), or at any of the Bristol Banks, at all of which Books are opened for the "Cathedral Nave Restoration Fund."

J.P. NORRIS
Canon in Residence and Sub-Dean

Following the notice in the Bristol newspapers, matters proceeded at remarkable speed. It is evident that many people in Bristol felt that their truncated cathedral was unworthy of such a prosperous and populous city, a great trading port and the '*metropolis of the west*'. *Canon Norris's initiative therefore provoked an immediate and enthusiastic response. In October 1866 a committee was formed under the chairmanship of Henry Cruger Miles of Kingsweston, with the public-spirited and generous corn-merchant William Killigrew Wait as its secretary. Wait was also chairman of the Liverpool and Lancashire Insurance Company, whose local office was in Corn Street, Bristol, where the meetings of the committee were held. As well as the chairman and secretary the committee included the Mayor, the Sheriff, and the Master of the Merchant Venturers and the following prominent and wealthy Bristolians:*

Phillip W.S. Miles	W.H. Wills
C.J. Monk, MP	C.S. Clarke
W.F. Mogg	Charles E. Ward
Francis Adams	W. Gale Coles
Charles Price	J.A. Cooke
J.B. Harford	J.S. Mitford
T.T. Taylor	Thomas Barnes

Within a few weeks subscriptions amounting to more than £11,000 had been contributed and early in November 1866 Cruger Miles wrote to the Dean and Chapter requesting their support.

B.R.O. DC/8/7 Chapter Minutes 28 November 1866

Letter to the Dean and Chapter from Cruger Miles dated 24 October 1866

Gentlemen,

For some years past it has been felt by many of the Citizens of Bristol of all classes that the imperfect state of your venerable Cathedral is to some extent a subject of reproach to the City and its Citizens and a hindrance to the full development of its usefulness.

This feeling has of late largely extended and the restoration of the Tower now in progress under your direction has brought the subject of the rebuilding of the Nave so prominently before the public, that a subscription list (at present only comparatively of a private character) has been commenced resulting in promised subscriptions to the extent of about £11,000 and the appointment by the subscribers of a provisional Committee for the purpose of communicating with you on the subject. As the Chairman of a Meeting of the Subscribers to the Fund held this day I have the honor to inclose you a List of the subscriptions with the names of the Committee and I feel confident that in so doing it would be impossible for me to give you a better proof of the general prevalence of the feeling to which I have alluded as existing amongst all classes of our fellow Citizens or a better guarantee of the influential support which the movement will receive as soon as an appeal is made to the public at large.

I have also the honor to inclose you a Copy of a series of Resolutions which have been passed at a Meeting of the Subscribers and in accordance with the fourth of such Resolutions I now beg to address you on behalf of the Subscribers of the Fund and to enquire very respectfully whether this movement will receive your sanction and confirmation.

In the event, as we confidently anticipate, of a favourable reply I have further to apply for a Meeting between you and the Committee as effecting the best mode of furnishing any further explanation that may be desired and of effecting arrangement with a view to obtain the report of some eminent Architect mutually satisfactory to yourselves and to the subscribers.

> I have the honor to be
> Gentlemen
> Your obedient Servant
> H. Cruger W. Miles

Kingsweston 24 October 1866

The response of the Chapter was at best lukewarm, and the Dean doubted whether sufficient funds would be subscribed to pay for a restoration of the nave. Nonetheless the Chapter agreed to meet Mr Cruger Miles and the Committee, and passed the following resolutions:

That the Dean communicate to the Chairman at that Meeting

1. That a majority of the Chapter is desirous of restricting the Nave to three or four bays as may be recommended on competent authority.
2. That if subscriptions be obtained which shall suffice to build more than this, the Chapter will readily assent.
3. That the Chapter is willing to leave all the arrangements as to choice of Architect to the Committee, but will have to request that the plans be submitted to it for its approval.
4. That the Chapter assume that the building will not be commenced until subscriptions be either received or guaranteed sufficient to complete whatever it may be contemplated in the first instance to build, whether the Nave in its old dimensions, or bay by bay.
5. Finally that the Chapter wish it to be understood that their consent is conditional on the new fabric being in the same style of Architecture as the old.

Thereafter, apart from Canon Norris who continued to be a principal driving force and a formidably successful fund-raiser, the Dean and the rest of the Chapter remained aloof, and took little part in the project. On 1 November 1866 The Bristol Gazette *reported that the Dean doubted whether Bristolians would contribute the necessary funds, but that if they did he would have no objection to the scheme. Undeterred by the indifference of the Chapter, the Committee pressed ahead with great speed, and in December 1866 appointed as its architect George Edmund Street. Street was already well-known for his Gothic designs for churches, schools and public buildings, and proved to be an inspired choice. Early in 1867 he wrote a long letter to the Secretary of the Fund-Raising Committee, William Killigrew Wait, in which he gave a brief account of the architectural history of the Augustinian abbey, and proceeded to outline his views on how the proposed new nave might best complement the remarkable 14ᵗʰ century work in the existing structure. The main points of Street's letter are as follows:*

The Ecclesiologist, 28, 1867

Letter from G.E. Street

......"We know, —-absolutely, one may almost say, what were the intentions of the architect who commenced the new nave [*i.e. during the 14ᵗʰ century*], with the exception of his treatment of the west front; and it remains for us to consider whether, knowing so much, we shall not be wise in respecting, as much as possible, his intentions. I am decidedly of opinion that this is the proper course to take –that which will be fairest to the old work, and which will really bring out most thoroughly the architectural beauties of the choir, as they were intended to be seen when they were first planned. This opinion will, however, apply with greater force to the planning, and proportioning, and general design of the building, than to its lesser architectural details.

"In my plan I have, therefore, drawn a nave as long and as wide as the fourteenth century men proposed to build theirs; and in the general design I should propose to follow very closely the work in the choir. Only I should wish to mark, by a few minor alterations, such, e.g., as the sections of mouldings, the design of window traceries, and the character of the sculpture, the fact that this new nave is really a work of the nineteenth century, not of the fourteenth. I feel confident that in this way a grand work may be legitimately accomplished; - one which will have enough novelty to make it something better than mere task-work to its designer, and yet so complete a harmony with the old work, that in the general coup-d'oeil no difference will be noticed between the two works.

"There are however, some portions of the work which will require an entirely original design, as there is no guide to them in the old work. These are the north porch and the west front. .....

"There was a north porch to the Norman nave, and its base was discovered when the road was last altered. It is probable (judging by the small fragment of it which was discovered) that this was so good a work, that the fourteenth century architect intended to preserve it; but scarcely a trace now exists of its design, and I propose therefore to build a porch to agree in style with the rest of the nave, but in the old position. This will vary the outline of the building, and give that light and shade to this part of the north front which is so desirable to obtain. It will be seen that I have made it lofty and large in its proportions, so that it may be fairly conspicuous in the general views of the church from the open space on the north side.

"Then as to the west front, I think it is probable that this was not intended to have steeples. It seems to me, however, that in so great a city as Bristol, it would be felt that the scheme ought to be of the most perfect kind, and that as we know nothing at all as to the intentions of the old architect in regard to the west front, we are practically at liberty to do whatever seems likely to be most effective. On this point I have no difficulty in expressing a decided opinion; for I believe that there is no question whatever that the cathedral will in all respects be a more striking and effective building if it is finished with two western steeples, than if it has simply a nave and aisles corresponding with, and very nearly repeating the outline of, the existing eastern portion of the church.

"With western steeples there can be no doubt that the building would have so mistakably the character of a cathedral church, that every one would at once be impressed with it. .....

"The planning of the western steeples is the only respect in which I propose to depart from the old ground lines. I feel that if I were to project them entirely beyond the old extent of the nave, I should bring the west front too near to the abbey gateway. I hope, however, that the plan which I *have* drawn will meet all views, because (as will be seen on reference to it) whilst I retain the exact length of the old central *nave*, I shorten each of the aisles by one bay in order to provide for the substructure of the steeples. This seems to me to be the best compromise to make; it allows of steeples of good scale, and will also allow of a fine western doorway, with a rose window above it in the west front. It gives exactly the original length to the centre, or nave, of the church, and only slightly alters, without really shortening, the aisles on either side. Such an arrangement of the plan will give also much varied perspective both inside and outside; and if it is really carried out thoroughly, I feel confident that your cathedral , differing though it does in its design from any other example, will nevertheless be a very noble work, and well worthy such a city as Bristol. I need hardly expatiate on the advantages of its situation. The views from the Green are so open and good, that the mass of the building will be seen to the greatest effect; whilst the near view from the south-west will be, owing to the fall of the ground, extremely good and picturesque. The addition of the nave and western steeples will give the whole a bulk and importance which will make the cathedral, as it ought to be, the most conspicuous object in the distant views of the city. ....

"In respect to the practical execution of the work I may here state that I propose to face the whole of the walls, inside and out, with Doulting stone wrought in the same way as the fourteenth century work in the choir. This will make a more lasting work, though slightly more costly than it would be if executed in Box stone; and it will harmonise thoroughly with the old work in course of time.

"I think I have put you in full possession of my proposals for this great work, and in conclusion I can only say that in no work that has ever been entrusted to me have I taken more interest than I do in this; and that not only shall I be most anxious to devote my earnest personal attention to the execution of the work in every part, but also I shall be most glad to explain my own views more fully if your committee wish me to do so, and at all times to consider most carefully any criticisms or recommendations which they or other persons interested in any way in the undertaking may make.

"I have prepared very careful working plans for the whole of this work, both inside and out; and I trust that an examination of these plans will suffice to explain any points which are not clear in this written explanation, if they do not do so, I shall be most glad to give any further explanations which may be required.

"Believe me to be yours very faithfully,
"GEORGE EDMUND STREET.

"To W.K. Wait, Esq., Honorary Secretary to the
Bristol Cathedral Restoration Committee."

Meanwhile the Committee continued to be extremely active and successful in raising money for the project which had obviously captured the imagination of many Bristolians. The most successful of the fund-raisers was Canon Norris. To many he appeared as a stern, scholarly figure, yet his infectious enthusiasm for the projects he espoused made him an exceptionally persuasive money-raiser. On I October 1867 a contract for executing the first part of the work according to Street's designs was agreed with George William Booth of Gosport, Hampshire, who had made a tender of £14, 270. Work proceeded rapidly under the supervision of George Wall, clerk of works, and by 17 April 1868 the foundation stone of the new nave was laid. The Bristol Times reported on the occasion as follows:

Cathedral Nave Restoration

Laying of the Foundation Stone

Yesterday afternoon was performed the ceremony of laying the foundation-stone of the new nave which it is intended to build in connection with our present Cathedral. The work, it is estimated, will cost nearly £35,000, of which £15,000 are already subscribed or promised. The event was looked forward to with some interest, because the Freemasons of the Province of Bristol had declared their intention of taking part in the ceremony; and it passed off yesterday very successfully, the weather, while not altogether propitious, being still satisfactory from 1o'clock until 4 – from the first assembling of the Freemasons to the laying of the stone – the neighbourhood of College-green was crowded by thousands of persons, while a large number of ladies testified their interest in the proceedings by being present, on hustings purposely erected for their convenience, inside the Cathedral railings. .... At the conclusion of the ceremony the procession re-formed, and returned to the Royal Hotel where over 200 ladies and gentlemen sat down to a cold collation, served in the new and elegant dining-hall, which was used for the first time on this occasion.

By 1871 £23,000 had been raised, of which £20,00 had already been spent and by 1874 the subscriptions totalled £39,500 and expenditure had reached £32,500, while 22 men were regularly employed on the building, with many more casual labourers [B.R.O. DC/F/4/1 Fabric Fund Account Book 1866–75]. Evidence of the enthusiasm for the project in Bristol is provided by the fact that a list of subscribers published by the Committee on 1 June 1875 contained over 300 names of persons who had donated a total of £40,750 [B.R.O. DC/F/1/3]. The amounts subscribed ranged from numerous donations of £5, through many of £100–£500, to a few very large sums. The names of most of the prominent citizens appear in the list. William Gibbs, J.J. Mogg and Sir Grevile Smyth each gave £2,000, W.K. Wait gave £1940, the Society of Merchant Venturers subscribed £1600 and 'anonymous' £1200. Several donations are listed as being received 'per Canon Norris', a tribute to his energetic and persuasive fund-raising. The whole list provides clear evidence of the enthusiasm which the project created in Bristol.

Controversy and Dispute

From the launch of the plan to rebuild the nave in 1866 and during the remarkably successful campaign to raise the necessary money and the rapid construction of the building, relations between all those involved had been harmonious. The Dean & Chapter were content to allow the Committee to proceed with the work, and, apart from Canon Norris, appeared to take little close interest in either fund-raising or building work. Certainly there are few references to this momentous feature of the cathedral's life in the Chapter Minutes from 1868 to 1876. This amicable situation was rudely shattered by a violent theological disagreement in 1876. The hard-working secretary of the Restoration Committee, William Killigrew Wait, had decided to add to the major contributions he had already made to the work by giving £1,200 for the building of the north porch. This had already been designed by Street, who had provided niches for statues around the entrance. Statues to fill these niches were made by the well-respected local sculptor, James Frank Redfern (1838–76), who had provided figures for several churches and for Salisbury cathedral. Six statues were required and the choice of subject was left to Redfern. For the apex of the porch he carved figures of the Virgin Mary alone and the Virgin carrying the Christ Child; lower down, around the arch of the doorway he carved statues of the

Fig. 13 The Statutes of the Four Latin Doctors of the Church, carved by James Redfern for the new north porch of the cathedral in 1876. They depict St Jerome, St Gregory, St Augustine of Hippo and St Ambrose, each distinguished by his traditional symbol – a cardinal's hat, a papal tiara, a burning heart and a scourge. This photograph must have been taken before the statues were installed on the porch. They were pulled down by order of Dean Elliot early on the morning of 6 April 1876.

*four Latin Doctors of the Church – St Jerome, St Gregory, St Augustine of Hippo
and St Ambrose. Each of the large figures could be identified by their traditional
attributes – respectively a cardinal's hat, a papal tiara, a burning heart and a triple
scourge. The porch was completed and the figures were installed in February 1876.
For some time all was well but during March, letters began to be published in local
newspapers protesting against what was viewed as the Roman Catholic symbolism
of the statues. Soon the papers were filled with Catholic denunciation of the statues
and demands for their removal. All the latent mid-Victorian protestant sentiment
and anti-papal feeling was roused to fury, and on 3 April 1876 a meeting was
convened in the Colston Hall, which had been built only a few years earlier. The
newspaper reports of this meeting provide a remarkable picture of the violent
passions which were aroused, the vigorous denunciation of the statues and the
intemperate language used by many of the speakers. Some of those present at the
well-attended meeting fell to blows, chairs were thrown and it seemed possible that
the meeting would end in rioting. Some speakers even claimed to detect in the statue
of St Jerome the features of the renegade cleric, John Henry Newman. Eventually
enough order was restored for a resolution to be passed 'to protest against the
imagery lately erected outside Bristol cathedral' and to demand the instant removal
of the offending statues* [Bristol Times 4 April 1876]. *Dean Elliot had been in Italy
with his wife when the statues were put up, but he had now returned and summoned
a meeting of the Chapter on 4 April, the day after the Colston Hall meeting. The
Chapter received a letter of protest against the statues from a deeply anti-Catholic*
Clerical and Lay Association for the Maintenance of Evangelical Principles, *and
also received a deputation from the previous day's meeting, led by Col. Savile and
the Revd. T.C. Price. They presented the resolution which had been passed by the
meeting. The intemperate wording of the resolution can be gathered from the special
exception which was expressed to the figure of the Virgin and Child in the apex of
the porch, which was described as 'Seated on the goddess, predominant above all
the saints, the object of special worship and adoration [Quoted by A.E. Street in the
biography of his father,* Memoir of George Edmund Street, *1888, 179].*

B.R.O. DC/A/8/7 Chapter Minutes 4 April 1876

[It was] Resolved that the Dean be requested to take such measures as he may think
fit for removing the objectionable Statues from the North Porch of the New Nave of
the Cathedral, namely those of the four Latin Fathers, the single figure of the Virgin
Mary, and the Virgin and Child above the door.

Canon Norris and Canon Wade presented the following protest:

The undersigned being dissentients to the above resolution desire to enter their
protest against it.

J.P. Norris
Nugent Wade

*In spite of their objection, the resolution was carried by three votes to two.
In the detailed notes which he made of the Chapter meeting, Canon Norris recorded
the following:*

B.R.O. DC/A/8/16 <u>Memoranda of Chapter by J.P. Norris</u>

The Dean read a statement of his own sentiments. He objected

1 To the Subjects
2 To the Treatment
3 To the manner in which they have been put up without approval.

Following the resolution of the Chapter, the Dean acted immediately. Without consulting the Restoration Committee, the Architect or the Donor, Mr W.K. Wait, he engaged a gang of workmen and early on the morning of 6 April they used ropes to pull the offending statues from their niches, smashing the figure of the Virgin Mary in the process. The other statues were later rescued by Street, who used them on the tower of a church he had designed at East Heslerton in Yorkshire. <u>The Bristol Times</u> *reported the removal of the statues on 7 April, and commented that:*

'a more rough and open exhibition of iconoclasm has not been seen in Bristol since the days of Oliver Cromwell'.

Later, the niches were filled with figures of the four Evangelists. The Dean's action produced a vigorous remonstrance from G.E. Street, who wrote to the Dean, to Mr W.K. Wait and to <u>The Guardian</u> *newspaper. In his long letter to the Dean he noted that drawings of the proposed porch and statues had been widely distributed and displayed in Bristol since 1867, and had provoked no comment. He continued*

B.R.O. DC/A/8/7 Letter to the Dean from G.E. Street 3 April 1876

But you will excuse my saying that seeing with what singular care you avoided discussing anything connected with the new works with me, I should have thought it a grave impertinence to ask your opinion of any of the details. I gathered from your manner you did not much like the work being undertaken, nor cared to make yourself in any way responsible for the character of any portion of it. You left all the responsibility, both for the cost and execution of my designs, to the Committee. ....
I never before in a long experience heard such an objection taken to such figures. They are great historical personages, interesting I should hope quite as much to Anglicans as to Roman Catholics, and in instructing the Sculptor to represent them in proper habits, I have been solely actuated by the desire to let it be seen for whom the statues are intended, though I may add that their appropriate costumes are very serviceable to the sculptor from an artistic point of view. I suppose no one in his senses would deny that many Popes have been good men and worthy of such a place as has been given St Gregory in this work, and if one is allowed to be represented it appears to me to be convenient to signify who is meant in an intelligible way, and I did not know or realise that in itself as a distinguishing badge a tiara could be more offensive than a mitre, for both are equally strange to modern English eyes, though both are equally understood as badges of certain conditions of life and offices.

Believe me to remain
Yours very faithfully
George Edmund Street

The unfortunate sculptor, James Redfern, was devastated by the passionate condemnation of his artistic work and the abrupt removal of the statues. Although only 38 years of age, he fell ill and died later in the year. Canon Norris was also deeply upset by the action of the Dean. His Memoranda *reveal that he seriously contemplated resigning as a canon at the cathedral. He was persuaded by his friends to remain, although only after an angry exchange of letters with the Dean, who was completely unrepentant about his action [For further details of the continuing disputes between Norris and the Dean, see* Joseph Bettey, 'Contrasting Clerics', in Joseph Bettey, ed., Historic Churches & Church Life in Bristol, 2001, 209–13].

Meanwhile the Restoration Committee felt gravely insulted by the Dean's precipitate action and by his reaction to the gift made by their Secretary, W.K. Wait, who had played such a major part in the successful fund-raising campaign. They wrote to the Dean demanding an apology, but when he replied justifying his attitude and actions, the whole Committee resigned, sending the following resolution to the Chapter:

B.R.O. DC/A/8/7   Chapter Minutes 18 April 1876

That as the Dean expresses no regret for the outrage which has been committed, or for the discourtesy offered as well to the donor of the porch as to the eminent architect who has been engaged in the work, but rather justifies the steps he has taken to carry out the resolution of the Chapter, the Committee do not feel called upon to give a detailed reply to the Dean's letter, or to discuss the question as to the propriety of the figures; that they feel the only course they can consistently take is to discontinue the work for which they were appointed, believing, as they do, that such friendly relations between themselves and the Dean and Chapter as would be necessary for the completion of the work have been rendered impossible by the circumstances which have taken place. ....

With the cathedral nave almost completed, the Dean & Chapter were left with no alternative but to undertake the management of the project themselves, and to attempt to raise the money necessary to finish it. A 'Cathedral Completion Fund' was opened with the Dean as treasurer, and an appeal was launched for the sum of £3,600 necessary to finish the work. Eventually the nave was completed and on 23 October 1877 the opening service was held before a great gathering of clergy and civic dignitaries, and the sermon was preached by Dr C.J. Ellicott, Bishop of Gloucester and Bristol. Sadly, apart from Canon Norris, the members of the Nave Restoration Committee whose efforts had ensured the successful completion of the work did not attend.

POSTSCRIPT 1877–1897

In the twenty years following the triumphant conclusion of the campaign for a new nave much more was accomplished. By 1888 the two western towers had been built and the cathedral was complete. A magnificent opening ceremony was held on 8 June 1888 before a congregation of some 3,000 people. The north-west tower was

GILBERT ELLIOT, DEAN OF THIS CATHEDRAL CHURCH 1850–1891

Fig. 14 Memorial effigy of Dean Gilbert Elliot (1800–91), commemorating the austere and staunchly low-church Dean who presided over the cathedral for 41 years during a period which saw the success of the ambitious and costly scheme to rebuild the nave. (Photograph by Philippa Johnson)

dedicated as a memorial to the eminent theologian, Bishop Joseph Butler, and the south-west tower to the great Bristol benefactor, Edward Colston. According to figures compiled by Dean Elliot, between 1868 and 1888 more than £80,000 had been spent on the new building, of which some £68,000 had been raised by public subscription [B.R.O. DC/F/1/4]. In spite of continuing disagreement with the Dean, and icy, though formally correct, relations between the two men, Canon Norris had continued to work tirelessly to raise subscriptions for the completion of the towers. It is pleasing to record that his wife, Mrs Edith Norris, was invited to lay the final stone on the north-west tower. George Edmund Street died in 1881, so he did not live to see the completion of the whole design for which he was chiefly responsible. His successor was John Loughborough Pearson (1817–97). Pearson's work on the cathedral included the completion of the western towers and the west front, the rearrangement of the choir, with a fine new marble floor, a new reredos for the High Altar which was now restored to its former position, and a new crossing screen. Street's plans for the western towers were followed, except that the two steeples which he had envisaged as adding height to each tower were omitted. Pearson's work on the west end of the cathedral inevitably involved the demolition of the building which was used as the Chapter office, and the destruction of Minster House which incorporated parts of the medieval Prior's lodging. The medieval Gatehouse survived and was carefully restored by Pearson. The completion of the spacious nave of the cathedral re-awakened calls for the restoration of a separate diocese and bishopric for Bristol. This campaign was wholeheartedly supported by Canon Norris, who was foremost in collecting subscriptions for it. The cause received a

Fig 15 Bronze plaque erected to the memory of John Pilkington Norris (1823–91) whose vision, enthusiasm and fund-raising skills ensured that the project to rebuild the nave received widespread support and was successfully completed. Without his involvement it is unlikely that the nave would have been built or that a separate bishopric and diocese for Bristol would have been restored.
(Photograph by Philippa Johnson).

boost in 1883 when a delegation led by Norris secured the support and a generous donation from the Prime Minister, W.E. Gladstone, partly as a result of Gladstone's admiration for the works of Bishop Butler. By July 1884, £20,000 had been raised, and an Act of Parliament authorising the establishment of a Bristol diocese and bishopric was obtained. The rights of the existing bishop of Gloucester and Bristol, C.J. Ellicott, had to be safeguarded, and it was not until 1897 that satisfactory arrangement could be made. On 28 October 1897 a large congregation saw Bishop George Forrest Browne enthroned in the cathedral as the first bishop of the newly-constituted diocese of Bristol.

Neither Dean Elliot nor Canon Norris lived to see the restoration of the bishopric, since both died within a few months of each other in 1891. During the last decade of his life, Dean Elliot, who was already over 80 years of age, seldom came to the cathedral from his residence in Clifton, although he kept a firm grip on the cathedral services and strenuously resisted any attempt to depart from the strictly low-church principles which he had espoused throughout his life. For both Elliot and Norris it was a grave misfortune that for 25 years they were closely linked together by mutual concern for the cathedral and for religious life in Bristol, and yet they differed so markedly in character, attitude and churchmanship, and were unable to avoid a continuing series of fierce disagreements.

BIBLIOGRAPHY

G. Amey   *City under Fire: The Bristol Riots*, (1979)

W. Barrett   *History & Antiquities of Bristol*, (1789)

G. Beachcroft &   eds., *Two Compotus Rolls of St Augustine's Abbey*,
A. Sabin,   Bristol Record Society, IX, (1938)

J.H. Bettey   *The Suppression of the Religious Houses in Bristol*, Bristol
Historical Association, (1983)
The Suppression of the Monasteries in the West Country,
(1989)
St Augustine's Abbey, Bristol, Bristol Historical
Association, (1996)
Bristol Cathedral: the Rebuilding of the Nave, Bristol
Historical Association (1993)
ed., *Historic Churches & Church Life in Bristol*, (2001)

J. Britton   *History & Antiquities of Bristol Cathedral*, (1830)

Browne Willis   *Survey of English Cathedrals*, (1727)

J. Caple   *The Bristol Riots*, (1990)

G. Cobb   *English Cathedrals: The Forgotten Centuries*, (1980)

E.S. Goodwin   'Bristol Cathedral', <u>*Archaeological Journal*</u>, XX, (1863),
38–63

David Higgins   *From the Catacombs of Rome to College Green, Bristol:
The Life of St Jordan of Bristol*, Bristol Historical
Association, (2007)

I.M. Kirby   *Records of the Diocese of Bristol*, (1970)

J. Latimer   *Annals of Bristol*, 4 vols., (1887–1900)

J.F. Nicholls &   *Bristol Past & Present:*, Ecclesiastical History II (1881)
J. Taylor

E. Ralph & J. Rogan   eds., *Essays in Cathedral History*, (1991)

J. Rogan	ed., *Bristol Cathedral: History & Architecture*, (2000)
A. Sabin	*Some Manorial Accounts of St Augustine's Abbey*, Bristol Record Society, XXII, (1990)
S. Seyer	*Memoirs Historical & Topographical of Bristol*, 2 vols., (1821–3)
M. Skeeters	*Community & Clergy*, (1993)
M.G. Smith	*Fighting Joshua: Sir Jonathan Trelawny*, (1985)
M.Q. Smith	*The Stained Glass of Bristol Cathedral*, (1983)
	Art & Architecture of St Augustine's Abbey, (1991)
A.E. Street	*Memoir of George Edmund Street*, (1888)
J. Wilson	ed., *Sermons Very Fruitful, Godly and Learned by Roger Edgeworth: Preaching in the Reformation c 1535–c1553*, (1993)

INDEX